The Old Norse–Icelandic
Legend of Saint Barbara

Edited by

KIRSTEN WOLF

This volume presents an edition (diplomatic and normalized) of the Old Norse–Icelandic legend of Saint Barbara extant in Stockholm, Kungliga Biblioteket Perg. 2 fol. from ca. 1425–1445 and also in Copenhagen, Det arnamagnæanske Institut AM 429 12mo from ca. 1500.

The introduction examines the origin and development of the Greek, Syriac, and Latin versions of the legend of Saint Barbara as well as vernacular translations and adaptations of the Latin versions of the legend and their reception by artists. Particular attention is given to Scandinavian and Icelandic adaptations of the legend and evidence of the cult of Saint Barbara in Northern Europe.

The analysis of the Old Norse–Icelandic rendering of the legend reveals that it is a close translation of a Latin version of the story represented by a manuscript in the Bibliothèque Municipale in Douai, Codex 838, the text of which is edited in an appendix to this study.

MASTER FRANCKE, *The Martyrdom of Saint Barbara* (ca. 1420)
from a series of scenes depicted in the retable from Kalanti
(by courtesy of the National Museum of Finland)

Studies and Texts 134

The Old Norse–Icelandic Legend of Saint Barbara

Edited by
KIRSTEN WOLF

PIMS

Pontifical Institute of Mediaeval Studies

TORONTO

PT
7299
.B3
O43
2000

Acknowledgements

This book has been published with the help of a grant from the Humanities and Social Sciences Federation of Canada, using funds provided by the Social Sciences and Humanities Research Council of Canada.

Canadian Cataloguing in Publication Data

The Old Norse–Icelandic legend of Saint Barbara

(Studies and texts, ISSN 0082–5328 ; 134)
Includes bibliographical references and index.
ISBN 0–88844–134–7

1. Barbara, Saint – Legends.   2. Christian saints – Biography – Early works to 1800. I. Wolf, Kirsten, 1959– .   II. Pontifical Institute of Mediaeval Studies.   III. Kungliga Biblioteket (Sweden). Manuscript. Perg. 2 fol., fol. 78rb–79rb.   IV. Arnamagnaeanske institut (Denmark). Manuscript. AM 429 12mo, fol. 76r–80v.   V. Series: Studies and texts (Pontifical Institute of Mediaeval Studies) ; 134.

PT 7299.B3O43 2000   270.1'092   C00–931221–8

PRINTED IN CANADA

In memory of
Margrethe Wolf and Christine Koch

Contents

Acknowledgements

This study of the Old Norse–Icelandic legend of Saint Barbara was funded by a grant from the Social Sciences and Humanities Research Council of Canada. I am indebted to the Council for its support of my research over the years and also to the University of Manitoba for granting me a sabbatical leave in the spring of 1996 to complete the main portions of this project.

During my sabbatical leave, my colleague Daisy Neijmann took over my duties as Chair and Head of the Department of Icelandic, for which I am grateful. Rory Egan kindly answered a number of questions concerning my edition of the Latin source text of the Old Norse–Icelandic legend, and Stefanie Würth was of assistance in making available to me rare German books. The Pontifical Institute's anonymous reader, who later revealed her identity as Marianne Kalinke, made several useful comments, especially on the translation of the Old Norse–Icelandic text. My warmest thanks are due to Phillip Pulsiano, husband, friend, and colleague, for his willingness to listen to my ideas and for reading the entire introduction.

Finally, I wish to thank Fred Unwalla and Jean Hoff of the Pontifical Institute of Mediaeval Studies for a pleasant collaboration and for their superb editing.

Introduction

1 THE LEGEND OF SAINT BARBARA

1.0 The Origin and Development of the Legend

The very existence of the virgin martyr Saint Barbara, one of the "quattuor virgines capitales,"[1] is doubtful. A patroness of miners, firework makers, artillerymen, architects, founders, stonemasons, gravediggers, fortifications, magazines, and a protectress against lightning, fire, sudden death, and impenitence, she was alleged to have been killed in the early Christian persecutions.[2] Historically, her life and martyrdom have not been verified. This, however, did not prevent the legend that grew up around her from becoming exceedingly popular.

The data of Saint Barbara's *vita* and *passio* derive from a legend composed in the seventh century, perhaps of Egyptian origin (Costelloe 1967: 86). That she was venerated long before is, however, evident from the fact that she was the patron saint of a monastery at Edessa in the fourth century, and that a Coptic basilica was dedicated to her in Cairo in the seventh century (Lapparent 1926: 6). The various later versions of her legend differ in certain details,

---

1. The other three "great virgins" are Saints Catherine of Alexandria, Margaret of Antioch, and Dorothy.

2. Kirsch (1907): "The emperor in whose reign the martyrdom is placed is sometimes called Maximinus and sometimes Maximianus; owing to the purely legendary character of the accounts of the martyrdom, there is no good basis for the investigations made at an earlier date in order to ascertain whether Maximinus Thrax (235–238), or Maximianus [286–305] or Maximinus Daza [308–313] (of the Diocletian persecutions), is meant" (285). Most critics, however, argue that she suffered martyrdom in 306 (Wimmer 1980: 1432). The *Greek Synaxary* and Emperor Basil's *Menology* support this opinion (Dunbar 1904: 1: 100).

and the traditions vary as to the place of her martyrdom; Nicomedia, Heliopolis, Tuscany, and Rome all claimed to be the place of her death.[3] The Bollandists (*Propylaeum ad Acta Sanctorum Decembris*) acknowledge the impossibility of establishing a critical text of her *passio* ("Quod peius, de loco ubi passa sit summa est dissensio, aliis eam Nicomediae, aliis Heliopoli vel etiam in Tuscia, immo Romae collocantibus" [1940: 564]); however, its main features may be summarized as follows.

Saint Barbara was the only daughter of the nobleman Dioscorus, a pagan and much devoted to the worship of idols. To protect Saint Barbara from the attentions of importunate suitors, Dioscorus built a tower in which he locked her. Nonetheless, many nobles, who had heard of her beauty but had never seen her, sought her hand in marriage. Saint Barbara, however, exasperated her father by refusing the hand even of eminent princes.

Dioscorus then went away on a long journey. Before his departure, he gave instructions for the building of a magnificent bath for his daughter. One day, Saint Barbara went to view the building and noticed that only two windows were being built in the southern side of the bath. In honor of the Holy Trinity, she ordered that a third window be added, promising the workmen that she would take upon herself her father's wrath at their disobedience to his orders. As she walked through the bath, she stroked the marble with her fingers; she traced the sign of the Cross on the marble as if engraved with a sharp tool. Also her footprints remained visible. In contempt, she spat on her father's idols on her way back to the tower.

Dioscorus returned from his journey and saw the third window in the bath. In answer to his questions, Saint Barbara rendered him an account of the significance of the three windows and acknowledged her faith. On hearing of her conversion to Christianity, he drew his sword in rage to kill her. A miracle saved the

3. Kirsch (1907): "These various statements prove, however, only the local adaptation of the veneration of the saintly martyr concerning whom there is no genuine historical tradition" (285).

saint, for the wall opened and closed again after she had slipped through the crack, and she was carried up onto a mountain, where two shepherds were keeping their flocks. Dioscorus pursued his daughter and asked the two shepherds if they had seen her. The good shepherd refused to betray the fugitive, but the wicked shepherd showed her father the saint's whereabouts by pointing with his finger. The deceitful shepherd promptly received his punishment: he was turned into stone and his entire flock into locusts.

Dioscorus dragged his daughter by the hair from the mountain and shut her up in a prison, whereupon he made known her crime to the prefect of the province, Marti(ni)anus. When brought before him, she refused to sacrifice to the heathen idols. Accordingly, he sentenced Saint Barbara to be tortured to make her recant, and he and Dioscorus supervised her flagellation. However, Saint Barbara remained firm in her faith, and during the night the Savior appeared to her, comforted her, and healed her wounds. The next day, Saint Barbara was subjected to renewed sufferings: burning torches were held to her sides, she was beaten on the head with a hammer, her breast was cut off, and she was led naked through the streets. But divine protection again guarded her against suffering, and the Lord covered her with a white garment. When the cruel tortures failed to force Saint Barbara to relinquish her faith, Dioscorus himself executed his daughter on a mountain. In punishment, he was struck by lightning as he descended, and his body was consumed so that not a trace of him was left. Another Christian, Juliana, suffered the death of martyrdom with her. A certain pious man called Valentinus buried the remains of Saint Barbara, and at her tomb many miracles took place.

The legend of Saint Barbara contains many elements which have parallels elsewhere. In fact, Weyh (1911–1912: 43) claims that the legend is merely a mosaic of commonly used topoi. According to Gad (1971: 72), the legend of Saint Barbara is no more than a variant of the legend of Christina and the legend of Joseph and Assenath, Potiphar's daughter. This may be an overstatement, although it is true that there are striking similarities between the legend of Saint Barbara and that of Saint Christina (*BHL* 4 Epitomae). Saint Christina, too, was born of parents of high rank and the object of many men's desire. And like Saint Barbara, Saint Christina was shut up in a tower by her father Urbanus,[4] where she was taught by the Holy Spirit, and showed her lack of respect for her father's idols by smashing them. The ensuing tortures of Saint Christina, first by her father, who, like Dioscorus, received divine punishment, and then by two wicked judges, Elius and Julianus, also recall the tortures of Saint Barbara (see chapter 5). Additional details in the legend of Saint Barbara, which cannot be traced to the legend of Saint Christina, are found in other tales. The building of a bath, for example, appears, according to Weyh (1911–1912), "in der arabischen Salomo- wie in der persischen Dschamsēdh-Sage" (42). Death by lightning appears in the legend of Saint George (*BHL* 3395). Concerning the punishment of a wicked shepherd, Köhler (1885: 299) notes the similarity between

---

4. Delehaye (1927: 33) notes that the enclosure of Saint Barbara in a tower is reminiscent of the story of Danae, whose father shut her up in a brazen tower. Gerould (1916) makes a similar observation: "Danae and her tower of brass furnished material for the legend of St. Barbara" (44). Delehaye (1927: 97) further draws attention to the similarity between the legend of Saint Barbara and that of Saints Juliana and Cyriaena, although in this case the legend of Saint Barbara appears to have been the one influencing the other. Cf. also Gerould (1916: 36), Günter (1949: 85), and the editors' comment in *Acta Sanctorum Novembris*: "Estne hæc nostra Cyriæna eadem quæ Barbara, celeberrima virgo et martyr, quæ die 4 decembris colitur? Causa suspicandi hæc est: sub Maximiano imperatore utraque martyrium fuisse legitur; idem supplicium, idemque de utraque miraculum narratur. Verberibus scilicet affecta Cyriæna, vestibus spoliata, per urbem nuda circumducitur, precibusque a Deo impetrat ne nuda conspiciatur. Eadem de Barbara virgine in Actis ejus apud Metaphrasten narrantur. Cyriæna martyrii socia adjungitur. Juliana quoque Barbaræ sociatur. Qua de re amplius inquiri poterit ubi de sanctæ Barbaræ martyrio agendum erit ad diem 4 decembris. Hic dubium movisse sufficiat" (i: 210). Weyh (1911–1912: 39), on the other hand, emphasizes the similarity between the Syriac Bassus legend and the legend of Saint Barbara. However, he considers it most likely that either the Bassus legend was influenced by the legend of Saint Barbara or that they both go back to a common source.

this episode in the legend and an ancient fable as well as a Swedish folk tale (Hallberg *et al.* 1967: 90).[5] Finally, Saint Barbara's miraculous escape to a mountain echoes, according to Günter (1949: 202–203), miracles in a number of legends, including the *Protevangelium Jacobi* and the legendary accounts of Jesus Christ's infancy.[6]

Saint Barbara's story along with accounts of miracles performed through her intercession, exempla revealing her power and glory, and the discovery and translation of her relics are recorded in Oriental (Syriac), Greek, and Latin manuscripts dating from the

5. Köhler (1885) says: "Jacob Grimm theilt in Haupts zeitschrift IV, 502 f. eine schwedische volkssage mit, wie ein mann, der auf seiner wiese mäht, einer vorüberfliehenden riesin verspricht gegen ihre verfolger zu schweigen, dies dann auch thut, aber mit dem wetzstein die richtung, in der die riesin geflohen, andeutet und dafür am folgenden tag von ihr durch einen steinwurf getödtet wird. In dieser und einer ähnlichen, ebenfalls mitgetheilten schwedischen sage findet Grimm mit recht in lebendiger volkslieferung die dem mittelalter schon geläufige, unter die phädrischen gestellte fabel: lupus, pastor et venator (appendix fab. a M. Gudio ex ms. Divionensi descriptarum nr. 23.), welche auch von Marie de France und von zwei mittelhochdeutschen dichtern (Reinhart Fuchs s. 328 und 348) behandelt ist. Wenn Grimm aber bemerkt: 'Aesop hat die fabel nicht', so irrt er, da sie sich allerdings als die fabel 'vom fuchs und vom holzhauer' bei ihm (ed. stereot. nr. 10) findet. Auch Babrius (nr. 50) hat sie behandelt, was Grimm freilich damals noch nicht wissen konnte. In beiden fassungen tritt kein wolf und kein hirte, sondern ein fuchs und ein holzhauer auf und sie unterscheiden sich außerdem besonders noch dadurch von der lateinischen fassung, daß der holzhauer den fuchs nicht durch winken mit dem auge, sondern durch deuten mit der hand zu verrathen sucht ... . Dadurch nähern sie sich der schwedischen sage, an welcher Grimm gerade den – wie er meint – fast wesentlichen zug des augenwinkens vermisst. ... Ich habe nun auch gefunden, daß die der schwedischen sage und den alten fabeln zu grunde liegenden züge uns zum theil auch in einer *legende* begegnen" (298–299).

6. Günter (1949) says: "*Bäume, Erde, Berge und Felsen* dienen dem Heiligen. Das Protevangelium Jacobi erzählt von Elisabeth, sie habe ihren kleinen Johannes vor der Verfolgung des Herodes ins Gebirge geflüchtet und, als sie kein Versteck fand, gebetet: 'Berg Gottes, nimm Mutter und Kind auf.' Da habe sich der Berg gespalten und sie geborgen. Und in den Kindheitslegenden Jesu öffnete sich ein Feigenbaum und barg Maria und das Kind vor Räubern" (202).

ninth century onwards (cf. *BHO* 132–134, *BHG* 213–218, *BHL* 913–971, and *BHL* Suppl. pp. 110–114).

Weyh (1911–1912) has examined *BHG* 213–217 (*BHG* 218, Archbishop Arsenios of Corcyra's *Laudatio*, was inaccessible to him). He argues that *BHG* 213/214 (ed. Viteau 1897: 89–105), *BHG* 215 (ed. Wirth 1892: 105–111), *BHG* 216, Simeon Metaphrastes's (ca. 900–after 984) *Martyrium beatae Barbarae*, which is included in his *Menologion*, a collection of 148 saints' lives, and *BHG* 217, Saint John Damascene's (ca. 657–ca. 749) encomium *Laudatio sanctae Barbarae* all go back to the same original,[7] which presents an abridged version of the legend: "Allmählich wurde die Legende am Anfange verkürzt, weil der Hauptnachdruck auf die Erzählung des eigentlichen Martyriums gelegt wurde, einige Züge am Anfang wohl auch theologische Bedenken auslösten" (14). According to Weyh, *Codex Vindobonensis hist. 61* (fourteenth century) and *Codex Messinensis 76* (twelfth century), both representatives of *BHG* 215, present the most original version of the legend. Unlike most of the later versions, they do not include mention of the persecution of Christians at the beginning of the legend and do not contain derogatory remarks about Saint Barbara's father; instead, they specify that he loved his daughter. They also state that Saint Barbara's father sealed up the door of the prison with a signet ring (whereas most of the later versions relate that he locked it with a key). Moreover, the two texts are the only ones in the entire Greek transmission of the legend that tell of Saint Barbara's bap-

---

7. "Die Angaben könnten den Eindruck erwecken, als ob es sich bei den ersten drei Nummern [*BHG* 213/214, 215, and 216] um drei verschiedene Fassungen der gleichen Legende handelte. Die ... Untersuchungen ... zeigen, dass sich alle diese Texte auf eine älteste Fassung zurückführen lassen. Freilich sind die Schwierigkeiten einer solchen Untersuchung gross. Es sind allgemeine, die bei allen hagiographischen Arbeiten zu überwinden sind. Zahlreiche Fassungen der griechischen Barbara-Legende sind noch nicht herausgegeben, zahlreiche Mittelglieder sind überhaupt nicht mehr erhalten, sodass es auch hier nicht mehr gelingt einen restlos sich fügenden Stammbaum zu konstruieren" (12).

tism in a suddenly erupting well. In the other later versions, Saint
Barbara's conversion or baptism is only implied by her sudden
offense at her father's idols on her way back to the tower.[8] Neither text includes the so-called Saint Juliana episode, which in
Weyh's opinion was not contained in the oldest form of the
legend, but which appears in a number of the later versions.

In this episode the God-fearing Juliana followed Saint Barbara
when she was brought forth from the prison where she had been
healed of her wounds by the Lord. When Juliana observed the
miracle that had been performed, she resolved also to become a
martyr. When the prefect sentenced Saint Barbara to be subjected
to renewed torture, Juliana grieved and complained. Upon inquir-
ing who she was, the prefect was informed that she was a Christian. Enraged, the prefect condemned her to similar torture. She
was imprisoned while Saint Barbara was led naked through the
city; and when Saint Barbara had been returned to the prison, the
prefect ordered them both to be executed. Saint Barbara was
decapitated by her father, Juliana by a soldier. According to Weyh,
the possiblity that a local saint by the name of Juliana might have
had her feast day on 4 December may explain the incorporation
of this episode into the legend. Since Saint Barbara's feast day fell
on the same day, their names, so close to one another in time and
space, were brought into a spiritual relationship. He points out as
a parallel and possible model the figure of Polychronia in the

8. "Nur in [Codex] Vind[obonensis hist. 61] und [Codex] Mess[inensis 76]
findet sich, im wesentlichen genau übereinstimmend, erzählt, dass bei Barbaras Besuch im Bad plötzlich Wasser aus dem Boden herausbrach und das
Becken füllte. Unter einem hymnusartigen Gebet auf Christi Taufbad im
Jordan und andere neutestamentliche Heilsbäder entkleidet sich Barbara, steigt
hinab und jubelt: 'Die Taufe empfängt Barbara im Namen des Vaters und des
Sohnes und des hl. Geistes!' Dann steigt sie wieder heraus, kleidet sich an und
kehrt in ihren Turm zurück, unterwegs den Götzenbildern ihres Vaters ihre
Verachtung durch Anspucken zeigend. In allen anderen Fassungen ist diese
Erzählung mehr oder weniger, meist bis zur Unkenntlichkeit, überarbeitet
worden und nur durch verschämte Nachträge angedeutet" (21).

legend of Saint George (1911–1912: 20). Denomy (1939: 166n71) draws attention to a similar relationship in the legend of Saint Agnes between Agnes and Emmerentiana.

Both *Codex Vindobonensis hist. 61* and *Codex Messinensis 76* are in Weyh's view independently derived from the same *Urtext*; the former, however, appears to be a more faithful representative of this *Urtext*, whereas the latter in some respects represents a later stage in the development of the legend, partly through abridgements (a portion of the dialogue between Saint Barbara and the workmen has been omitted), partly through expansions (a prayer spoken by Saint Barbara before her imprisonment has been added, as has a voice from heaven promising the fulfilment of Saint Barbara's prayer at the end of the legend, and the account of her visitation by the Savior in the prison has been amplified).[9]

The Byzantine hagiographer Simeon Metaphrastes's *Martyrium beatae Barbarae* (= *BHG* 216) and the *BHG* 213/214 version of the legend show strong affinities. Thus, in contrast to the texts of *Codex Vindobonensis hist. 61* and *Codex Messinensis 76* (*BHG* 215), *BHG* 216 includes mention of the persecution of Christians and gives topographical information about Dioscorus's place of residence. It also contains the Saint Juliana episode. As in *BHG* 213/214, Saint Barbara is beheaded by her father and Saint Juliana by a soldier, and as punishment both Dioscorus and the prefect are consumed by fire. On the other hand, *BHG* 216 specifies that the door of the prison was bolted and sealed (and not locked). It should also be noted that *BHG* 216 contains a number of features that have no parallel in *BHG* 213/214 (and *BHG* 215). Thus, Metaphrastes relates that Saint Barbara gave as her reason for the

---

9. "Zwischen [Codex] Vind[obonensis hist. 61] und [Codex] Mess[inensis 76] besteht enge Verwandtschaft, die so zu erklären ist, dass sie auf eine gemeinsame Quelle zurückgehen, deren Darstellung in Vind. getreuer, also ursprünglicher vorliegt, während Mess. die Erzählung teils verkürzt, teils durch typische Wunderzüge erweitert hat, also eine jüngere Entwicklungsstufe der Legende vertritt" (16).

construction of the third window that more light would be admitted and that the building would be more beautiful. Moreover, according to Metaphrastes, it was only after the bath had been built, when she often used to come there to meditate, that one day she was filled with the Holy Spirit. Weyh (1911–1912: 31) dates the exemplar of *BHG* 216 to the mid-tenth century.

The *Laudatio sanctae Barbarae* (*BHG* 217) differs from *BHG* 213–216 in that Saint John Damascene indicates that Saint Barbara was already a Christian when she learned of the proposals of marriage, and that she rejected the proposals because she wished to remain a virgin and *sponsa Christi*.[10] As one would expect of an encomium, a number of details are also omitted: there is no topographical information and no mention of Saint Barbara's finger and foot imprints in the bath or of her baptism, and the episode concerning the shepherds is not included. On the other hand, a prayer is added in which Saint Barbara prays for a place where her relics may be preserved. Aside from these divergences, the core of the legend agrees so closely with that of *Codex Vaticanus 866* (eleventh century; = *BHL* 215) that Weyh (1911–1912: 30–31) believes that Saint John Damascene's exemplar must also have been the exemplar of *Codex Vaticanus 866*, which he dates to the first half of the eighth century.

As far as the Syriac version(s) of the legend of Saint Barbara are concerned, Weyh (1911–1912) limits his analysis to *BHO* 134 (ed. Bedjan 1890–1897: 3:345–355). He believes that *BHO* 134 is a translation from Greek but is reluctant to single out a specific version as its source. He points out that the Syriac legend contains features characteristic of the *BHG* 213/214 version, including the Saint Juliana episode, the mention of the persecution of Christians at the beginning of the legend, and the statement at the end that both Saint Barbara's father and the prefect were killed. *BHO* 134

---

10. Cf. Weyh (1911–1912): "Die beiden Züge begegnen uns auch … bei Symeon Metaphrastes; das zeigt, dass er, obwohl er sonst eine jüngere Legendenform benützte, doch auch die Lobrede des Johannes von Damaskus beizog" (31).

also has certain older and more original characteristics not found in *BHG* 213/214, however. Thus, the statement that Dioscorus loved Saint Barbara very much is, as noted above, found only in *Codex Vindobonensis hist. 61* and *Codex Messinensis 76* (= *BHG* 215). Moreover, in connection with the imprisonment of Saint Barbara, only *Codex Vindobonensis hist. 61* and *Codex Messinensis 76* (and Metaphrastes) specify that Dioscorus sealed up the door of the prison with a signet ring; *BHO* 134 too relates that the prison was sealed and not locked up. Weyh (1911–1912) concludes that *BHO* 134 "einen Typus zeigt, der manchen alten Rest treu bewahrt hat, welcher auf [Codex] Vind[obonensis hist. 61] und [Codex] Mess[inensis 76] hinweist, der aber im ganzen eine Entwicklungsstufe darstellt, wie sie in der jüngeren Gruppe P [= *Paris. 770* (1315)] R [= *Codex Pii papae II 22* (eleventh century)] Vat. 803 [*Codex Vaticanus 803* (eleventh century)] bei Viteau vertreten ist" (35). He notes, however, that *BHO* 134 does contain elements not found in any of the Greek versions. Thus, *BHO* 134 says that Dalason, the home of Dioscorus, in the province of Aliopolis, is twelve miles from Antiochia, whereas other versions use Euchaita as the point of departure, and that the prefect resided in Alparos, not Heliopolis. Moreover, according to *BHO* 134, both the traitorous shepherd and his flock were turned into locusts; in the other versions, the shepherd was turned into stone. *BHO* 134 further relates that Dioscorus and the prefect were killed by hail-stones, not fire.[11] Finally, the Valentinus episode and the information about the burial of Saint Barbara's remains are not included.

BHO 133 (ed. and trans. Lewis 1900) is virtually identical with *BHO* 134. The opening of the legend in *BHO* 133, however, differs from that of *BHO* 134 in that the legend is said to have taken

---

11. Cf. Weyh (1911–1912): "Getötet werden Barbaras Vater und der Statthalter und zwar ganz einzigartig durch Hagel, nicht durch Feuer. Obgleich wir den nämlichen Uebergang auch in der Georgslegende finden, wo nach Georgs Gebet Dadianus und seine Könige durch Feuer getötet werden sollen, wofür zwei orientalische und eine lateinische Fassung Hagel eintreten lassen, so möchte ich doch nur einen Lesefehler Bedjans oder Schreibfehler der Kopisten annehmen, die das syrische ñurā verlasen" (37).

place during the reign of Maximianus, the Aximus of this narrative, and the government of Aquinus; it also relates that Dioscorus
was a Greek in the city called Heliopolis, who lived in a village
named Glasius twelve miles from Euchaita (cf. *BHG* 213/214).
Moreover, *BHO* 133 includes no mention of Saint Barbara's footprints in the bath or the New Testament references to the Lord's
baptism by John the Baptist (Matthew 3:16, Mark 1:9, Luke 3:21),
to the blind man who washed in the pool of Siloe and received
sight (John 9:7), to the pond at Jerusalem (Bethsaida) in which a
paralyzed man was healed (John 5:2-9), and to the Samaritan
woman who requested water from Jacob's well (John 4:7-26). In
contrast to *BHO* 134, *BHO* 133 specifies that the prefect and Dioscorus were consumed by fire and not killed by hail-stones.
Finally, *BHO* 133 relates that when Saint Barbara was led naked
through the streets, the Lord came, seated on the chariot of cheru-
bim, and sent the angels and clothed her with a white garment.
This is, according to Weyh (1911-1912: 24), a late feature (*Codex
Vindobonensis hist. 61*, for example, says that an angel sent by the
Lord covered Saint Barbara with a white garment, and *BHO* 134
merely states that at God's command she was covered with a white
garment) and is found also in *Codex Vaticanus 866* (= *BHG* 215)
and in a number of *BHG* 213/214 texts (*Codex Ottobonianus 1*
[eleventh-twelfth century], *Paris. 770*, *Codex Pii papae II 22*, and
Codex Vaticanus 803).

The various Latin versions of the legend of Saint Barbara
would also seem to be based ultimately on Greek sources. As with
the Syriac versions, it is, however, difficult to single out a specific
version or versions that may have served as sources for the translations and to assign a date, even an approximate one, for Saint
Barbara's entry into the West. Nonetheless, it is certain that before
the ninth century she was publicly venerated (Kirsch 1907:
285).[12] Her feast day (*dies natalis*, that is, [heavenly] birthday) on

---

12. The reference to Saint Barbara in John the Deacon's life of Saint
Gregory the Great (book 4, ch. 89) from the late eighth or early ninth
century is probably one of the earliest literary references to the veneration
of Saint Barbara. See Gordini and Aprile (1962: 763-764).

4 December, which was celebrated since the twelfth century (Melchers 1965: 781), but which was expunged in the new Roman calendar published in 1969 after the Second Vatican Council (1962–1965), does not appear in the original recension of the *Martyrologium Hieronymianum* (ed. Rossi and Duchesne 1894),[13] that is, the *Codex Bernensis, Codex Epternacenis,* and the *Codex Wissenbergensis,* however, but was added at a later date and is found in the *Breviarium Richenoviense,* which assigns the place of her suffering to Rome ("In Rome. barbarae uirginis" [Rossi and Duchesne 1894: 150]). This notice may be due to the presence of her relics in Rome (see n31) and not unlikely at the Santa Maria Antiqua, which boasts her first known representation, an eighth-century fresco (Denomy 1939: 149n7; Grüneisen 1911: 100, 220, fig. 169, plate XVIII). Her feast day is not mentioned in the Venerable Bede's martyrology, dating from around 720 either, although it is found in later redactions, which include the works of an anonymous cleric at Lyons, who around 800 compiled a new martyrology by adding numerous notices to those of Bede (Paris, Bibliothèque Nationale lat. 3879; see Quentin 1908: 131–221), and the deacon Florus of Lyons (d. 860), who around 850 completed the former's work.[14]

In fact, the first notice of the feast day of Saint Barbara occurs in the historical martyrologyies of Rabanus Maurus (776/784–856), Archbishop of Mainz, and Ado (ca. 800–875), Archbishop of

---

13. The *Martyrologium Hieronymianum,* falsely attributed to Saint Jerome (ca. 341–420), was drawn up in northern Italy in the second half of the fifth century. The oldest manuscripts of this work date from the eighth century and depend upon a single Gallican recension that was made in Auxerre between 592 and 600 or at Luxeuil between 627 and 628. The original text was compiled from three principal sources: the work of the *Chronographer of 354* (an almanac containing, along with other listings, a *Depositio Episcoporum* and a *Depositio Martyrum*) continued to 420, the *Syriac Breviary* or *Calendar of Antioch* compiled between 362 and 381, and an African calendar, as well as other as yet unresolved sources (Brun 1967: 317).

14. Ed. Dubois and Renaud (1976). For a discussion of Florus's martyrology, see Quentin (1908: 222–408, 683).

Vienne. The former, which was based on Bede's work, martyrolo-gies and passionals, the *Liber Pontificalis*, the *Dialogues* of Gregory the Great (ca. 540–604), and the works of Gregory of Tours (539–594), was written between 843 and 854. Concerning Saint Barbara, Rabanus Maurus evidently derived his notice from the *passio* of the saint, possibly a version of the *Menologion* of Simeon Metaphrastes (Costelloe 1967: 86):

> Natale Barbarae martyris, quae temporibus imperatoris Maxi-miani passa est pro Christo. Nam pater eius nomine Dioscorus diues ualde sed paganus et colens idola ipsam filiam suam uni-cam, eo quod nollet nubere et deos falsos colere, multis tor-mentis affligebat. Nouissime uero precepto presidis a suo patre decollata est, et conpletum est martyrium eius in bona confessi-one cum sancta Iuliana. Descendente uero patre eius a monte, descendit ignis de celo et conbusit eum, ita ut nec puluis eius inueniretur. (Rabanus Maurus 1979: 123–124)

Aldo's martyrology was compiled between 853 and 860 "ut sup-plerentur dies qui absque nominibus martyrum, in martyrologio quod venerabilis Flori studio in labore domni Bedae accreverat, tantum notati erant" (quoted in Quentin 1908: 17). Nine-tenths of this martyrology was taken from Florus of Lyons; the remaining text Ado claimed to have derived from an ancient collection copied by him in Italy at Ravenna, but this portion of the text has been condemned as sheer forgery on Ado's part. In contrast to the Greek Calendar, the Syrian Menologies, and his Western prede-cessors, who give the date of Saint Barbara's feast day as 4 Decem-ber, Ado gives the date as 16 December and situates the legend in Tuscany. Gaiffier (1959: 40) suggests that Tuscany (Tuscia) may, in fact, be a misreading of Antioch, a name found in the oldest Latin version of Saint Barbara's *passio* (*BHL* 913; see below)[15] and in a Syriac version (*BHO* 134): "Il est certain qu'à Rome et dans la

---

15. This is according to Zaccaria's (1781) edition of the *BHL* 913 version, but not Maliniemi's (1957) edition, in which no name is given. See n19 below.

région voisine de la Ville éternelle, le culte de Ste Barbe était assez vivace dès le IXe/Xe siècle. Adon, ayant remarqué cette vénération sur le sol italien, n'aurait-il pas eu sous les yeux un manuscrit qui portait *Antiocia*, écrit assez indistinctement et, par suite d'une mauvaise lecture, interprété *Intuscia*?" (40). Ado's text is as follows:[16]

> In Tuscia, natale sanctae Barbarae virginis et martyris, sub Maximiano imperatore. Haec primum a patre suo Dioscoro diu afflicta sub dira custodia, dein tradita praesidi Marciano, expoliata, nervis et taureis valde caesa, discerpta est, et cilicio plagae eius defricatae. Inde reclusa in carcere, ubi luce divina consolata est, mox circa latere eius lampades ardentes applicatae, et caput eius malleis caesum, et mamillae eius praecisae. Deinde nuda per plateas ducta, et flagellis diutissime afflicta est. Ad extremum gladio data martyrium consummavit XVII Kal. Ian. (Dubois and Renaud 1984: 418)

Ado's work exercised much influence and was used by Usuard (d. 877), monk at Saint-Germain-des-Prés in Paris, who conflated the texts of Florus of Lyons and Ado. In fact, Usuard depends so much on Florus and Ado that it may be considered an abridged edition of their works, although he appears to have borrowed also from Pseudo-Jerome, Bede, and the anonymous martyrologist at Lyons. Like Ado, Usuard gives Saint Barbara's feast day as 16 December and claims Tuscany to be the place of her martyrdom:

> In Tuscia, passio sanctae Barbarae virginis, sub Maximiano imperatore. Haec post diram carceris macerationem et nervorum occisionem, # ac lampadarum adustionem mamillarumque praecisionem, atque aliorum tormentorum cruciationem, # ad extremum gladio data martyrium consummavit. (Dubois 1965: 360)

---

16. Dubois and Renaud (1984: 418) note that it is impossible to determine the text used by Ado. Cf. also Quentin (1908: 493).

Usuard's work became the model for every later Roman martyrology and the direct ancestor of the one published as official for the universal Church by Pope Gregory XIII (1572–1585) in 1584 with the bull *Emendatio*.[17] Unlike Usuard (but like Rabanus Maurus), the *Martyrologium Romanum* gives the date of Saint Barbara's feast day as 4 December and claims Nicomedia to be the place of her death:

> Nicomediae passio sanctae Barbarae virginis et martyris, quae in persecutione Maximini, post diram carceris macerationem lampadarum adustionem, mamillarum praecisionem atque alia tormenta, gladio martyrium consummavit. (1940: 564)

Gaiffier, attempting to explain the location of Saint Barbara's martyrdom in Nicomedia, a name which does not appear until the eleventh century (see n23), proposes the following hypothesis: "Plusieurs recensions donnent à Ste Barbe une compagne de martyre, Julienne; or, il existe une victime célèbre de la persécution de Maximien, Julienne de Nicomédie" (1959: 40–41).[18]

The most widespread and at the same time the oldest Latin version of the legend of Saint Barbara in the West is *BHL* 913, the oldest manuscript of which is the *Codex Augiensis XXXII* from the first half of the ninth century. The text of *BHL* 913 is represented

---

17. The *Martyrologium Romanum* was republished under Pope Sixtus V (1585–1590) with the notes and treatise on the martyrology by the cardinal and church historian Baronius (1538–1607). It was frequently revised, especially in 1630 under Pope Urban VIII (1623–1644), who reorganized its structure and introduced recently canonized saints, but also under Pope Clement X (1670–1676) in 1681 and Pope Benedict XIV (1740–1758) in 1748. The revision in 1924 is characterized by attempts at a complete reform. The more recent editions have merely added new feasts and newly canonized saints.

18. Gaiffier (1959) says further: "Le nom de *Civitas Solis*, traduisant le grec Héliopolis, laissait sans doute perplexes les hagiographes. Mais c'est seulement à l'époque moderne que Nicomédie a évincé pour le bon les autres noms de lieu. Baronius, constatant la diversite; de vocables, donna la préférence à cette cite; parce qu'il la trouvait mentionée dans un manuscrit ancien; or, celui-ci n'est autre que le codex X de la Vallicellane, qui ... représente un abrégé (*BHL*. 917f) de la longue Passion du diacre Pierre (*BHL*. 921)" (41).

by SKB A 56 (*Breviarium Aboense*) from ca. 1500 (ed. Maliniemi 1957: 179–184).[19] Gaiffier points out that "[l]a Passion *BHL*. 913 est une version assez maladroite du grec," but admits that "[d]ans l'état actuel de nos connaissances, il serait téméraire de vouloir préciser exactement de quelle recension grecque elle dépend, mais pour le fond, il est certain qu'elle coïncide avec *BHG* 213, 214 et 215" (1959: 15n3).

The various Latin versions differ from each other in a number of details. Generally, they may be divided into two main categories, the primary difference between the two being the manner in which Saint Barbara's baptism takes place. In one, represented by *BHL* 914 (ed. Mombrizio 1910: 1:138–140), Saint Barbara baptizes herself in "piscina aquæ" (138);[20] the other, represented by *BHL* 916 (Jacobus de Voragine's [ca. 1230–1298] *Legenda Aurea* compiled between 1252 and 1260 [ed. Graesse 1890: 898–902][21]) tells that

---

19. So *BHL Novum Supplementum*. In *BHL*, the edition by Zaccaria (1781: 137–142) is cited as a representative of *BHL* 913. The two texts are virtually identical.

20. *BHL* 913 and 915 belong to this category (Gaiffier 1959: 28n1).

21. The legend cannot be ascribed to Jacobus de Voragine, but was added to the *Legenda Aurea* by a later author or authors (in Graesse's edition, the legend is relegated to a sort of appendix ["legendae superadditae"]; see n26 below). The *Legenda Aurea* seems to have continually expanded to include additional lives. Cult interest is, of course, a major reason for these additions, but the specific needs of the monastic communities must also have been an important factor. Legends were the most commonly used literature in daily communal readings, and the "original" corpus of the *Legenda Aurea* could provide only 170 at the most for this purpose. Indeed, Williams-Krapp (1986: 231) notes that an anonymous printed edition of the Latin *Legenda Aurea* from around 1470 contained no fewer than 448 saints' lives. Reames (1985) draws attention to the fact that the promise in the legend of Saint Barbara that those who honor her memory will receive remission of their sins at the Judgment seems inconsistent and incompatible with Jacobus de Voragine's characteristic purification of the old legends: "One can hardly imagine Jacobus himself promising, as the chapter on Barbara does (p. 901), that devotion to the saint will ensure the remission of all one's sins at the Judgment. Instead he insists on the necessity of penance, illustrating the greatest mercy of the Virgin and other intercessors with stories in which an unhappy male-

Saint Barbara corresponded with Origen of Alexandria (ca. 184–252) and was baptized by Origen's messenger.[22]

In contrast to *BHL* 914, which, like the Greek and Syriac legends and the earliest Latin ones, locates the story in Heliopolis (that is, "in regione orientali quæ uocabatur Solis ciuitas" [138]; see n18 above) at the time of the persecution of Christians, *BHL* 916, like the *Martyrologium Romanum*, claims Nicomedia to be the place of Saint Barbara's martyrdom[23] and includes no mention of the persecutions. According to *BHL* 916, Saint Barbara pondered the difference between her parents' anthropomorphous gods and the creative power on which the existence of the earth and the sky depends. Her reason told her that the gods of her parents were created things, had had an existence like her own. That existence they owed to an uncreated being. Therefore she despised the pagan gods and longed to know the true God.[24]

---

factor is restored to life long enough to fulfill this requirement" (160). She draws attention to the fact that when Nicholas of Cusa (1401–1464) set out to reform the diocese of Brixen in the Tyrol around 1450, he forbade his clergy to teach the people such "superstitiosa" as were found in the *Legenda Aurea* accounts of Saints Barbara, Blaise (*BHL* 7 Epitomae), Catherine of Alexandria (*BHL* 1667), Dorothy (*BHL* 2324), and Margaret of Antioch (*BHL* 5309) (see also Schreiner 1966: 41–42).

22. In *BHL* 913a, the baptism was performed by an unknown saint. *BHL* 917 and 921 identify this saint with Origen's messenger, and *BHL* 916 with Valentinus (Gaiffier 1959: 28n1). For a discussion of *BHL* 920, see below.

23. So also *BHL* 915, attested in copies from the eleventh century (Gaiffier 1959: 21n3).

24. *BHL* 916: "Erat autem beata Barbara ingeniosa et a tenera aetate vanas cogitationes relinquens coepit divina cogitare. Cum enim semel templum intraret, videns simulacra parentibus suis ait: quid sibi volunt hae similitudines hominum? Respondent parentes: taceas, non hominum, sed Deorum sunt et volunt adorari per illud, quod nescitur et quod non videtur. Barbara dixit: fuerunt quondam homines, quos nunc colimus? Respondent: ita. Ex hoc beata Barbara die noctuque replicabat tacita dicens: si homines fuerunt Dii nostri, ergo nati sunt ut homines, mortui sunt ut homines; si Dii essent, nec nati fuissent nec mortui, quia deitas, ut mihi videtur, nec coepit nec desinit esse. Homo etiam habet originem terrae, quia terra est materia ejus, si ergo homo de terra est et homo Deus est, ergo aliquid praecessit eum, quod ejus origo

A rumor came to Nicomedia that in Alexandria there lived a very wise man, Origen by name. It occurred to Saint Barbara that he was the very man who could teach her the truth, who could confound the pagan Gods, and she considered how she might contact him. Since her father was "nobilis et valde potens" (898), she did not reveal her secret to him, and since she had no "curator" (898) who could speak on her behalf, she resolved to send a letter to Origen asking the questions she had contemplated concerning the true God. Origen responded: "[S]cire debes, quod unus est verus Deus in substantia et trinus in personis, scilicet pater et filius et spiritus sanctus" (899). He entrusted a priest, Valentinus, with the letter. In Nicomedia, Saint Barbara's father was told that Valentinus was a skilled physician from Alexandria, a man who could cure souls. He was allowed to visit and converse with Saint Barbara. He instructed her in the Faith and baptized her. We hear nothing futher of him.

Next follows the account of Saint Barbara's confrontation with her father about her suitors, her father's journey, the windows, and her flight. Unlike *BHL* 914, according to which both the treacherous shepherd and his cattle turned into a marble statue, only the shepherd turns into stone, whereas his cattle are changed into locusts. (This may, however, have seemed somewhat exaggerated for the compiler, for he adds that "[h]oc apocryphum est" [900].) The account of Saint Barbara's torture, healing, and renewed torture is virtually identical with that of *BHL* 914, except that there is no mention of Saint Juliana.[25]

---

dicitur; sic aptius dicerem terram Deum. Sed quia nec terra a se est nec coelum a se nec aër a se nec aqua a se, ex quibus quatuor elementis constat homo, sed creaturae sunt, necesse est his esse creatorem. Ecce quanta sapientia in tam juvenili puella. Tandem tradita studiis liberalibus alta transscendebat, sed defuit ei notitia veri Dei, vanos autem Deos oculte sprevit, et cum vidit Diis, scilicet lignis et lapidibus, flectere genua sensibilia insensibilibus mutis, animo valde correxit" (898).

25. *BHL* 914: "Quædam uero mulier domini cultrix et timens dominum. nomine Iulliana sequebatur beatissimam Barbaram et uidens mirabilia domini: quæ fiebant in ea: et plagæ eius qui sanatæ sunt: tradidit. semetipsam ad flagellandum" (139).

The conclusion of the legend differs from *BHL* 916 in a few details. According to *BHL* 914, the prefect ordered Saint Juliana to be imprisoned and Saint Barbara to be led naked through the entire region and flogged. "Respiciens uero in cælum beata Barbara martir christi ait: Qui operis cælum nubibus esto adiutor et protector meus: et protege me a facie impiorum: qui me affligunt" (140). The prefect then commands Saint Barbara and Saint Juliana to be beheaded. But this version is also marked by the reappearance of Dioscorus in the narrative. In his fury, he again assumes control over his daughter and brings her to a mountain. "Martyr autem chrysti orabat dominum: ut coronam certaminis sui consumaret cum beata Iulliana. Et facta est illi uox dicens: Veni dilecta mea Barbara: et requiesce in regno patris mei in cælis cum Iulliana socia tua et amabili mea" (140). Saint Barbara is subsequently executed by her father. Saint Juliana suffers a similar fate, carried out by "Centurione in eodem loco" (140). "Passa autem est sancta Barbara una cum sancta Iulliana pridie nonas Decembris" (140). When Dioscorus descends from the mountain, he and the prefect are struck by lightning and extirpated so that not even their ashes were found. But a certain pious man named Valentinus obtains the saints' remains and "posuit ... in Ciuitate in habitaculo religioso" (140), and at the grave many people are cured.

By contrast, *BHL* 916 relates that when Saint Barbara was ordered to be led naked through the region, she prayed: "[D]omine Deus, qui operis coelum nubibus, adjutor et protector meus esto et tege nudatum corpus meum, ne videatur ab oculis impiorum virorum" (900). God's angel then came and covered her body with a white garment. Seeing this, the prefect commanded that she be killed. Dioscorus took her and brought her to a mountain. Again, she prayed: "[D]omine Jesu Christe, cui omnia obediunt, praesta mihi hanc petitionem, ut, si quis memor fuerit nominis tui et famulae tuae faciens memoriam passionis meae, domine, ne memineris peccatorum ejus in die judicii, sed propitius esto ei, tu enim scis, quia caro sumus" (901). Her request was at once answered by a voice from heaven, and she obtained from God the privilege that her worshippers would not die without having received the Eucharist: "Et facta est vox de coelo ad eam dicens: veni, pulcherrima mea, requiesce in cubilibus patris mei, qui est in coelis, quod postulasti, donatum est tibi" (901). She was subsequently beheaded by Dioscorus, who himself was struck by lightning as he descended the mountain. "Finita est autem sancta martir Christi Barbara cum sancta Juliana quinta die mensis Decembris imperante Maximiano et praesidente Marciano" (901).

Both *BHL* 914 and 916 are based ultimately on *BHL* 913, but it is clear that *BHL* 916 also made use of other sources.[26] Thus, the idea that Barbara had corresponded with Origen while she was imprisoned in the tower and might even have been converted through his intervention cannot be attributed to the compiler of *BHL* 916, but originated with the work of a deacon named Peter, an eleventh-century writer who is the author of the legend found in *BHL* 921 and also of a hymn in honor of Saint Barbara (Blume 1908–1909: 1:166–168, nos. 144 and 145; Gaiffier 1959: 18–19).

According to *BHL* 921, the legend of Saint Barbara takes place during the reign of Maximinus Thrax.[27] To provide the narrative with a historical frame, the author reproduces a passage allegedly from Bede, which celebrates the merits of the mother of the

---

26. Concerning *BHL* 916, Gaiffier (1959) says: "Nous n'en connaissons qu'un témoin manuscrit: l'Ottobonianus 223, qui comprend la Légende dorée (fol. 1–256ᵛ, XIVᵉ siècle) et une série de courtes Vies de saints (fol. 257–261, XVᵉ siècle, cf. *Catal. Lat. Vatic.*, p. 419). Parmi celles-ci figure en tête l'abrégé (*BHL.* 916) suivi de deux miracles (*BHL.* 971, 956). Ces trois textes furent imprimés avec d'autres *Legendae superadditae* dans de nombreux incunables de l'œuvre hagiographique de Jacques de Voragine. Ces *Legendae superadditae* ne sont pas toujours les mêmes ni imprimées dans le même ordre. Th. Graesse [1890] a reproduit en appendice de sa *Legenda aurea* la série qui se lit dans l'incunable décrit sommairement par F. A. Ebert [*Allgemeines bibliographisches Lexicon*, t. I (Leipzig, 1821) col. 872, nº 10672ᵇ]" (37–38). Gaiffier argues that the imprint may be identified with the edition which appeared between 1474 and 1476 in Basel. This is among the earliest editions of the *Legenda Aurea*; Seybolt (1946: 328) lists it as number six.

27. For the discussion of *BHL* 921, I rely on Gaiffier (1959: 20–22).

Emperor Alexander Severus (222–235), Julia Mamaea. Curious about religious matters, the princess has the learned Origen ("Origenes Alexandriae, immo toto orbi clarus habetur") brought to her. Peter then turns to the history of Maximinus's persecutions, which were directed especially against the clergy and the family of Julia Mamaea "praecipue propter Origenem." Just as Origen, responding to Julia Mamaea's demands, offered instructions in the Faith, so Origen initiated Saint Barbara into the mysteries of the Christian faith. Moreover, in order to lend lustre to the conversion, Peter describes first Saint Barbara's doubts about the pagan gods, who are enumerated on the basis of a passage in Isidore of Seville.[28] Saint Barbara's brief letter is principally a panegyric to Origen and a criticism of the pagan gods; Origen's much longer letter is in essense a treatise on God, the Trinity, the Incarnation, and the Redemption. Peter also modifies the topographical data and passes over in silence all the many names in the Greek texts and in *BHL* 913, except one: Thalassis;[29] Heliopolis, it should be noted, has been replaced by Nicomedia. Peter appears not to have been the first to introduce this change (see n23), but is, nonetheless, anxious to be precise about this matter of locality: "Hoc imperante [Maximino], Marcianus presidebat Nicomedie, que civitas a Nicomede rege Bithinie et condita et vocata est." Moreover, in order to provide details about the voyage of Saint Barbara's envoy, he notes: "Est autem Alexandria in confinibus Aphrice et Aegi < p > ti constituta, caput regionis illius; Nicomedia vero in provincia Phenicis que est Siria ab oriente habens Arabiam, a meridie Mare rubrum. Quia ergo hee due urbes longe altrinsecus distant, dubitat Barbara nec sperat rei effectum."

28. See *Etymologiae* 8.11 (PL 82:314). This passage was reproduced by Rabanus Maurus in his *De universo* 15.6 (PL 111:426–436).

29. Cf. *BHL* 913: "Igitur milites circumduxerunt eam in predium, quod vocatur Delasium, in loco Solis" (Maliniemi 1957: 183) / "Igitur milites circumduxerunt eam in prædium quod vocatur Dalasium in loco solito" (Zaccaria 1781: 141). Thalassis corresponds to Dalasius, but Heliopolis has been omitted.

BHL 916 also derives some of its information from *BHL* 920, which forms part of a grand encomium on Saint Barbara composed in the last decades of the fourteenth century by a Flemish Augustine monk called John of Wakkerzeel (a village north of Louvain).[30] As Gaiffier (1959: 37) observes, this version can thus be dated to the end of the fourteenth century. John of Wakkerzeel's work comprises, according to Gaiffier (1959), a prologue (*BHL* 918), the legend proper (*BHL* 920), a description of the translation of Saint Barbara's relics from Egypt to Rome and from Rome to Piacenza (*BHL* 926),[31] an account of twenty-three miracles performed by Saint Barbara (*BHL* 932–955), and an *Informatio ex sacra scriptura de genealogia sive origine beatissime virginis ac martiris Christi sponse Barbare* (*BHL* 919); this text, a series of testimonies by Origen or *Dicta Origenis de beata Barbara*, cannot be ascribed to Wakkerzeel, but is the work of an anonymous author.

John of Wakkerzeel, a theologian and an important figure in his order (he took his vows as a professed religious in 1370, twice

---

30. Here and in the following I rely primarily on Gaiffier (1959), but also on Derolez (1991).

31. Cf. Derolez (1991): "The history of the relics of Saint Barbara is confusing. According to one tradition [*BHL* 922–924] her relics were brought from the East first to Constantinople, and then to Venice and Torcello. John of Wakkerzeel, on the other hand, contends that her body was transported to Rome and deposited in the Cemetery of Calixtus. On Charlemagne's request the body was taken to Saint Sixtus's monastery in Piacenza, but Pope Honorius I retained the head in Rome" (208). On Saint Barbara's relics, Weale (1872–1873) comments: "Nous disons Sainte Barbe *de Nicomédie*, parce qu'il est certain qu'il y eut plusieurs saintes de ce nom qui ont été confondues ensemble, de telle sorte qu'il est excessivement difficile si non impossible de distinguer entre elles et d'arriver à la vérité sur l'histoire de chacune. Le corps d'une sainte de ce nom est conservé à Kiev ... Celui d'une autre ... se trouve à Torcelli. Le corps d'une troisième Sainte Barbe dont le culte remonte à une époque fort réculée repose à Riéti ...; un autre, à Plaisance, et un autre dans l'ancienne église des Jésuites, à Venise. En 985 une partie considérable des reliques de S. Barbe fut apportée de Rome à l'abbaye de S. Bavon, à Gand. En 1150 la main gauche (laeva exsiccata) et une partie du bras furent transférés à l'église de S. Basile, à Bruges, et de là, en 1643 à celle des Augustins, dont le dernier survivant, Bernard de San, la présenta à l'église de S. Jacques en 1810" (11–12n5). Weale's view is shared by Hallberg *et al.* (1967: 190).

held the position of provincial of the province of Cologne [1390, 1397], and in 1392 lectured on the *Sentences* of Peter Lombard at the University of Bologna) appears to have undertaken the work primarily out of devotion to Saint Barbara[32] and out of his desire to make available a *vita* that did not treat her *passio* only "superficialiter," but that also detailed her conversion, the translation of her relics, and her most significant miracles:

> Licet enim nonnulli legendam de beatissime virgines et martyris Barbare passione superficialiter conscripserunt seu ediderunt, pauci tamen modum mire conversionis aut eius sacre translationis vel innumerabilium eius miraculorum enodationis ad spiritualem exercitationem nostre devotionis nobis in scripturis tradiderunt; quinymo huiusmodi materia, videlicet de eius conversione et translatione, in certis mundi partibus nullatenus reperiri potest. (Gaiffier 1959: 6n1)

Wakkerzeel claims to have expended great effort in obtaining as many sources and as much information as possible, making inquiries and having inquiries made on his behalf in Rome and Piacenza, and receiving assistance from a conveniently unnamed helper who also suggested that he write the legend.

As for the sources for his legend of Saint Barbara, Gaiffier (1959: 15) argues that Wakkerzeel conflated the texts of *BHL* 913 and *BHL* 921 and reproduced virtually all the details he could find in *BHL* 921, except for Origen's long letter, of which he presents only a section: "Sed quia longum est tam multis intendere," he has Origen write, "ad narrationem unius rei redeamus." The phrasing seems somewhat clumsy and, as a result of this omission, Origen makes no allusion to the Incarnation and the Redemption. However, the author is not as preoccupied with condensing his text as might first appear, for he fills this lacuna with new episodes added to the *passio* (cf. below).

---

32. On 26 November 1397, he instituted a daily mass at the altar of Saint Barbara in the church of the Augustinian convent in Ghent.

John of Wakkerzeel tried to find a solution to the conflicting topographical data in *BHL* 913 and *BHL* 921, but the resulting compromise testifies to his uncritical attitude to his sources. He begins by identifying the Heliopolis of *BHL* 913 not with the Syrian but the Egyptian city of that name: "fuit in Oriente apud Egiptum dux illustris ... qui in civitate residebat nomine Solis ad quam Ioseph cum dulcissimo puero Ihesu et matre benedicta eius gloriosissima virgine Maria propter metum Herodis regis veteri dinoscitur historiographorum confugisse testimonio. Insuper et de qua Isaie XIX legitur." He then claims that Heliopolis was founded by the Bithynian King Nicomedes: "Alioquin invenitur ipsa [civitas Solis] a Nichomede rege Bythinnie fore condita etiam quia Nichomedia vocata." Later, when he recounts the Christians' military expeditions in Egypt, he again affirms the identity of the two cities: "Christicola dicta turma ad urbem nomine Solis seu Nichomedia pervenit." Yet he also repeats the remark of Peter the deacon that Saint Barbara's envoy had to make a long journey from Nicomedia to Alexandria, but without omitting or modifying the statement that his Nicomedia (= Heliopolis of Egypt) is not very far from Alexandria: "Et quia hee due urbes, Alexandria videlicet et Nicomedia, altrinsecus longe distant, dubitat perspicuosissima virgo Barbara ... nuncium ... debitum sortiri effectum."

John of Wakkerzeel also appears to have used sources other than *BHL* 913 and 921, although his references are vague: "Prefatus insuper venerabilis doctor plura de sancta Barbara iam dictis [*BHL* 921] superaddidit que in urbe sancta litteratorie eidem viro insinuavit se veridice vidisse et legisse in diversis et antiquis valde repperisse scripturis." However, in the account of Saint Barbara's parents, he adds: "Dux iste [Dioscorus] itaque nobilissimam sibi genere duxerat uxorem, antiqua quadam narrante historia, de radice Yesse, que nobis ad salutem Dei et hominis Genitricem dignissime fructificavit, procreatam et coronam cuiusdam regni a progenie in progenies ei exinde successam possidentem."[33] Moreover, he gives

---

33. See also Villemot (1864: 20–21).

Saint Barbara's mother the title of queen and claims that she died when her daughter was very young: "regina pia matre eius defuncta." Gaiffier (1959: 24–30) argues that the "antiqua historia" that traces Saint Barbara's maternal lineage to David's father may be the *Liber de amore Christi ad virginem matrem* attributed to Origen, a work to which John refers, and from which he borrows, in his *Informatio* (*BHL* 919). As Gaiffier (1959: 30) observes, not a single copy of this extraordinary *Liber* survives, and may have existed only in the imagination of a fifteenth-century compiler.

As to the *Dicta Origenis,* its peculiarly scholastic style has lead scholars to believe that it was composed toward the end of the Middle Ages. The text is found in only three manuscripts: two from the Benedictine abbey of Saint Trond in Belgium dating from the first half of the sixteenth century (Brussels, Bibliothèque Royale 21003 and 21004) and a manuscript from the Beguinage of Herentals in Belgium dating from the 1470s (Yale University, Beinecke Rare Book and Manuscript Library, Marston 287).[34] The two Belgian manuscripts and the *Informatio* correspond in several

---

34. Marston 287 has been discussed by Derolez (1991). He notes that to John of Wakkerzeel's corpus of texts, the compiler Nicasius de Pomerio, a priest and chaplain of the Altar of the Holy Ghost in the Beguinage of Herentals, a small city in Belgium, east of Antwerp, added a series of Latin hymns, anthems, verses, and collects in honor of Saint Barbara. He also added two more extensive texts: a genealogy of Saint Barbara (an expansion of the *Informatio*) and a second legend of Saint Barbara. Derolez points out that "[t]his Life is different from the Wakkerzeel version, insofar as here Origen has no role at all in Barbara's conversion (which is in accordance with the Genealogy, where she is said to have been superior in scholarship to the Greek Church Father), and as there is no mention here of Barbara having been visited by the Child Jesus or by Saint John the Baptist. On the other hand the text, which is said to have been transmitted by reliable persons 'ex partibus Napulie [!],' does not mention the country where Barbara lived and was put to death (this contrasts with Wakkerzeel, who states that Barbara lived in Heliopolis, also called Nicomedia, a city in Egypt), but it says that in beauty she did not have her equal in 'Apulia, Naples, Sicily or Rome,' which suggests that the anynomous author situates the story in Italy" (204). On the final pages of the manuscript is a long list of gifts bequeathed by God to Barbara as well as a scholarly homily on the Annunciation.

details: Saint Barbara is said to have belonged to the family of Jesse and to have been baptized by John the Baptist; Christ is also said to have revealed himself to her in her tower in the form of a young child.[35]

It is precisely on these points that John of Wakkerzeel departs from the text of *BHL* 921 and chooses instead to follow the order and presentation used by pseudo-Origen. Like him, he begins by relating the visit of an angel: "Declaravit utique ei angelus universa fidem orthodoxam concernentia, ut prius efficacissime ex prehabitis Origenis legationibus fuerat edocta. Et super hec omnia, narrante ei angelo, de incarnatione Christi." Given the last clause, it should be no surprise that the part of Origen's letter that dealt with the Incarnation is omitted: clearly, instruction by a celestial messenger renders an excursus on the subject superfluous. To Saint Barbara, then, appears "illico Dominus in similitudinem pulcherrimi pueri in quo, magis quam exprimere sufficit, delectabatur." The angel then reveals to her the torments suffered by the Savior, and the Child Jesus stands transformed: "Mutatus est puer quasi totus passus et sanguinolentus." In this way is she initiated into the mystery of the Redemption. The miraculous intervention of John the Baptist from the *Informatio* is also related here, although John of Wakkerzeel's list of exempla is drawn from the legends of Saints Agatha,

---

35. See Gaiffier (1959: 27–28). The *incipit* of this text reads: "Origenes in multis libris scribit multa mirabilia de progenie et vita beatissime regine Barbare. Specialiter namque edidit unum librum qui nuncupatur: *Liber de dilectione et amore*. Hunc enim librum edidit de beatissima et supergloriosissima virgine Dei genitrice Maria, qua scilicet dilectione dilexit filium suum Iesum Christum, et de eius virginitate, etiam de eius excellenti gratia. In libro quoque prefato scripsit multa de virgine Barbara" (ibid. 27). Derolez (1991) notes that "[t]he Beinecke manuscript [Marston 287] stands apart in having the following title for this text: 'Incipit breviloquus epilogus de progenie, vita, passione et prerogativa excellentissime < et > gloriosissime virginis et martiris Christi Barbare.' Its text is otherwise close to the one in the Brussels manuscripts, but it offers some remarkable variant readings. One is that an ancestor of Barbara is called *rex de Bohemia* in the Beinecke manuscript, while the Brussels manuscript 21003 reads *rex de Babilonia*" (213n15).

Martin, Nicholas, and Augustine, whereas the compiler of the *Dicta* draws parallels from the Old Testament.

John of Wakkerzeel's grand encomium seems to have been popular and is found in a number of manuscripts and printed editions from the fifteenth, sixteenth, and seventeenth centuries: Gaiffier (1959: 9–11) lists no fewer than eighteen.[36] Moreover, it was translated and published in French, German, and Dutch. By the end of the fifteenth century, there were three editions of the French version, three of the Low German, and two of the Dutch. In addition, John of Wakkerzeel's work found its way into two printed editions (one German, the other Dutch) of the *Legenda Aurea* and also served as the basis for the *Vita vel tragoedia beatae Barbarae virginis et martyris, filia* [sic] *Dioscori regis Sisten in Palestina, sub Maximiano imperatore*, a mystery play preserved in a fifteenth-century manuscript, and inspired *Le mystère de sainte Barba*, a Breton play from the mid-sixteenth century (ed. Ernault 1885). It was also used in a little book, *Acta S. Barbarae virginis et martyris, patronae morientium* (Augsburg, 1703), written by the Jesuit Nicolas Müller.[37] Finally, it also seems to have had considerable influence on the cult of Saint Barbara and have given it new impetus.

Above all, it increased the prestige of Saint Barbara as a patroness of a good death, for all the miracles in John of Wakkerzeel's collection strengthen the belief that those who honor her memory will not die without having received the Sacrament of Penance and the Eucharist. In this respect, his version of the legend does not differ from the earlier versions, however, for these also contain a

---

36. Derolez (1991: 202) draws attention to the fact that while the first four parts of John of Wakkerzeel's work (*BHL* 918, 920, 926, 932–955) occur in a series of manuscripts and in a fifteenth-century printed edition, the *Dicta Origenis* are known only through three manuscripts (cf. above).

37. This learned Jesuit refers (p. 7) to a Czech translation of Wakkerzeel's compilation, published in Prague in 1670 and reprinted in 1700 and 1754. Gaiffier (1959: 12n2) notes that it was dedicated to authorities in the town of Kuttenberg (Kutná Hora), where a church was built with Saint Barbara as its patron.

phrase in which Saint Barbara promises that her worshippers will receive remission of their sins at the Judgment. In *BHG* 215, for example, the promise is made in Saint Barbara's last prayer, which *BHL* 913 renders as follows: "[P]resta michi Domine peticionem hanc, et da famule tue graciam, vt si quis memorauerit nominis tui et nominis famule tue, dierum martirii mei, ne memineris peccatorum eorum in die iudicii, sed propicieris peccatis eorum" (Maliniemi 1957: 183).[38] What is novel about John of Wakkerzeel's legend is that he attributes to the intervention of Saint Barbara a much more precise efficacy: "ut omnes ... qui mei memoriam agentes fideliter te invocaverint largiflua tua pietate consolentur, et precipue passionis mee diem annua devotione ad laudem tuam recolentes quatenus morte non preveniantur improvisa, sed vera confessione conterantur, habito tamen munimine perceptionis sacrosancti corporis et sanguinis tui, ne a diabolo illaqueati faciali gloria tua priventur; Domine, ne memineris peccata eorum in die iudicii, sed propitiare eis."

Passages such as these, corroborated by accounts of the many miracles, reinforce this devotion: Saint Barbara was, according to the text of a prayer, "singulare morientium solatium." Even the image of the sudden death of her father, Dioscorus, appears to have served as an incentive to invoke the saint in order to escape a similar fate. Indeed, the promise of her efficacious intercession at the hour of death meant that Saint Barbara came to be included among the fourteen or fifteen holy helpers. These holy helpers or auxiliary saints (in missals called "auxiliatores," "adiutores," and "legitimi adiutores") constitute a group of saints who enjoyed a collective cult in the Rhineland in the fourteenth and especially the fifteenth centuries. From the Rhineland area the cult spread to the rest of Germany, Hungary, and Scandinavia (the devotion

---

38. "[P]ræsta mihi petitionem hanc, et da famulæ tuæ gratiam, ut siquis memoravit in nomine tuo nomen famulæ tuæ, faciens nomen martyrii mei, Domine, ne memineris peccata ejus in die Judicii, sed propitiare ejus peccatis" (Zaccaria 1781: 142).

seems to have had little following in France and Italy.) The names and number of the saints varied from place to place, but the principle of their inclusion seems to have been their power to intercede against various diseases, especially their power to grant to the devoted a revelation of their salvation at the hour of death. The list generally comprises Saints Acacius, Barbara, Blaise, Catherine of Alexandria, Christopher, Cyricus, Denys, Erasmus, Eustace, George, Giles, Margaret of Antioch, Pantaleon, and Vitus. For one or other of these were sometimes substituted Anthony, Leonard, Nicholas, Sebastian, Roch, or, in areas of Germany and Scandinavia, Dorothy (Franz 1902: 171–172).

1.1 The Legend in the Vernacular

Vernacular retellings of the legend of Saint Barbara, in hymns, odes, prayers, stories, and drama, appear to have been popular in France and Belgium, where her cult was particularly strong. Her cult in Belgium is attested as early as 985. According to the *Annales sancti Bavonis Gandensis* for the year 985, the venerable monk, later abbot, Erembold "brought from Rome relics of Saint Barbara and those of Saint Pancratius together with those of many other saints to the Monastery of Saint Bavon," and on the first Kalends of August 1080, these relics were translated to the Monastery by the abbot Wichmannus, "possibly after the completion of the work of enlarging the Church and Choir, begun by Abbot Odwin in the year 985" (Denomy 1939: 154).

An Old French poetic version of the legend, the *Vie Sainte Barbe* (ed. Denomy 1939: 157–175), is preserved in Brussels, Bibliothèque Royale 10295–304, copied by a certain Jehan Vagus between the years 1428–1429 in the district of Hainault. On the basis of a linguistic analysis of the poem and the poet's use of the *Legenda Aurea*, Denomy (1939: 156) dated the poem to the end of the thirteenth century or the beginning of the fourteenth. Gaiffier (1959: 38n3), however, remained sceptical: "Trouvant la Passion abrégée *BHL.* 916 dans l'édition de Graesse, quelques érudits ont cru qu'elle remontait à l'époque de Jacques de Voragine, par exemple

... A.J. Denomy ... Ce n'est pas ici la place d'étudier la date de cette version, mais il paraît difficile d'admettre, à la suite ... de Denomy, qu'elle soit de la fin du XIIIᵉ siècle." In fact, it is doubtful that *BHL* 916 can be regarded as the source. The poet's rather free treatment of the legendary material makes it difficult to pinpoint a specific version; the lack of any mention of Saint Barbara's correspondence with Origen points to a version that stems from *BHL* 914, whereas her baptism by John the Baptist ("La vint messire sains Jehans, / Baptistre Dieu et boin sergans; / La damoisielle a batisie" [vv. 143–145]) points to *BHL* 920. Indeed, the poem stakes a claim for novelty. This is to be a story different from accounts of Ogier, Roland, and Oliver: "Histore voel conter nouvelle, / Piecha n'oïstes la pareille. / Sachies que ce n'est pas d'Ogier, / Ne de Rolant ne d'Olivier, / Mais d'une sainte damoisielle / Qui par tant fu courtoise et belle" (vv. 3–8). Certainly it does contain interesting details not found in other adaptations, Latin or vernacular, of the legend. Thus, Dioscorus, prior to his trip, tells masons to consult his daughter concerning the bath ("Puis a sa fille visetee / Et solatie et confortee. / A pardefin mout li pria / Que de l'ouvrage bien pensast, / Souventes fois en la semaine / Alaist veïr l'oevre hautaine" [vv. 89–94]). At her death, the virtues of Saint Barbara are compared to those of Saints Catherine of Alexandria, Agnes, Agatha, and Margaret of Antioch (vv. 392–436); the poet then adds the account of a miracle about a beheaded knight whose head is rejoined to his body before he expires, following confession and extreme unction (vv. 437–500). The poem concludes with a prayer to Saint Barbara.

Another version in verse, the *Vie de tres glorieuse vierge madame sainte Barbre martire* (ed. Williams 1975: 161–165), is found in Avignon, Musée Calvet 615, a manuscript from the sixteenth century. The poem differs from the *Vie Sainte Barbe* in a number of ways. It begins with a prayer seeking favor for the devotees of the saint (st. 1–3), and whereas the *Vie Sainte Barbe* does not localize the story in time or space, the *Vie de tres glorieuse vierge* situates it in Nicomedia (st. 4). Unlike the *Vie Sainte Barbe*, the *Vie de tres glorieuse vierge* also relates that Dioscorus allowed his daughter to have an additional window installed in the tower (st. 11–12); there she is visited by the voice of God, which also baptizes her (st. 20). Moreover, in the *Vie de tres glorieuse vierge* Saint Barbara's mother appears trying to change her daughter's new religious inclinations (st. 21–29). The poem terminates abruptly (in mid verse) after the burial.

Three minor Old French poems on Saint Barbara have also been preserved in books of hours or prayer books from the fifteenth century. The first poem (ed. Denomy 1939: 172–175) is preserved in Paris, Bibliothèque Nationale nouv. acq. lat. 615, a prayer book in use at Autun, from the end of the century, and is followed by a rhymed prayer to Saint Barbara (ed. Denomy 1939: 175). The second poem (ed. Denomy 1939: 176–177), preserved in Paris, Bibliothèque Nationale fr. 24865, is followed by a Latin hymn (ed. Blume 1922: 96, no. 79), an anthem, versicle and response, and the prayer. The third poem (ed. Denomy 1939: 177–178), preserved in Paris, Bibliothèque Nationale lat. 1321, a prayer book in use in Paris from the end of the century, is a hymn of intercession. It is followed in the manuscript by a commemoration, versicle and response, and the prayer, and then by another commemoration, versicle and response, and prayer in Latin.

A prose version of the legend found in Paris, Bibliothèque Nationale fr. 975 (ed. Williams 1975: 166–183), which once belonged to Jeanne de France (1464–1504), dates from the late fifteenth or early sixteenth century. Williams (1975) maintains that the source is *BHL* 916: "This unknown author follows basically the Latin version of Jacobus de Voragine's *Legenda Aurea* which he translates in the usual medieval manner: changing, contracting, expanding, supplementing" (158). However, several details, including the opening of the story, point to *BHL* 920. Thus the author begins with an etymologization of Saint Barbara's name and then sets the story in the time of Maximianus and in the Egyptian city of Solis now named Nicomedia: "Au temps que l'empereur Maximien, filz Dioclesien qui persecutoit durement la foy de Jhesu

Crist, regnoit ung parvers satrape nommé Dioscorus qui estoit moult noble duc et riche, mais paien estoit et adorait les ydoles. Lequel demouroit es parties d'Egipte vers orient en une cité nommee Solis. De laquelle cité parle Ysaie au XIXe chapitre de son livre en laquelle nous lisons que Joseph mena la vierge Marie avecques son enfant Jhesus pour doubte de Herode. Laquelle cité, comme nous trouvons, est de present nommee Nichomedie a cause de Nichomede qui en fut roys" (167). Like *BHL* 920, the prose version traces the lineage of Saint Barbara's deceased mother to the line of Jesse, from which sprang also the Virgin Mary ("de la racine de Jesse, dont la benoite vierge Marie, mere de Dieu, est issue" [167]), and relates how Saint Barbara was visited by Jesus Christ in the form of a child ("Et quant vint au point de l'incarnacion, nostre seigneur Jhesu Crist s'aparust a elle en semblance d'un petit enfant tres bel" [171]), and was baptized by John the Baptist ("la bien eureuse vierge receut sur son saint chief le saint sacrement de baptesme par la main du glorieux precurseur de nostre Seigneur, mon seigneur saint Jehan baptiste" [172]). Finally, this prose version follows *BHL* 920 in several other details: the legend concludes with an account of the erection of a temple where miracles took place, the forging by the people of Nicomedia of a suspended and illuminated shrine, the restoration to life of dead crusaders brought to her tomb, the removal of her body to Rome, the later translation (minus the head) by Charlemagne to the Benedictine monastery of Saint Sixtus in Piacenza, and the claim that God granted Saint Barbara's prayer to permit her devotees to leave this world only after confession, repentance, and last rites.

The legend of Saint Barbara is also included in the Franco-Italian writer Christine de Pizan's (ca. 1365–ca. 1430) *Livre de la cité des dames* (ed. Curnow 1975) written between 1404 and 1407. One of the most important contributions to the early fifteenth-century "querelle des femmes," the work is an explicit and systematic defence of women against the standard charges of the misogynistic tradition by adducing some two hundred examples of extraordinary achievement by women in virtually every area of human endeavor. The form of the work is significant: it is an allegorical dream vision in which the three personified virtues reply to the criticisms of women and provide Christine with directions and building material for the *Cité des dames*. In the first part, Dame Raison ennumerates a range of extraordinary women in politics, law, war, and the arts and sciences; Dame Droiture continues in the second part with a list of women who display exemplary moral virtue; and Dame Justice ends the work by relating stories of women who are exemplary in the spiritual realm, that is, female saints and holy women. It is in this third section that Dame Justice narrates the story of Saint Barbara (chapter 9.2; Curnow 1975: 998–999). While Boccaccio is considered the primary source for the first two parts, it is generally believed that Vincent of Beauvais's (ca. 1190–1264) *Speculum Historiale* (in Jean de Vignay's French translation, ca. 1282-after 1340) and possibly also Jean de Vignay's *Légende Dorée*, a French version of the *Legenda Aurea* made at the request of Jeanne de Bourgogne, queen of Philippe VI de Valois (1293–1350), in 1333–1334, provided the material for the third part, although Christine relied also on other sources, including Boccaccio's *Decameron* and *De casibus virorum illustrium*.

Three dramatic treatments of the legend of Saint Barbara have survived in the large corpus of medieval French religious drama: a five-day play,[39] a two-day play (reprinted no fewer than ten

---

39. Frank (1960) offers the following description of this long play, which had no fewer than one hundred roles: "The longer play indicates, sometimes in Latin, sometimes in French, how the elaborate production was to be staged and how the scenery was to be transformed from one day to the next. Like other saints, Barbara protests against the teaching of her pagan masters (who, strangely enough, require her to read Boccaccio among many other authors). But it must have been the peculiarly sadistic treatment of the young virgin that aroused the emotions of the audience: bound to a stake, naked, she is beaten, burned, and her breasts are torn off; at the instigation of her own father she is rolled in a barrel studded with nails and dragged by the hair over a mountain before being finally decapitated. A *stultus* improvised quips and drolleries during the performance which was otherwise relieved by

times between 1520 and 1602; ed. Seefeldt 1908: 1–57), and a fragment of another play.[40] Seefeldt (1908: ix–x) draws attention to the fact that between 1448 and 1539 more than a dozen performances of the legend of Saint Barbara in French took place, which, as Muir (1986: 165) notes, makes the legend of Saint Barbara the most frequently performed of all saint plays in France between 1450 and 1550.[41] The performance in Laval in 1493, which appears to have been especially good, earned the praise by the contemporary chronicler, dramatist, and actor Guillaume le Doyen: "il n'estoit honneur qu'en Laval" (Muir 1986: 164).[42]

Dramatic versions of the legend were not limited to France. Battelli (1924: 339–354, esp. 348) refers to an unedited Italian play based on *BHL* 916 performed in Florence in 1588 (Williams 1975: 156n6), and, among the saints' plays performed in Spain, Crawford (1967: 146) mentions an *Auto del martyrio de Santa Barbara* (ed. Rouanet 1901: 2: 78–89) and Lapparent (1926: 36) an *El Prodigio de los montes y martir de cielo* by Guilhem de Castro. Saint Barbara plays are also known to have been performed in Dutch and German, but they have not survived (Lockwood 1953–1954: 29).

---

various amusing touches (in it, for instance, wives and young girls were reproached for faults as prevalent today as in the fifteenth century), but on the whole the play makes dreary reading with its succession of brutal episodes, its long theological disquisitions, and its unimaginative style" (200).

40. Seefeldt (1908: xv–xvi) argues that all three plays seem to be independently derived from the same source, which he considers to be *BHL* 916.

41. The plays were performed in Amiens (1448), Compiègne (1475 and 1476), Angers (1484), Metz (1485), Decize (1489), Laval (1493), Nancy (1505), Domalain près La Guerche (1509), Limoges (1533), Péronne (1534), Saint-Nicolas-du-Port (1537), and Tirepied near Avranches (1539). To the thirteen mentioned by Seefeldt, Muir (1986: 179n122) adds another two performances, both at Mons (1459 and 1491). See also Julleville (1880: 2: 20, 38, 44, 48, 63, 87, 94, 120, 123, 134, 137).

42. Muir (1986: 164–165) notes that the painted wooden panels installed some twenty years later in a roof over the chapel of Saint Barbara in the church of St.-Martin-de-Connée about forty miles from Laval may have been influenced by this dramatic retelling of the legend.

Saint Barbara enjoyed considerable popularity in other parts of Europe as well. Williams-Krapp (1986: 394–395) lists eleven collections in which the legend of Saint Barbara is included, in Germany and the Netherlands,[43] and notes also twenty-one texts independent of these legendaries.[44]

Versions in verse appear to have been especially popular. A *Barbaren passie* is preserved in three manuscripts (Munich, Bayerische Staatsbibliothek Cod. Germ. 478; Dessau, Zweigstelle der Universitäts- und Landesbibliothek Sachsen-Anhalt Cod. Georg. 4 4to; and UUB C 497, all from the fifteenth century) and was printed many times in the sixteenth century. The edition published by J. Koelhoff in Cologne in 1498 and that published by Heinrich von Nuyss in Cologne in 1513 form the basis of Schade's edition (1854: 52–65); the Low German version published by Simon Mentzer in Magdeburg in 1500 was edited by Wegener (1878: 1–7). Reuter (1977: 602) notes that the lack of a thorough study of the relationship among the various manuscripts and editions of the poem makes it very difficult, if not impossible, to determine the poem's date of composition and its provenance. As his source, the translator mentions a book in which he read the story ("als ich in dem boiche las" [Schade 1854: v. 42]; "Alse ick in eynem boke lasz" [Wegener 1878: v. 38]), and from the phrase "zo duitsche ... beduden" (Schade 1854: v. 28; "recht beduden" [Wegener 1878: v. 18]) one must assume that it was in Latin. Schade (1854: 39) considers *BHL* 916 to be the most likely source, but admits that in a few details the poem differs from *BHL* 916. The lack of any mention of Origen and the location of the story in "die ... stat Sola" (Schade 1854: v. 5; "eynes stad ... Sola" [Wegener 1878: v. 32]),

---

43. The legendaries are: *Legendar des Marquard Biberli, Bebenhauser Legendar, Das Buch von den heiligen Mägden und Frauen, Darmstädter Legendar, Die elsässische Legenda Aurea, Der Heiligenleben Hermanns von Fritzlar, Der Heiligen Leben, Der Heiligen Leben (Redaktion), Mittelfränkische Heiligenpredigt, Die niederdeutsche Legenda Aurea,* and *Schwäbische Heiligenpredigt.*

44. Only one of the texts independent of these legendaries has been edited; see Reuter (1977: 603) and Williams-Krapp (1986: 395).

however, point to a version closely related to *BHL* 914 as the source, which, like the *Barbaren passie*, also specifies that the miraculous transformation of the shepherd's cattle is visible "usque in hodiernum diem."

Three other versions of the legend in verse are extant, but have not received scholarly attention (Reuter 1977: 603). One is found in Klosterneuburg, Stiftsbibliothek 1079, from the end of the fifteenth century, which also contains poetic retellings of the legends of Saint Margaret of Antioch and Saint Dorothy. The beginning of the poem in honor of Saint Barbara is as follows: "Gots genaden manigvalt / vns ist vor menig vngezalt" (Diemer 1853: 45). Another, *Von sant Barblen*, in High Alemannic, is preserved in St. Gallen, Stiftsbibliothek 592, a mid-fifteenth-century manuscript of *Die elsässische Legenda Aurea* (Kunze 1970: 273). The *incipit* of this text is as follows: "in gottes namen billich werd / in himel doert vnd hie vff erd / och willen han ze sagen hie / waz gelitten het vnd wie / sant barbra nach der geschrift ..." (Reuter 1977: 603). The third is preserved in Engelberg, Stiftsbibliothek 240, from 1478 (Williams-Krapp 1986: 40–41), which begins with the words: "Sant Barbara du edels vas / werd du als ich las / vol tugenden beliben / Als ich han geschriben" (Reuter 1977: 603).

Of note in this connection is also the Dominican Johannes Kirchschlag's sermon (ed. Eis 1959: 198–199) delivered on Saint Barbara's feast day to the nuns in the Saint Catherine convent in Nürnberg in 1486:

> Der wirdig vater Johannes de kirchslag, czu der czeit prior vnd leßmaister, predigt dicz an S. Barbara tag jm 86 jar.
> Die selbig iunckfraw S. Barbara, als jr lengere legent sagt, so hieß sie den tempel, den jr vater bestelt hett seinen aptgotten czu pawen, mit solcher vntterscheidt machen: Mitten scholt er weitt sein vnd scholt tzwo ab seytten haben. Daz betewttet nach jrer meinung, daz ein einiger got sey, der aller ding gewaltig wer. Daz betewt daz selbig weit im mittel; dy tzwo abseytten betewtten, daz den selben waren got wirt gedint in wurcken vnd beserychlichen leben. Vnd iij venster,

die ob allen andern venstern an hoh, groß vnd weitt gegen den auffgang der sunnen wern, daz czu bedewtten die heiligen drywaltigkeit, die da alle dinck erlewchten wer. Von den venstern allein sagt jr kurcze legent.

Nw mercket was von jrer großen marter. Jr vater czum ersten slug er sie selber mit rymen oder andern vnd hieß sie durch die gancze stat nacket zychen. Doczu preyttet sich jr schonnes hor vnd bedeckt allen jrn leib. Dar nach richt er sich mit guttem an sie. Da das nicht halff, zoch er sein swertt auß vnd wolt sie ertodt haben. Do thet sich die mawrn auff vnd entpfing sie denn. Der ein hirtt verriet sie, als jr gemeine legent sagt. Do sie ir vater vantt, zoch er sie pey dem hor vom perg vnd slug sie ser vnd antwurtt sie dem richter. Dier hieß sie auch grewlichen ser slahen mit..., also daz aller ihr leib verwuntt wartt, vnd die selben wunden mit heren tuchern zu reyben vnd in kercker stoßen. Do trostet sie vnser herr etc. Darnach hieß er sie pey den fußen auff hencken vnd mit krewllen allen jrn leib zu reißen vnd in jr wunden fewrige fackeln pusch oder sam lampen an allem jrn leib halten, und zu dießem ir hawbt mit einem hamer zu slahen, daz ir daz plut zu mundt, naßen, augen vnd oren außging. Darnach must sie auff scharpffe, ploße swert gen. Vnd nach dem allen todt sie ir eygen vater. Daz wir durch jr gepet zu ewigen vaterlant komen, des helff vns got. Amen.

As Eis (1959: 199) points out, the sermon is interesting in that it shows that Johannes Kirchschlag knew of a "lengere legent," a "kurcze legent," and a "gemeine legent" of Saint Barbara, and that he presupposed knowledge on the part of his audience of these versions. Eis notes, however, that the three-legend versions to which Kirchschlag refers cannot be identified until all the extant versions of the legend from the end of the fifteenth century have been examined.

A further testimony to Saint Barbara's popularity in Germany are the many folk beliefs associated with her feast day. Bender (1957: 1236) notes that on Saint Barbara's feast day, miners in the area of Salzburg received so-called "Barbarabrot" (Barbara-bread), and on "Saint Barbara's night" they put out food and drink for the

"Bergmandl."[45] To protect themselves from death in the mines, they lighted a so-called "Barbaralicht" (Barbara-candle).[46] Even today, according to Bender, cherry twigs ("Barbarazweige") are cut and placed in water so that they will flower by Christmas. The custom in Bohemia is to cut the twigs with one's back to the tree and dressed only in a shirt. In several places, including Austria, name tags are hung on the twigs; the one whose twig is the first to flower is believed to be assured good luck in the following year.[47] Peine (1896: 11) and Lapparent (1926: 29–30) also mention a herb with healing powers which was named after Saint Barbara, and Heilfurth lists a number of Saint Barbara songs (1956–1957: 18–23, 36–38, 40, 44, 49–53, 58–63).

The cult of Saint Barbara received more muted observance in England than on the Continent. Lockwood (1953–1954) notes that "[t]here is only one certain church dedication in her honour, that of Ashton-under-Hill, near Tewkesbury, but even this is to be attributed to French Augustinian monks at one time settled in neighbouring Beckford, whither they had moved from the convent of SS Martin and Barbara in Normandy. Only in the Norfolk area does a popular cult appear to have existed to any appreciable extent, though

45. See also Kirnbauer (1952: 32–33) and Heilfurth (1956–1957: 16–17).
46. See also Kirnbauer (1952: 32) and Heilfurth (1956–1957: 16).
47. Peine (1896: 1) and Kirnbauer (1952: 36) quote a verse by Martin Greif entitled "Barbarazweige." Küppers (1968) comments: "In Wirklichkeit hat der Barbarazweig eine ganz andere Herkunft. Wenn im November das Vieh von der Weide getrieben und in die Ställe geführt wurde, dann schnitt der Bauer Zweige von den Bäumen, um sie im warmen Stall oder in der Wohnstube zum Blühen zu bringen. Eine festgelegte Zeit bis zum Blühen war nicht vorgeschrieben, wohl aber versuchte man eine möglichst kurze Zeitspanne herauszuholen. Je nach der Schnelligkeit des Blühens und vor allem je nach dem Reichtum und der Fülle der Blüten schloß man auf den Segen in der Landwirtschaft für das kommende Jahr. Seit dem 15. und 16. Jahrhundert brachte man nun die Sitte des Zweigeschneidens mit dem bevorstehenden Weihnachtsfest in Verbindung und gab den hervorsprießenden Blüten eine spezielle Deutung auf das Christgeburtsfest hin. Da aber das Knospen und Blühen in den warmen Stuben oft sehr beschleunigt wurde, wählte man für den Termin des Einsteckens in Wasser das Fest der heiligen Barbara am 4. Dezember" (12–13).

this, too, may well have owed its origin to foreigners, in this case to the Flemings, ancient immigrants in East Anglia" (23).[48]

The legend of Saint Barbara, however, does make an appearance in the *Gilte Legende* and in William Caxton's *Golden Legend*. The *Gilte Legende*, a collection of 178 legends, is a translation made around 1438 of Jean de Vignay's *Légende Dorée*. Several later manuscripts of the *Gilte Legende* included saints' lives not found in the original. One of these lives is the legend of Saint Barbara found in London, Lambeth Palace Library 72, which also contains three other items not found in any other *Gilte Legende* manuscripts. These are, according to Görlach (1972: 19), a variant "Jerome," "Cayme," and the "Three Kings of Cologne." Görlach (1972: 19) notes that whereas "Cayme" is inserted at its appropriate place in the Old Testament history and merely reflects a general tendency to enlarge the biblical portions of legendaries, the other three texts are easily recognizable as additions by their disproportionately lengthy texts and their division into chapers, which are introduced by subheadings or résumés underlined in red: "Here begynneth the lyfe of seynt Barbara virgyn and martyr of crist and also of her kynrede in xvi chapiters And this is the fyrst folowynge ... ." Görlach (1972: 19) also argues that the legends of Saints Jerome and Barbara "frame" the manuscripts London, British Library Addit. 11565 and 35298, which contain all the texts of London, Lambeth Palace Library 72 except the four.[49] In Görlach's opin-

---

48. Lockwood (1953–1954) further draws attention to the dedication to Saint Barbara of Haceby Church near Grantham: "The meagreness of the records of this old church leaves room for doubt as to the authenticity of the present dedication to St. Barbara, as quoted, for example, in Crockford's *Clerical Directory* for 1951–2, but it is worth noting that as early as Domesday Book land at *Hazebi* was held by the powerful adventurer Gilbert de Gand who came over with the Conqueror" (23).

49. Görlach (1972) says: "[T]he legends of *Jerome* and *Barbara* 'frame' the *ALL* [London, British Library Addit. 11565 and 35298], *Jerome* preceding them on 188v-, and *Barbara* following after *Becket* on 251v; the *Three Kings of Cologne* are appended at the end of MS L [London, Lambeth Palace Library 72], ff. 437r–461r: all are thus found in makeshift positions typical of later additions" (19).

ion, the legends of Saints Jerome and Barbara and the "Three Kings of Cologne" were composed before the *Gilte Legende* and were copied without any deliberate alterations into the ancestor of London, Lambeth Palace Library 72.

The legend of Saint Barbara is also preserved in Durham, University Library Cosin V.iv.4. Görlach (1972), who notes that there are only minor verbal differences between the text of the legend in London, Lambeth Palace Library 72 and that of the legend in Durham, University Library Cosin V.iv.4, says about this version: "Like *Jerome* the legend has an original preface, which specially mentions Augustine and Brigit, and therefore seems to have been written for Syon; as in the case of *Jerome*, the L [London, Lambeth Palace Library 72] compiler omitted the preface when he included the legend in the *Gil[te Legende]*, but otherwise did not alter the text" (20n6).

The French *Légende Dorée* was modified twice during the fifteenth century: first around 1420 when forty-two "Festes Nouvelles" were added, and again sometime in the last decades of the century, when the traditional order of the chapters was altered and several additional saints' lives were incorporated. It is this revised collection that William Caxton (ca. 1422–1491) set out to translate in his *Golden Legend,* the last full-scale hagiographical compendium published in England before the Reformation, which was first issued from Caxton's press at Westminster in 1483. Although the *Légende Dorée* forms the basis of the *Golden Legend,* it is clear that Caxton also made use of the *Gilte Legende*, that is, one of the expanded versions – and one closely related to London, British Library Addit. 35298 – and the *Legenda Aurea*, especially for texts not contained in the *Légende Dorée*. Concerning the legend of Saint Barbara, it seems that he did not rely on the *Légende Dorée* or the *Legenda Aurea*, for the legend exhibits virtually all of the features characteristic of the *BHL* 913 or 914 versions, above all the lack of any mention of Saint Barbara's correspondence with Origen.

1.2 Artistic Representations of the Legend

Saint Barbara became a favorite subject especially of Flemish and Italian, but also German, artists in the fifteenth and sixteenth centuries. Jan van Eyck (1390–1441), Matteo di Giovanni (1433–1495), Rosselli di Cosimo (1439–1507), Botticelli (1445–1510), Hans Holbein the Elder (ca. 1465–1524), Tilmann Riemenschneider (ca. 1468–1531), Albrecht Dürer (1471–1528), Lucas Cranach the Elder (1472–1553), Lorenzo Lotto (ca. 1480–1556), Jacopo Palma Vecchio (1480–1528), Raffael (1483–1520), Bernadino Luini (d. 1532), and Giovanni Battista Moroni (ca. 1525–1578), to mention but a few, all represented Saint Barbara in their art. The painting of her by Jan van Eyck in the Musée Royal des Beaux-Arts at Antwerp and the fresco by Matteo di Giovanni in the Chiesa di S. Domenico in Siena are probably the most famous representations.

Saint Barbara is usually presented as a well-dressed young woman (in keeping with her father's legendary status). Braun (1943: 115) notes that until the late fifteenth century, at least in Germany, Saint Barbara is depicted in a belted, ankle-length dress with a cape draped over her shoulders. The influence of specific fashions of dress is not noticeable until after the end of the fifteenth century. Around that time, she also begins to appear with a headdress, whereas previously she had been depicted bareheaded (Petzoldt 1973: 305).

In most of the later representations of Saint Barbara, she is wearing a crown, as in Raffael's painting in the Gemäldegalerie in Dresden (Küppers 1968: 55, fig.),[50] or, occasionally, a diadem or a wreath of flowers, as in Jan van Eyck's famous representation (Bol 1965: 70, fig.; Küppers 1968: 35, fig.). A palm also makes its appearance now and then as one of her attributes, as, for example, in Giovanni Battista Moroni's painting in the Pinacoteca di Brera in Milan (Gordini and Aprile 1962: 761–762, fig.). The crown and the palm both symbolize her martyrdom. A book, as in Jan van Eyck's representation or on the triptych in the Wallraf-Richartz-Museum in Cologne by the "Master of the Holy Family," where

50. Cf. Gaiffier (1958: 22).

Saint Barbara appears in the company of Saints Bruno, Dorothy, and Hugh of Lincoln (Braun 1943: 154, fig. 69; Küppers 1968: 51, fig.), does not appear until the late fifteenth century and is rather uncommon.[51] Of a fairly late date is also a sword.

As far as Saint Barbara's more specialized attributes are concerned, the oldest representation of the saint, an eighth-century fresco in the Santa Maria Antiqua, associates her with the peacock (Grüneisen 1911: 100, 220, fig. 169, plate XVIII), a symbol of apotheosis and immortality. Her best known emblem, however, is a tower, as exemplified by Stephan Lochner's (d. ca. 1451) painting in the Wallraf-Richartz-Museum in Cologne (Küppers 1968: 47, fig.). The tower, which may be either round or square, often has three windows symbolizing the Trinity. Sometimes Saint Barbara is holding a miniature tower in her hand, as in Raffael's painting, at other times a large tower is placed next to or behind her, as in Jacopo Palma Vecchio's representation in the Santa Maria Formosa in Venice (Küppers 1968: 59 fig.; Mariacher 1968: 16 fig.).

While the tower is both the oldest and the most common of Saint Barbara's more individual attributes, a chalice with or without the host, symbolizing her protection against sudden death, that is, before having received the Eucharist, is not uncommon, but does not appear regularly until the fifteenth century.[52] Sometimes Saint Barbara is holding the chalice in her hand, as in Lucas

51. Braun (1943: 115) believes that the book represents the Gospels. Hallberg *et al.* (1967: 123) think that the book refers to Saint Barbara's keen study of Scripture and/or her correspondence with Origen.

52. Cf. Weale (1872–1873): "Ce sont des allusions à la faveur qu'elle reçut au moment de son martyre, que tous ceux qui invoqueraient le nom de Jésus en se recommandant à elle, obtiendraient la grâce d'une bonne mort. Or, comme ceux qui meurent avec les derniers sacrements ont le plus d'espoir d'être sauvés, Sainte Barbe fut invoquée à cette fin. Un miracle remarquable arrivé à Gorcum en Hollande le 28 Août 1448, contribua beaucoup à l'adoption de cette pratique" (13). A man named Henry Kock was nearly burnt to death in a fire at Gorkum. He called on Saint Barbara, to whom he had always shown great devotion. She aided him to escape from the burning house and kept him alive until he could receive the last sacrament (Villemot 1864: 146–147; Kirsch 1907: 285).

Cranach the Elder's famous painting in the Gemäldegalerie in Dresden (Gordini and Aprile 1962: 765–766, fig.; Küppers 1968: 67, fig.), at other times it appears in the window or door opening of the tower, as in Lucas Cranach the Elder's woodcut in the Wittenberg *Heiltumsbuch* from 1509 (Schade 1980: fig. 31b). Braun (1943: 116) comments that if Saint Barbara is depicted with both a tower and a chalice, she is usually holding the chalice in her hand while the tower is placed next to her, as on the inner wing of the altar in Oberstadion, Oberamt Ehingen (Württburg), from 1458 (Braun 1943: 76, fig. 30). Exceptions are found, however, as on the painting of Saints Ursula, Gertrude of Nivelles, Apollonia, Catherine of Alexandria, Barbara, Dorothy, Bridget of Ireland, and Cecilia by the "Master of Saint Severin" in Cologne from the end of the fifteenth century, where the chalice is placed in the door opening of a miniature tower in Saint Barbara's hand (Braun 1943: 154, fig. 68).

Less common attributes are a burning torch and the figure of Saint Barbara's father Dioscorus at her feet. Both of these attributes are, naturally, derived from her legend. The former refers to the scene in which the prefect holds burning torches to her sides; the latter symbolizes her victory over paganism. A burning torch appears in a tapestry, where Saint Barbara is found in the company of Saints Benedicta, Christina, Apollonia, Catherine of Alexandria, Reparata, and Fausta, from Neuburg an der Donau from around 1425, now in the Kunstgewerbemuseum in Cologne (Braun 1943: 118, fig. 50; Küppers 1968: 23, fig.). Braun (1943: 116) notes that this is the only example known to him in Germany; in Italian depictions of Saint Barbara, several examples are found (see Petzoldt 1973: 306–307). The figure of Dioscorus is found on the wing of a triptych in Aachen, Münster, from around 1510, where Saint Barbara appears in the company of Saints Antonius of Rivoli and Sebastian (Braun 1943: 100, fig. 43) and in Rosselli di Cosimo's painting in the Galleria dell'Accademia in Florence (Lapparent 1926: 29 fig.; Gordini and Aprile 1962: 763–764, fig.). This attribute does not appear until the late fifteenth century and turned out to be shortlived.

In the Low Countries, Saint Barbara is sometimes depicted holding the feather of either an ostrich or a peacock.[53] The attribute appears to be unique to this area.[54] Gaiffier (1958) argues that it has its origin in the *Dicta Origenis de beata Barbara*, which reports that the Savior appears in the likeness of a child to the future martyr and gives her as a symbol of virginity the feather of an ostrich, which, according to Origen, surpasses all other animals in dignity. In Gaffier's view "[c]es textes éclairent parfaitement le problème iconographique. ... Barbe porte une plume d'autruche comme symbole de sa virginité et de son élection aux divines épousailles. Ce n'est guère que dans les Pays-Bas que se rencontre l'attribut de la plume d'autruche sur les peintures consacrées à sainte Barbe" (22).[55]

Some artists focused on individual episodes from Saint Barbara's legend. The most common scenes are: Saint Barbara's baptism, the construction of the tower, the addition of a third window, Saint Barbara's argument with her father, Saint Barbara's escape, the shepherd's betrayal, the trial, the tortures of Saint Barbara, and Saint Barbara's execution (Petzoldt 1973: 309). Of these, the oldest is Saint Barbara's execution, which often appears on altarpieces. These typically show Saint Barbara kneeling with her father with his sword raised and pagan priests, who attempt to force her to worship an idol, at her side, as in Lorenzo Lotto's "Storia delle vita di santa Barbara" in the Capella Suardi in Trescorre (Bergamo) (Küppers 1968: 27, fig.).

53. See Petzoldt (1973: 306).
54. Cf. Braun (1943): "Für die Angabe, die Heilige werde auch mit Pfauenfedern in der Hand abgebildet ... ist mir im Bereich der deutschen Kunst kein Beleg begegnet" (118).
55. Cf. Petzoldt (1973): "Nach anderer Erklärung (nicht i. d. Leg. belegt) sollen sich d. Ruten b. d. Geißelung i. Federn verwandelt haben" (306). See also Weale (1872–1873: 16–18).

2 SAINT BARBARA IN THE NORTH

2.0 The Cult and Legend in Scandinavia

There is little evidence of the veneration of Saint Barbara in Scandinavia before the mid-fourteenth century.[56] The earliest recording of her feast day (4 December) is in the *Vallentuna Missal* from around 1198 (ed. Schmid 1945: 94, 129). In the charters, Saint Barbara's feast day is not attested until 1348 in the archdiocese of Lund and 1352 in the diocese of Strängnäs. It is clear, however, that by then the cult of Saint Barbara was well established in Lund. When on 1 September 1145 the high altar and the right-hand side altar were consecrated in the cathedal of Lund, relics were deposited in both (*SRD* 8: 448, 452); a relic of Saint Barbara was deposited in the side altar dedicated to Saints Vincent and Alban (*SRD* 3: 456; Weibull 1923: 92; Hallberg *et al.* 1967: 101). Saint Barbara's feast day is also found in virtually all of the Latin rhymed calendars (cisiojani) preserved in Scandinavia (see Odenius 1959) and is included also on the runic calendar from Gotland from 1328 (NkS 203 8vo; ed. Lithberg and Wessén 1939: 13, 111) as well as on later Swedish runic sticks (see Lithberg 1934: 77–94) and Danish and Swedish pictorial calendars.[57] Despite these references, Saint Barbara does not appear regularly in the liturgical sources until after 1400. Her feast day is not included in the *Linköping Ordinary* from around 1400 (ed. Helander 1957), and the exclusion of Saints Barbara and Bridget in the *Hemsjö Manual* (ed. Johansson 1950) leads its editor to postulate the late fourteenth century or the early fifteenth century as the date of its composition (74).[58]

---

56. Here and in the following I rely on Hallberg *et al.* (1967: 100–106).

57. For example, NkS 901 8vo from 1513 (see Børthy 1966: 79 fig.), Stockholm, Statens Historiska Museum nos. 21280–21282, UUB A 307a, and Linköping, Stiftsbibliotek J 79 (see Hallberg *et al.* 1967: 101n25). On these, Saint Barbara's feast day is marked with a tower.

58. Concerning Saint Barbara, Johansson (1950) says: "Den definitiva tidsbestämningen ge två viktiga helgon, som saknas i HM [*Hemsjö Manual*], nämligen *Barbara* och *Birgitta*. Den förstnämnda tillhör de tidigare omtalade

A letter of 8 December 1411 written at Queen Margrethe's (1353–1412) request provides an interesting example of the increase in Saint Barbara's popularity in Scandinavia in the early fifteenth century. In this letter, Abbot Salomon and Abbot Niels of the Cistercian monasteries in Esrom and Sorø, respectively, promise in return for a handsome sum of money to send pilgrims to no less than forty-four named places of pilgrimage in Denmark and abroad and to have these journeys completed within two years. One person, according to the letter, was to be sent to where Saint Barbara reposes ("thiit som sancta Barbara ligger").[59] Liebgott (1982: 38) comments on the unusual nature of this pilgrimage and notes that if indeed it was carried out, a small number of pilgrims would presumably have visited several places of pilgrimage en route; if forty-four pilgrims were sent out simultaneously, a couple of monasteries would easily have been depopulated. That at least one Dane, the nobleman Christen Skeel (1603–1659), made it to Italy and viewed Saint Barbara's relics is known from his travelogue from 1619–1627 (ed. Tomner 1962). In 1626, he visited the "Templum Mariæ Annunciatæ" in Naples, where in the sacristy he saw twelve reliquaries in the form of head and shoulder portraits of

---

quattuor virgines. Redan det faktum, att tre helgon av denna grupp äro med i litanian, medan den fjärde saknas, tyder på, att HM bör vara sammanställt vid en tidpunkt, då kulten av denna helgongrupp håller på att slå igenom. Barbara är med i Strängnäskalendarier från 1300-talets slut och förekommer i dateringar vid 1400-talets början. Hennas namn saknas dock ännu i sådana tidiga litanior som [SKB] A 97 [= *Missale Lincopense*] och [UUB] C 421 [= *Collectarium Dominicanum diocesis Aboensis*] men är sekundärt insatt i den senare. Icke heller i finska kalendrar återfinnes hon vid denna tid. I Skara stift har hon livligt dyrkats. I målningar från 1400-talets senare hälft är hon representerad, och i breviariets litania har hon åkallats" (73).

59. Liebgott (1982: 38) considers this place to be Rome. Hallberg *et al.* (1967: 189), however, argue in favor of Venice, which was widely known for its relics of Saint Barbara, and refer among other things to GkS 3041 8vo from the 1490s. This manuscript contains a section on "De reliquiis pretiosis et uenerandis que habentur Veneciis," and in this section it is related that in a monastery in Venice Saint Barbara's body is preserved ("in quo corpus sancte barbare requiescit in quadam capella marmoreo quodam sarcophago").

saints ("12 skabe med Helligers brystbilleder aff sölff oc forgylt" [73]). One of these he describes as Barbara whose head smells from having been embalmed ("Barbaræ martyris, huiss hoffuedt luchter aff ded, ded er balsomieridt" 73; Hallberg *et al.* 1967: 189).

Around the same time, that is, the early fifteenth century, Saint Barbara's feast day begins to appear in letters of indulgence among the days on which the privileges of the indulgences are to be granted. Among the many examples listed by Hallberg *et al.* (1967: 107–110) can be mentioned a letter of 4 May 1418, in which seven cardinals in Konstanz each granted an indulgence of one hundred days at the altar of Saint Bridget in Vadstena. The indulgence was to be granted on the feast days of, among others, Saints George, Catherine of Alexandria, Barbara, and Margaret of Antioch. For the benefit of the Saint Gertrude chapel outside of Kalmar, the bishop of Linköping granted on 31 March 1444 a forty days' indulgence, and also in this letter Saint Barbara's feast day is mentioned. The same bishop granted in a letter of 16 December 1447 the same privilege on Saint Barbara's feast day to devout visitors to the church of Norra Vi.

A further testimony to the increase in Saint Barbara's popularity in the fifteenth century is the establishment of altars dedicated to her.[60] In 1461, Hartvik Krumedike of Akershus established for his wife and other family members an altar in the cathedral in Oslo in honor of Saints Bartholomew and Barbara, at which votive masses were to be said on Sundays, Wednesdays, and Fridays for all Christian souls:

> Fore alla gudz winer som nw åro ådher her efter fødhas kungiør ek Hartik Krummedik riddare oc høuitzman vppa Akersshws at gudi till lof oc ære fore myna oc mynnæ kære hustrv frv Kadrin Marquardzdotter Marquardh Buk hustrv Sigriidh Olaff Buk oc alla andra beggis wara forelder siæle, haffuer ek nu mæd birath moodh betheinkt at stikta eit altare

---

60. Here and in the following I rely on Hallberg *et al.* (1967: 107–110).

i Oslo domkirkio i sancti Bartholomei oc sancte Barbare heidher ther hwar wiko mæd sunnodagx møsso skulu holdes møssor hwar odensdagh oc hwar fredagh æwinneligha fore alla crisna sæle (*DN* II 838: 627–628).

At the initiative of Canon Mogens Kempe, her mass was introduced on 27 October 1476 in the cathedral of Lund, in which, according to the diocese's printed calendar, it was celebrated as a duplex. From a letter of 9 May 1505, it is known that Canon Olof Esbernsen planned to establish an altar in that cathedral in honor of the Virgin Mary and Saints Christopher and Barbara. This interest in Saint Barbara in Lund is no doubt due to the presence of her relics in the cathedral. One such relic was mentioned above; another relic was kept in one of the three reliquaries on the high altar. Barbara Brahe, the wife of Stig Olufsen Krognos of Bollerup and one of the first women in Scania known to carry Saint Barbara's name, personally did much to promote the veneration of her name saint: she donated to the cathedral a picture of Saint Barbara made of silver, which contained several valuable relics of various saints (cf. *SRD* 8: 455: "In ymagine argentea sancte barbare, quam contulit nobilis matrona domina barbara relicta domini stigoti militis"), and was also responsible for the introduction of three masses at Saint Barbara's altar in the Franciscan monastery church in Malmö. Other churches containing altars dedicated to Saint Barbara include Saint Peter's church in Malmö, the Carmelite monastery church in Landskrona, the cathedral in Åbo, the Marian church in Åhus, Saint Nicholas's church in Halmstad, the cathedral in Ribe, the cathedral in Roskilde, and the Marian church (Vor Frue Kirke) in Copenhagen. The last-mentioned church, which owned more than 200 relics, possessed five relics of Saint Barbara (*SRD* 8: 260–268; Liebgott 1982: 118–128). One of these relics was preserved in a glass reliquary ("In amphora vitrea") also containing relics of Saints Mary Magdalen, Apollonia, Ursula, Dorothy, and Margaret of Antioch. Another was kept in a tower dedicated to Saint Anthony ("In turri Sancti Anthonii cum cristallo & una campana"), which contained relics of also a number of other saints, including Saints Bridget and Christopher. While the sources do not specify the nature of these relics, it is known from an inventory of around 2 July 1517 of the relics of the cathedral in Stavanger that the cathedral owned a piece of "sancte Barbare kyortil" (*DN* IV 1074: 790), which Bishop Hoskold himself had brought home from Rome.[61] It is further known that the Franciscans in Copenhagen owned three relics of Saint Barbara, including a lock of her hair ("De capillis Sanctæ Barbaræ Virginis" [*SRD* 8: 283]). And the Franciscans in Roskilde, who had in their possession no fewer than six relics of Saint Barbara, were proud owners of a piece of her head ("Item de Capite Sanctæ Barbaræ" [*SRD* 8: 274]), which was kept in a richly ornamented shrine ("In Scrinio cum lapidibus & ymaginibus cum littera F.").

The Saint Barbara guilds in Scandinavia date from the latter half of the fifteenth and the sixteenth centuries. From two letters dated 6 February 1497 and 10 February 1498 (ed. Nyrop 1899–1900: 231–235, nos. 36 and 37), it is known that there was a Saint Barbara guild in Randers. In the former letter, the provincial of the Franciscan province of friars in Denmark gives the members of the Saint Barbara guild a share of the order's good deeds; in the latter, the prior of the so-called Helligåndshus in Randers includes the members of the guild in the circle of those who have benefited from the hospitallers' good deeds. Three Saint Barbara guilds are known to have existed in Sweden: one in Stockholm, first mentioned in 1452,[62] another in Halmstad, first mentioned in 1500, and a third in Nyköping, first mentioned in 1546 (Hallberg *et al.* 1967: 113).

Saint Barbara is frequently depicted in Scandinavian churches. Normally, she is wearing a crown and surrounded by a halo; representations of Saint Barbara bare-headed and with her hair down, as on the little figurine in the altar cabinet in the church of Amsberg, Dalarna (Hallberg *et al.* 1967: 126, fig. 20), are rare. She

61. See Hallberg *et al.* (1967: 190).
62. For a discussion of this guild, see Brun (1917: 72–78).

is usually holding a tower, as in one of the oldest representations of Saint Barbara in Scandinavia, a fresco from around 1300 in the tower of the church of Tingstäda, Gotland (Hallberg *et al.* 1967: 99, fig. 7). As is common in the oldest depictions of the saint, the tower is small and narrow and usually has a pointed spire (the cupola on the fresco in Tingstäda is an exception), as on the inside of one of the doors of a sacrament-niche in the choir of the church of Gothem, Gotland (Curman and Roosval 1959–1964: 87, fig. 107; Hallberg *et al.* 1967: 102, fig. 8) from the early fourteenth century. Later representations of Saint Barbara show a tendency to make the tower more naturalistic, for example by making it larger and by placing it behind Saint Barbara, as on the door of the altar cabinet in the church of Västra Ed, Småland, from 1526 (Hallberg *et al.* 1967: 145, fig. 27). In some instances, the tower is furnished with a little front building, which is obviously the bath house mentioned in the legend, as in the fresco in the now demolished church in Bunkeflo, Scania (Hallberg *et al.* 1967: 152, fig. 34). The tower (or bath house) is often depicted with three windows, as on the door of the later altar cabinet in the cathedral of Strängnäs (Hallberg *et al.* 1967: 139, fig. 25); sometimes a chalice, with or without the host, is placed in the window or door opening of the tower, as on the door of a reliquary cabinet in the church of Västra Ed (Hallberg *et al.* 1967: 144, fig. 28). Occasionally, Saint Barbara is holding the chalice in her hand, as on the fresco in the choir in the church of Hald, Jutland, from ca. 1520 (Saxtorph 1967: 302); Hallberg *et al.* (1967: 121) note, however, that this is a late feature.

Quite often, Saint Barbara is depicted holding also the palm of martyrdom, as on the fresco in the cathedral in Århus (Liebgott 1982: 79, fig.; Saxtorph 1967: 342) or the above-mentioned door of the altar cabinet in the cathedral of Strängnäs. A book is also relatively common, as on the door of a reliquary cabinet in the church of Västra Ed (see above).

A rather uncommon attribute is a sword. When it does appear, it never serves as the only attribute, however, and is usually accompanied by a tower, as on the fresco in the church of Kumla, Västmanland (Hallberg *et al.* 1967: 152, fig. 35), or a palm and a book, as on the engraving on the foot of the chalice in the church of Ärentuna, Uppland (Hallberg *et al.* 1967: 114, fig. 15).

Often Saint Barbara is depicted in the company of other female saints, usually the three other "virgines capitales," as in, for example, the church of Tortuna, Västmanland (Cornell and Wallin 1953: 11, fig. 4), the church of Hattula in Finland (Nilsén 1986: 379, fig. 250), or the church of Tensta, Uppland (Cornell and Wallin 1933: 79, fig. 1). She is also found together with other saints, however, as in, for example, the church of Kongens Lyngby, Zealand, where the Trinity is surrounded by Saints Dorothy, Barbara, Ursula, and an unidentified female saint (Saxtorph 1967: 90); the church of Råby, Jutland, where she appears together with Saints Apollonia, Christina or Agatha, Catherine of Alexandria, Dorothy, Gertrude, and Juliana (Saxtorph 1967: 308); and in the church of Bunkeflo, Scania, where she is found together with the Virgin Mary and Saints Catherine of Alexandria, Dorothy, Margaret of Antioch, Ursula, and Mary Magdalen (Rydbeck 1904: 68). Saints Dorothy and Catherine of Alexandria seem to be rather frequent companions of Barbara. Saint Barbara and Saint Dorothy are depicted on, for example, the inside of one of the doors of a reliquary cabinet in the choir of the churches of Gothem, Gotland (see above), and Sorunda, Södermanland (Lindblom 1916: 27, fig. 16), on the altar cabinet (now lost through fire) in the church of Aspeboda, Dalarna (Hallberg *et al.* 1967: 127, fig. 22), and also on the altar cabinets in the churches of Romfartuna, Västmanland (Hallberg *et al.* 1967: 147, fig. 29), Ekerö, Uppland, and Tierp, Uppland (Hallberg *et al.* 1967: 140). In the three last-mentioned examples, Saints Barbara and Dorothy are depicted on each side of the Madonna; a similar arrangement appears also on the altar cabinet of the church of Valö, Uppland (Hallberg *et al.* 1967: 109, fig. 12), although here they are in the company of also the two other "virgines capitales." Saint Barbara and Saint Catherine of Alexandria appear together on, for example, the frescos in the churches of Löt in the Mälar area (Nilsén 1986: 116, fig. 58), Nødebo, Zealand, and Lem and Åle, Jutland (Saxtorph 1967: 97, 304, 338).

Some artists focused on individual episodes from the legend of Saint Barbara. Her execution is depicted, for example, on an altar cabinet in the church of Kuddby, Östergötland (Hallberg *et al.* 1967: 94, fig. 4), and was frescoed also by the painter Johannes Ivan in 1451 in the church of Vendel, Uppland (Hallberg *et al.* 1967: 91, fig. 3). The most famous depiction is, however, the retable from Kalanti (earlier Nykyrko), now in the National Museum of Finland in Helsinki, made around 1420 by the famous painter in Hamburg, Master Francke. A triptych with double wings, it contains a pictorial series in eight parts depicting the legend of Saint Barbara on the inner panels of the outwings and on the outer panels of the inner wings (illustrated in Pylkkänen 1966 and Küppers 1968: 15). When the inner wings of the retable are opened, a series of scenes from the life of the Virgin Mary are revealed. As Pylkkänen (1966) observes: "Although the liturgically more valuable series of reliefs of the life of the Virgin Mary were displayed on festive occasions, the retable has become famous for the painted pictorial series of Saint Barbara." The series depicts: (1) Saint Barbara arguing with her father about the three windows; (2) her miraculous escape through the wall from Dioscorus, who clenches his fist and raises his sword; (3) Dioscorus's pursuit and the shepherd's betrayal; (4) her imprisonment; (5) her trial; (6) her tortures (a burly executioner beats the saint with a knotted cord while another slices off her breast); (7) her hanging at the gallows and being scorched by burning sheaves of straw; and, finally, (8) her execution.

No church bells carrying Saint Barbara's name are in evidence in Scandinavia. It should be noted, however, that her name appears on the rim of the Mary Magdalen bell cast in 1462 by the founder Herman for the Saint Nicholas church in Burg (Femern) (Uldall 1982: 191). Moreover, a depiction of what is probably Saint Barbara is found in the inscription of the Virgin Mary bell built in

1490 by the same Herman for the church of Garyp in Friesland. The bell is now in the Saint Nicholas church in Bested (Åbenrå); she is depicted holding a tower in her left hand and what is possibly a book in her right hand (Uldall 1982: 194).

A female saint holding a tower on the seal of Olæf Laurensøn, priest in Førsløff in Ringsted parish (1459), has lead one scholar to identify the saint as Barbara (Petersen 1883: no. 407). This is the only extant seal bearing witness to the veneration of Saint Barbara in what is now Denmark. In Sweden, several seals have been preserved.[63] The oldest seal is that of Barbara Thomasdotter, the first person in Scandinavia known to have carried the saint's name.[64] Her seal, which consists of a large crowned B, was used in 1390 (Hallberg *et al.* 1967: 172, fig. 50a). The second oldest seal is that of Ivar Eriksson, priest at Kopparbjerget, used in 1427. It is more ornate, depicting a crowned Saint Barbara standing beneath a Gothic baldachin with a tower in her left hand (Hallberg *et al.* 1967: 172, fig. 50b). On the seals of Sven Magnusson, dean in Uppsala (1470, 1472, and 1475), Helge Pettersson, dean in Strängnäs (1467, 1482, 1483, 1484, 1485, 1487, and 1491), Alf Henningsson, canon in Stockholm (1475), and Sven Eriksson, priest in Snöstorp (1494), Saint Barbara is also shown holding a palm (Hallberg *et al.* 1967: 173–174, fig. 52a–b, 54b). The first two mentioned are almost identical and may have been fabricated by the same person (Hallberg *et al.* 1967: 155–156). The seal of Sven Eriksson is striking for its depiction of Saint Barbara trampling on Dioscorus. Depictions of the saint with her less common attributes – a chalice, or a branch with flowers, or a book – are also found on the Swedish seals of Olof Eriksson, priest in Bälinge, Uppland (1487), and of Nicolaus Olaui, prior of the Dominican monastery in Sigtuna (1492) (Hallberg *et al.* 1967: 174 fig. 54a and 55a). The most

63. Here and in the following I rely on Hallberg *et al.* (1967: 154–160).
64. Otterbjörk (1981: 144). In Denmark, the name is not attested until 1437 (Knudsen and Kristensen 1936–1948: 1, 95). Norwegian occurrences of the name are all of a later date (Lind 1905–1915: 110).

impressive of the extant seals is, however, the seal of Birger Mag-
nusson, Bishop of Västerås (1462–1464), used in 1463 (Hallberg *et
al.* 1967: 172, fig. 51). The Virgin Mary holding the Child Jesus
occupies the center of the seal; both figures are surrounded by
church buildings with towers and chapels. John the Baptist and
what is most likely Abbot David of Munktorp are shown standing
in the entrances of the buildings on either side of the Madonna.
Saint Barbara appears under a round arch beneath the Virgin
Mary's feet; she is surrounded by a halo, and holds a palm in her
right hand and a chalice in her left.

Saint Barbara's popularity in Scandinavia may be attributed to
her status as one of the holy helpers, whose cult was, as noted
above, particularly strong in the fifteenth century. The extant
Scandinavian books of prayers and hours include a number of
prayers to the holy helpers, all of which include Saint Barbara.[65]
Indeed, *Anna Brade's Prayer Book* contains a prayer to Saint Barbara specifically in her function as a holy helper (ed. Nielsen 1946–
1963: 2, no. 298):

> hær efftherscriues een bøn aff then værdighe nødhhielperske
> *sanc*ta barbara for brad dødh
>
> O Glædes *sanc*ta barbara forthi tw æst eth blomster effter
> iomfru maria*m* / tek openbared*is* all the hellige trefollighedh

---

65. *Johanne Nielsdatter's Book of Hours* (SKB A 42 from ca. 1480) contains
"ien mygh*et* god bøn aff the xv nødhielpær" (ed. Nielsen 1946–1963: 1, no.
59), which lists the following: George, Blaise, Erasmus, Pantaleon, Vitus,
Christopher, Denys, Cyricus, Eustace, Magnus, Giles, Catherine of Alexandria, Margaret of Antioch, and Barbara. She is also included among the holy
helpers in the prayer "Aff the xv nødhhielpere hwo them pakaller i syn nødh
me*th* gudelighedh tha fanger han hielp til vissæ til liiff oc siæl" in *Anna
Brade's Prayer Book* (Thott 553 4to from 1497; ed. Nielsen 1946–1963: 2, no.
328) and in similar prayers in *Karen Ludvigsdatter's Book of Hours* (LUB 25
8vo from ca. 1500; ed. Nielsen 1946–1963: 1, no. 152), Christiern Pedersen's
Bønnebog i at høre messe (1514; ed. Nielsen 1946–1963: 4, no. 1174), and
Ingegärd Ambjörnsdotter's Prayer Book (SKB A 43 from the beginning of the
sixteenth century; ed. Geete 1907–1909: no. 166).

/ tw vast slagen m*eth* tiwræ senær / oc gneden m*eth* harclæde offue*r* thit legemæ / och gøden m*eth* blodh / thine spene afskorne oc vthførdh aff thine clæder / vden thw iførdis skynnende hwide clæder tilborne aff ænglene Tw pyntes oc plagdes aff thin fader dyoscoro / Mæn tw glæd*is* nw m*eth* vor herræ ih*es*u *christ*o / vær for oss til gudh een myldh fortalerske

Versiculus O iomf*ru* sa*n*cta barbara gudz vtualde fyne pærlæ bedh for oss til gudh / Ath wi matte vorde værdige *christ*i nadhe

colle*c*ta

O herre gudh wi bedhe / ath sa*n*cta barbara iomfrues oc thin æræfullæ martir*is* bøn skal beware oss af ondæ vanfrydh / oc the*n*ne værildens fattigdom / oc aff bradh oc vforsynligh dødh / oc aff allæ genwordige tingh / ath wi for he*n*nis bøn matte forskylde værdelighe ath fange vor herris ih*es*u *christ*i legemæ oc blodz vnfangelse / Veth then sa*m*me vor herræ ih*es*um *christ*um Ame*n*

Other prayers to Saint Barbara are found in Danish and Swedish prayer books. The longest prayer is the one contained in *Visdoms Spejl* (AM 782 4to from the beginning of the sixteenth century; ed. Nielsen 1946–1963: 3, no. 535).[66] The legend of Saint Barbara told in this prayer appears to be based on a source closely related to *BHL* 916. Thus Nicomedia is said to be the place of Saint Barbara's martyrdom, and, as in *BHL* 916, Saint Barbara is baptized by the priest Valentinus. In contrast to *BHL* 916, however, the prayer in *Visdoms Spejl* includes reference to Diocletian. Moreover, we learn that when Saint Barbara's father in his anger wanted to kill her, the tower bent down for her, so that she could walk out of the window and flee to the desert: "men tornyth bøyde sygh neder thil iorden med teg, oc thw gick vth at vindwet oc flyde for tÿn fader vdy ørkenet och skwlde teck the*r*" (186).[67]

66. The prayer is found also in AM 784 4to.
67. This scene is depicted in tempera on wood from ca. 1470 by an unknown German artist (see Kirnbauer 1952: 26, fig.). Accordingly, the detail about the tower bending down for Barbara must have appeared in versions

Finally, the prayer omits any reference to Saint Barbara's return to and execution by her father; it merely states that the judge ("ræt-ter") ordered her head to be cut off with a sword: "lod hand hwgge tith hoffwet aff m*eth* eth swærd" (187). The account con-cludes with a plea for Saint Barbara's intercession ("Bed for oss iomfrw sancta barbara at vÿ motte vorde verdige at fange hemer-iges glæde" [187]) and a "collecta": "Gwd thw som haffwer giffwet the*nn*e hellige iomfrw sancta barbara som thith naffn haffwer bekent oc stor martir oc pine haffwer lyth for tyn skyld, vy bede deg alle at vy for hendes verskyld motte fange nade at frelses aff all vkristelig død oc fraa all nød bode thil lyff oc siell, amen" (187).

Shorter prayers to Saint Barbara are found in *Johanne Niels-datter's Book of Hours* (ed. Nielsen 1946–1963: 1, no. 65), *Karen Ludvigsdatter's Book of Hours* (ed. Nielsen 1946–1963: 1, no. 161),[68] AM 418 12mo from around 1500 (ed. Nielsen 1946–1963: 2, no. 383), AM 75 8vo from ca. 1500 (ed. Nielsen 1946–1963: 3, no. 418), AM 72 8vo from the fifteenth century (ed. Nielsen 1946–1963: 4, no. 1075), *Ingeborg Predbjørnsdatter's Book of Hours* (ed. Nielsen 1946–1963: 4, no. 916),[69] and *Märita Thuresdotter's Prayer Book* (SKB A 37 from ca. 1500; ed. Geete 1907–1909: no. 181).[70]

---

of her legend circulating in Germany and Scandinavia. Indeed, Heilfurth (1956–1957) cites the episode "[n]ach einem Legendar aus dem späten 15. Jh., vgl.: Der Heiligen Leben und Leiden anders genannt das Passional. Leipzig 1913, Bd. I, S. 188" (6n8).

68. This prayer is also found in *Johanne Nielsdatter's Book of Hours, Else Hol-gersdatter's Book of Hours*, GkS 1615 4to, and *Marine Issdatter's Prayer Book*.

69. This book of hours also contains "Ien annen mygh*et* god bøn aff s*an*cta katerina, s*an*cta barbare m*eth* andre iomfru*æ*r" (ed. Nielsen 1946–1963: 4, no. 903).

70. The prayer is perserved also in a number of other manuscripts; see Geete (1907–1909: xcii). Hallberg *et al.* (1967) note that to the nine texts of the prayer mentioned by Geete, SKB A 78 can be added: "Denna handskrift innehåller en av Vadstenamunken Laurentius Petri (invigd 1542) verkställd översättning av lektioner avsedda för icke latinkunniga nunnor i klostret; till denna bekostade Christina Gunnarsdotter (invigd till nunna 1526) pappret. Pärmarna till denna lilla codex bestå av två överklädda pergamentsblad med fornsvensk text. Bladet, som utgör stommen i bakpärmen, innehåller förra och bladet i frampärmen senare delen av bönen till S. Barbara" (93n15).

In the last-mentioned prayer, Saint Barbara is called "the wtualdha paradisi rödha rosen, og renleksins lilia ... thät söta winbärit oc alzs kons dygda källa" (391), and her humble devotee prays: "war mik naadugh baadhe liffwandis oc dödhe, oc bidh for mik at jak matte faa for my*n* död synda angher oc scriftamal oc gudz wärdogha licama j mino*m* ythersta thima" (392).[71] Finally, it should be noted that a passage in AM 784 4to urges us to honor the Virgin Mary and the virgin saints Catherine of Alexandria, Barbara, Dorothy, Margaret of Antioch, Gertrude, Agatha, Odilia, Apollonia, Clare, Cecilia, Thecla, Concordia, Petronilla, and the 11,000 virgins on Saturdays (ed. Nielsen 1946–1963: 4, no. 1113a, cf. no. 1125g):

> Om løffuerdaghen skal ma*n* tencke paa hemerig*is* glede ock ere iomfrue maria m*eth* alle hellige iomfruer, s*a*nctam Katherina*m*, s*a*nctam Barbara*m*, s*a*nctam Doroteam, s*a*nctam Margaretam, s*a*nctam Gertrude*m*, s*a*nctam Agatam, s*a*nctam Otiliam, s*a*nctam Appolonia*m*, s*a*nctam Clara*m*, s*a*nctam Ceciliam, s*a*nctam Teclam, s*a*nctam Concordiam, s*a*nctam Petronilla*m*, the xi twsende iomfruer bede for [oss] ewindelig. Ame*n*

Two versions of the legend of Saint Barbara have been preserved in Old Swedish. One is found in SKB A 110 (*Codex Oxenstiernianus*) from Vadstena. It consists of 300 leaves and is not a single book as such, but rather a collection of six manuscripts. The Swedish *Sermo angelicus*, a collection of miracles, and a translation of

---

71. As evident from this prayer, Saint Barbara, in addition to her functions as a patroness and protectress, also serves as a model of virtuousness and purity. Hallberg *et al.* (1967: 93) draw attention to the fact that in Henricus de Hassia's (d. 1397) work on the chaste life, which, presumably under the influence of the Brigittines, was translated into Swedish in the beginning of the sixteenth century, she is mentioned in a list of virgin saints, who valued chastity to such an extent that they willingly suffered torture and death: "wars herra wälsignadha modh*er* jo*m*ffru maria war oc san fatikdomse*ns* älskerska, oc först io*m*ffrudome*n* loffwade oc hwlt, äpth*er* huilka otaleka hälga io*m*ffrwr swa renleken älskadho, at the för ha*ns* skuld wildho lidha dödhen oc wtläghe oc pinor, swa so*m* kateri*n*a, margaritta, barbara, appollonia, cecilia, lucia, cristina, agnes, agata, dorathea, oc otaleka andhra" (Dahlgren 1875: 20).

the Acts of the Apostles form a unit, the oldest, from 1385. The second book is incomplete and somewhat later; it contains a translation of the *Vitae Patrum* and a life of Saint Bridget. The legend of Saint Barbara is found along with the Gospel of Nicodemus, a section of Saint Bridget's revelations, and a number of other saints' lives in the third book, written in a hand no later than the beginning of the fifteenth century (ed. Klemming 1877–1878: 307–314).[72]

Several details in the version of the legend in *Codex Oxenstiernianus* suggest that it was probably based on *BHL* 916: Saint Barbara is said to have been baptized by the priest Valentinus ("Sidhan kom valencius präster ok döpte hona" [307]) and Juliana is not mentioned until the end of the legend ("Vm sama dagh ok i sama stadh pintes ivliana" [311]). Saint Barbara's final prayer is also considerably closer to *BHL* 916 than to *BHL* 914, in as much as it attributes much more precise efficacy to the intervention of Saint Barbara: "Hon badh mz tarom gratande ok sagdhe. Herra ihesu christe hör mina böön. at hwar thän som minnes vppa mina pino. at han skuli ey dröfwas i dödzens tima. vtan mz skriptamalom. ok gudz likama, ledhas til ärwärdhelika äro. Tha tedhes christus hänne sighiande. Kom miin vtwalda. Thy at iak girnas thinna siäl fäghrind. Alt hymerikis härskap vänter thik. ok astundar at thu skuli koma. Ok thz som thu beddes. är thik gifwit" (311). Finally, *Codex Oxenstiernianus*, like *BHL* 916, relates that after being stripped of her clothes and ordered to be led naked through the city, an angel covered Saint Barbara with a white garment ("Tha tedhes hänne ängelen ok holde hona mz hwito klädhe. swa at hon syntes ey vm thre tima" [311]).

Other details, however, point to *BHL* 914. Contrary to *BHL* 916, *Codex Oxenstiernianus* locates the story in Heliopolis ("I enom stadh som het solampne" [307]) at the time of the persecution of Christians ("J dyocleciani ok maximiani daghom. var swa stoort haat ofwer cristna män. at i enom manadhe pintos sywttan thusand" [307]). Moreover, as in *BHL* 914, there is no mention of Saint

72. See Carlquist (1996: 29).

Barbara's correspondence with Origen, and, as in *BHL* 914, it is stated at the end of the legend that Valentinus buried Saint Barbara's and Saint Juliana's bodies ("Valencius präster som döpt hafdhe sanctam barbaram. gik til marcianum. ok beddes thera kroppa. ok iordhadhe them. i ödhmyuko*m*. ok laagho*m* stadh" [311]).

These divergences in *Codex Oxenstiernianus* from *BHL* 916 point to a version representing an earlier stage in the development of the legend, that is, a precursor to *BHL* 916. As noted above, *BHL* 916, like *BHL* 914, is based ultimately on *BHL* 913, but incorporates information from *BHL* 921 and *BHL* 920. The location of the story in Heliopolis ("solampne" [307]) excludes *BHL* 921, which situates it in Nicomedia, as the source of *Codex Oxenstiernianus*, but makes *BHL* 920 a likely candidate. *BHL* 920's candidacy is further strengthened by the fact that in *Codex Oxenstiernianus* Heliopolis is situated in Egypt ("i egyptolande" [307]), to which Joseph fled with the Child Jesus and the Virgin Mary during Herod's massacre of the innocents (Til hwilke*n* stadh iosep flydhe mz ihesu christo ok hans modher. that herodes drap meenlöso barnen" [307]). Further details in *Codex Oxenstiernianus* that have parallels only in *BHL* 920 include a reference to Barbara's age (she was fifteen years old: "fämta*n* aara gambla" [307]) and to the angel that visits her in the tower ("Tha tedhes gudz ängel hänne. ok bewiste hä*n*ne ok sagdhe, at gudh skop al thing. ok huru gudz son took mandom af iomfru marie. ok frälste os mz sino*m* dödh. ok sagdhe Troo stadhelika a christum. Thy at thik tilbör at thola mykit for hans nampn skuld" [307]). According to *Codex Oxenstiernianus* as well, Saint Barbara "gömde sik i enne skrubbo" (308) after having fled from her father, a detail to be found only in *BHL* 920 ("in montemque transiens cavernosum"); and when Saint Barbara traces the sign of the cross with her thumb on the stone pillars of the tower, the stones "blotnadho swa som veeght wax" (308)[73] – again, a detail that points to *BHL* 920. The end of the

---

73. *BHL* 920: "In columnis marmoreis quasi in molli cera dextero pollice vivifice crucis impressit signa ut intuentium mentes incitarentur."

legend in *Codex Oxenstiernianus*, with its account of the miracles that took place at Saint Barbara's grave, the removal of her body by heathens to a temple, the discovery by Christians of her relics and their transportation to Rome, also reveals an affinity with John of Wakkerzeel's grand encomium. Finally, a miracle appended to the legend in *Codex Oxenstiernianus* (in *BHL* 914 about a decapitated merchant and witnessed by three Cistercian abbots) also shows a dependence on the work of John of Wakkerzeel.[74]

In comparison with *BHL* 920 the legend in *Codex Oxenstiernianus* is, however, much abridged, and many details have been omitted. There is no mention of Saint Barbara's distinguished lineage, nor any account of the miraculous transformation of the wicked shepherd into a marble statue or of his cattle into locusts. The description of the saint's baptism also appears to have been abbreviated. Omitting any reference to her correspondence with Origen, *Codex Oxenstiernianus* begins by relating the visit of an angel. The subsequent visitation of the Savior in the form of a young child is not mentioned, nor is the baptism of Saint Barbara by John the Baptist. Instead the baptism of Saint Barbara is performed by the priest "valencius" (307), who suddenly and without any introduction appears in the tower – and in the narrative.

On one more point, *Codex Oxenstiernianus* differs from *BHL* 920. In the Latin text, when Dioscorus drew his sword to kill

74. Hallberg *et al.* (1967) note that "[e]n latinsk version av detta mirakel återfinnes i kapitlet De extrema unccione av en inom birgittinmiljö tillkommen sakramentsutläggning från 1400-talets början, De septem sacramentis. Enligt Carl-Gustaf Andrén, som nyligen utgivit denna ur flera synpunkter viktiga skrift, förhåller den sig mycket självständig till den av Robert Geete ederade fornsvenska utläggningen om 'siw sacramenta', som eljest utgör den fornsvenska bearbetningen av den latinska texten. I 'siw sacramenta' saknas också miraklet om den halshuggne köpmannen" (87). They further draw attention to the fact that "[e]n latinsk version av texten i Codex Oxenstierna föreligger i Cod. Ups. C 1 (tidigare under signum I 6° 6us tillhörig Vadstena kloster), nedskriven under 1300-talets senare del (f. 181v–183r *Rubr.* Barbare virginis. *Inc.* Tempore maximiani et diocleciani imperatorum fuit apud egiptum dux quidam illustris). Även denna avslutas med miraklet om den halshuggne köpmannen" (89).

Saint Barbara the wall opened and closed again after she had slipped through the crack: "Mox igitur pater furore repletus gladium arripuit ut filiam tam sibi dilectam transfigeret. Ipsa vero non mori Christo rennuens, sed genitori compatiens oravit ad Dominum, et mira Dei gestina clementia; statim abscisus est marmor eam intus suscipiens." According to *Codex Oxenstierni-anus*, the tower bent down, enabling her to flee: "Tha bögdhe sik tornet nidher. ok satte iomfruna lätlika a iordhena. ok hon flydhe til et biärgh" (308). That this is not an invention on the part of the compiler of the *Codex Oxenstiernianus* is evident from the inclusion of the same detail in the Danish prayer to Saint Barbara in *Visdoms Spejl* (see n67).

It is possible, if unlikely, that the compiler of *Codex Oxenstiernianus* conflated two or more versions of the legend of Saint Barbara. Given the popularity and dissemination, in manuscript and print, of John of Wakkerzeel's encomium, variant versions probably came into existence. Indeed, Derolez (1991) notes that in the Marston 287 manuscript of this work, there is no mention of Origen in connection with Saint Barbara's conversion, nor is there any mention of Saint Barbara having been visited by the Child Jesus or by John the Baptist (see n34). While these divergent details in *Codex Oxenstiernianus* cannot be ignored, they do not significantly exclude *BHL* 920 as the source of the Old Swedish legend.

The other version of the legend appears in *Siælinna thrøst* from around 1420, which survives in a Vadstena manuscript, SKB A 108 from ca. 1430–1450 (ed. Henning 1954: 196–199).[75] The work is a translation of a Low German adaptation of the *Legenda Aurea*, *Der große Seelentrost*, from the mid-fourteenth century, but augmented with material drawn from the Vulgate, Peter Comestor's *Historia Scholastica*, and a number of Swedish works. It consists in the main of an exposition of the Ten Commandments,

---

75. See Carlquist (1996: 28). The work had previously been edited by Klemming (1871–1873). A modern Swedish edition of the legend of Saint Barbara is found in Fogelklou *et al.* (1917: 1: 41–44).

which are explained through various biblical and profane legends, miracles, and the like. The legend of Saint Barbara is found in the exposition of the Fourth Commandment. A translation from the original of the Swedish *Siælinna thrøst* into Danish (*Siæla trøst*) survives in the fragments UUB C 529 and SKB A 109, both from around 1425 (ed. Nielsen 1937–1952). The two fragments do not cover the legend of Saint Barbara.

The legend of Saint Barbara in *Siælinna thrøst* is, according to Thorén (1942: 75) a compilation of *Der große Seelentrost* (ed. Schmitt 1959), *Codex Oxenstiernianus*, and a Latin text, most likely *BHL* 916. Thorén argues that the German text has been used only to a small degree. That the legend in *Siælinna thrøst* is based, at least in part, on *BHL* 916 is evident from the location of the story in Nicomedia ("I Maximiani keysara daghum war een man j nichomedia mæktogher och riker heeth dioscorus" [196]), the lack of any mention of the persecution of Christians, and the transformation of the wicked shepherd into stone and his cattle into locusts ("oc han vmskiptis genstan j een sten oc all hans faar wordho locuste" [197]).[76] Moreover, Saint Barbara's last prayer points to the *BHL* 916 type:

Herra ihesu *christe* skapare hymilz oc iordz / thera frælsare och helare oppa thik thro / hør mina bøn oc giff mik thinne thiænisto qwinno som for thina skuld hafwer thessa pynor lidhit the nadh at thu wili werdhoghas giffwa allom them som oppa thit nampn kalla / oc hafwa afminnilse aff minne pyno tyma / Alla synda forlatilse / Oc minz thera synder alregh meer / Oc lath them ey forfaras j dødzsins tyma / Vtan lat them faa scriptamaal / oc thin wælsighnadha lykama / oc ledhas til æwinnelika æro. (199)[77]

---

76. It should be noted, however, that this statement is found also in *BHL* 920: "Nam eius [Deus] ultione mutatus est pastor ilico in statuam marmoris, ovesque eius facte sunt locuste." According to *Der große Seelentrost*, the shepherd "wart ... to eime stene vnde darto al sin queck" (131).

77. Saint Barbara's request that her worshippers will not die without having received the Eucharist is found also in *Codex Oxenstiernianus*, but the prayer in *Siælinna thrøst* is closer to that in *BHL* 916. In *Der große Seelentrost*

Particular features can be traced only to *Codex Oxenstiernianus*: Saint Barbara was fifteen years old ("xv ara gambla" [196]); when she traced with her finger the sign of the Cross on the stone pillars of the tower, the stones "blotnadho so*m* a*n*nat wax" (196); and after having fled from her father, she "gømde sik j ene skrubbo" (197). The sparsity of detail surrounding Saint Barbara's baptism – *Siælinna thrøst* merely states that while Dioscorus was away Saint Barbara was baptized – also points to *Codex Oxenstiernianus*.[78]

In comparison with both *BHL* 916 and *Codex Oxenstiernianus*, the legend in *Siælinna thrøst* (and *Der große Seelentrost*) is much abbreviated. The episode about the three windows is omitted; there is no mention of Juliana and Valentinus; and the details about Saint Barbara's miraculous escape from the tower are not included. The compiler was concerned not with the details of Saint Barbara's life, but rather with Saint Barbara's exemplary obedience to the Fourth Commandment.

A further reference to saint Barbara in Old Swedish literature is found in the medical sections of UUB C 601, written at the end of the fifteenth and the beginning of the sixteenth century. In a passage on bloodletting, we read, among other things: "Jtem om sancti benedicti apto*n* oc sancte pede*r*s ad vincula oc sancte barbare virginis later sik late thz är dödzins tekn" (Klemming 1883–1886: 64; Hallberg *et al.* 1967: 94).

Saint Barbara's prayer is as follows: "Do vel se vp ere kne vnde helt ere hende vp to gode vnde sprak: 'Here god alweldige, eyn schepper hemelrikes vnde ertrikes, eyn heylant vnde eyn trost aller lude, wente ik dorch dynen willen, leue here, desse marter lide, so bidde ek dij vor al de lude, de myne marter eren, dat du en rukes to vorgeuen alle ere sunde, also dat du er nummer mer gedenkest'" (132).

78. According to *Der große Seelentrost*, Saint Barbara baptized herself: "Do stunt dar eyn vath, dat was ydel. Do bat se vnsen heren god, dat he dat vath lete werden vul wateres. To hant was dat vul myt watere. Do dankede se vnseme leuen heren vnde bat en anderwerue, dat he dat water segenen vnde benedien wolde in deme namen der hilgen dreuoldicheit. Dar na trad se in dat water vnde dofte sijk suluen" (131).

2.1 The Cult and Legend in Iceland

That the female virgin martyrs were recognized as a particular group of saints and celebrated as such is clear from the *Old Norwegian Homily Book* (ed. Indrebø 1931) dated to around 1200. The female virgin martyr saints are not mentioned by name, however, but simply referred to as "helgar meyjar" in connection with instructions for which saints and groups of saints are to be celebrated "in die omnium sanctorum":

> En er sia hotið halden hælgum møyum þæim er gengo í spor hæilagrar Marie drotningar. *ok* hafnaðo ollum licams munuðum fyr aost guðs. *ok* vildu hældr þiona himnescum bruðguma í ollu at-hæfe an saurgasc af iarðlegre munuð. (145)

This group of female saints, we assume, included Saint Barbara.

That Saint Barbara was well established in Iceland within a century of the composition of the *Old Norwegian Homily Book* is evident from the preserved calendars, most of which appear to be derived from the *Niðaróss Ordinary* of the early thirteenth century (ed. Gjerløw 1968).[79] Her name ("Barbare uirginis") appears in AM 249c fol., an Icelandic liturgical calendar written in the late thirteenth century.[80] As Gjerløw (1980: 125) observes, AM 249c fol. is in effect two documents in one, for at the line-ends of each day, a cisiojanus or rhymed calendar runs parallel with the calendar. This cisiojanus (ed. Odenius 1959: 96–97) contains for December the following feasts:[81]

---

79. "*Jn natali sancte barbare uirginis et martyris. Ant. super psalmos* Jn honore huius uirginis. *Psalmi de die. Cap.* domine deus meus exaltasti. *Umn.* Virginis proles. *V.* Diffusa est gratia. *Ant. in ev.* Aue gemma. *Ps.* Magnificat. *Oratio propria*" (297).

80. Gjerløw (1980) comments: "Árni Magnússon's note attached to it says that it was prefixed to a 'mutilo Ψalterio Latino ä Skardi ä Skardzströnd', which he received as a gift in 1708. As pointed out by J. Þorkelsson ... the calendar was, however, a late-comer to Skarð. An analysis of the obits, entered c. 1400, points to the great family of Oddi and its ramifications" (125).

81. The cisiojanus in AM 249c fol. had previously been edited by Beckman and Kålund (1908–1918: 2: 225–228).

P*ost* deq*ue* barba nicho ueniunt victo lu nichasi
O sapi cu*m* thoma thola natalis domini fit

She is also included in the calendars AM 249d fol., dated to ca.
1300;[82] AM 249e fol., dated to the thirteenth century;[83] AM
249f fol. dated to the beginning of the thirteenth century;[84] AM
249m fol. from the second half or the last quarter of the fourteenth century;[85] AM 249n fol. to the thirteenth century, AM

82. See Kålund (1889–1894: 1: 227); Gjerløw (1980: 105, 122–124). Gjerløw notes that "[t]he calendar *MS AM 249d fol.* ... originally belonged with
the psalter *C* [= AM Access. 7d. Psalter VII]. A note by Árni Magnússon, attached to it, says that he had received it as a gift from Mag. Björn Þorleifsson
(bishop of Hólar 1697–1710) in 1703, prefixed to a Psalterium Latinum, and
that it might have come from (the church of) Skinnastaðir. ... This psalter was
dated c. 1360–1370 by Árni Magnússon. ... This date may be too early" (105).
  83. Kålund (1889–1894: 1: 227); see Gjerløw (1980: 103, 122–124, 126).
Gjerløw draws attention to the fact that "[t]he calendar *MS AM 249e fol.* ...
originally prefixed to the psalter *B* [= AM Access. 7d. Psalter II; Lbs. fragm.
60], has attached to it a note by Árni Magnússon: 'Fra Eyri i Skutilsfirde.
Framan vid altare slitur'" (103).
  84. Kålund (1889–1994: 1: 228); see Gjerløw 1980: 110, 122–124, 126.
Gjerløw notes that "[t]he calendar *MS AM 249f fol.* ..., written by the same
scribe (except for one leaf), was formerly prefixed to *F* [= AM Access. 7d.
Psalter XI from the first quarter of the fourteenth century]. The provenance
of this calendar is known; a note attached to it by Árni Magnússon says that
it came from the church of Vallanes (S. Múl., diocese of Skálholt), and that
it was bound together with a psalter: 'Fra Vallaness kirkiu | var i spiólldum
| og Ψalltari aptanvid.' Among the numerous additions to this calendar is the
dedication by Bishop Oddgeir of the church of Vallanes to St. John the Baptist on St. Alexis' day, 17 July, 1367. ... The calendar consists of three bifolia,
ff. 1–6, and a separate leaf, f. 7. F. 1r is blank, ff. 1v–6v contain the months
January–November. F. 7 with the month of December on the recto, and a pascal
table on the verso, possibly a replacement of a lost leaf, is written in a later hand,
with Arabic numerals for the days from 14 to 31 December" (110).
  85. See Gjerløw 1980: 117–118, 122–124. The calendar, containing the
months April–December, has attached to it a note by Árni Magnússon: "Þetta
mun vera fra Eyri i Skutilsfirde." Gjerløw (1980) thinks that AM 249m fol.
"may possibly have belonged with MS *s* [= AM 209 8vo]" (101). It contains,
in the lower margin of each month, the same cisiojanus as AM 249c fol. with
some Icelandic additions.

249o fol., dated to ca. 1300, and AM 249p fol., dated to the thirteenth century;[86] and the fragments of AM 249q fol., that is, those that cover the month of December, dated to the thirteenth-fifteenth century.[87]

Saint Barbara is also listed in two calendars dating from after the Reformation: AM 249g fol. (dated to the latter half of the sixteenth century)[88] and AM 249i fol. (dated to around 1600),[89] as well as in the calendar AM 249l fol. (dated by Kålund [1889–1894: 1: 230] to the end of the twelfth century). According to Kålund, the last-mentioned calendar belonged to the same codex as GkS 1812 4to; Cormack (1994) comments that "they [AM 249l fol. and GkS 1812 4to] contain entries for nearly every day and cannot be said to represent general Icelandic usage" (13n2). The same applies to AM 249a fol. from the end of the thirteenth century (ed. Wormald 1966: 176–180),[90] AM 249b fol. from ca. 1200 (ed.

---

86. On the dating of AM 249n, 249o, 249p see Kålund (1889–1894: 1: 231). See also Gjerløw (1980: 95–96, 122–124); she observes that "the calendar *MS AM 249p fol.* has been identified as belonging to our *MS A* [= AM 241a fol. Psalter] by Professor Louis-Jensen" (101).

87. See Kålund (1889–1894: 1: 231). Concerning the calendar AM 249q fol. I, which, however, consists of only one leaf and contains only the month of January, Gjerløw (1980) comments that it "seems to have been written c. 1400 or somewhat later" (118). She believes that AM 249q fol. I may have belonged with AM 209 8vo.

88. Kålund (1889–1894) comments: "Kalendariet er muligvis udført af eller for en sön af den skålholtske biskop Gísli Jónsson, Árni Gíslason, om hvem en notits med navns underskrift findes under 20. juli (fra år 1585)" (1: 229).

89. Kålund (1889–1894: 1: 229). On a note attached to the manuscript, Árni Magnússon provides the following information: "Þetta er Calendarium þad sem stod framanvid Grallarann er eg feck af Ragneidi Markusdottur i Storadal, qvem alibi descripsi & postea discerpsi."

90. The calendar was formerly prefixed to a psalter which came from England and belonged to the Church of Skálholt. According to Wormald, "the manuscript to which it was attached was certainly in England in the first half of the sixteenth century" (174). Saint Barbara is not included in this calender.

Gjerløw 1980: 193–204),[91] AM 249h fol. from ca. 1160–1189,[92] and AM 249q fol. VII from the late fifteenth century (ed. Gjerløw 1980: 208–210),[93] all of foreign origin. Finally, it should be noted that the calendar AM 249k fol., dated by Kålund (1889–1894: 1: 129) to the fourteenth century, is fragmentary and covers only the months February–October.

Although the liturgical sources do not specify the status of her feast day, it appears that it was that of a *leyfisdagr*, that is, a day of relaxed observance on which it is permitted to work. A manuscript of *Grágás*, *Skálholtsbók*, contains the following list of saints' days, identified as *leyfisdagar*:

> Þessir eru leyfis dagar. Sebastiani. Vincencij. blasij. agathe. Johannis ante portam latinam. Barnabe. Viti. Johannis et Pauli. Commemoracio Pauli. vij. fratrum. Marie Magdalene. Aduincula Petri. Inuencio stephani. Sixti. Ypoliti. Octaua Marie. Augustini. Decollacio Johannis baptiste. Mauricij. Cosme et Damiani. Remigij. Dionisij. Gereonis. Luce. virginum. Seuerini. Briccij. Theodori. Barbare. Leyfi er tuimællt at hafa Barbaro Messo ef æigi stendr a föstu deghi. (*Grágás* III: 36)

According to Cormack (1994: 16n13), the note on Saint Barbara's mass ("if not on a Friday") presumably reflects the fact that it fell during Advent. A reference, in the same manuscript, to permitting the eating of meat on the feast of Saint Barbara may, according to Cormack (1994: 19n26), reflect a local observance:

---

91. According to Gjerløw (1980: 205), the main source of this calendar, which includes Saint Barbara, was a German martyrological calendar chiefly based on Usuard's martyrology. Its original provenance is still in doubt.

92. According to Magnús Már Lárusson (1963: 106), the calendar, which lists Saint Barbara, is south German in its structure.

93. The manuscript consists of two fragments which together make one leaf containing the months September–December. The calendar includes Saint Barbara. Gjerløw (1980: 208) believes that it was probably written in Germany.

Iola föstu eigu*m* w*er* at hallda. w*er* sk*ul*u*m* taka til at w*ar*na
wið kiöti an*n*an dag viku þa*nn* e*r* drottins dag*a*r eru .iij. æ
millu*m* o*k* jola dags hins fy*r*sta. þa sk*al* æ*igi* eta kiöt æ þ*ei*rre
stundu nema an*n*an hu*er*n dag j viku þ*r*iðia o*k* fimta o*k* þuatt
dag o*k* d*r*ottins daga o*k* M*e*ssodaga alla lögtekna. o*k* Barbaro
M*e*sso. (*Grágás* III: 37)

References to Saint Barbara's feast day or mass appear relatively frequently in Icelandic documents. Apart from the mention
of her mass in *Rímbegla*, the common name for the Icelandic com-
putistic treatises collected in *Rím I-III* (ed. Beckman and Kålund
1908–1918: 2: 1–64, 83–178, 181–222),[94] in which it is stated that
"Iola fasta skal hefiazst avallth drottins daginn nęsta fyri Barbaro
messo" (*Rím I*, 24; cf. *Rím II*, 85, 156),[95] these references appear
in the charters. Thus Brother Ásbjörn Vigfússon (d. 1439), Abbot
at Þingeyrar, specifies that his letter of 4 December 1437 was
written on "Sanctæ barbare virginis et martiris dag" (*DI* IV 612:
573), Sigríður Grímsdóttir that her letter of 4 December 1569 was
written "ä Barbarumessu" (*DI* XV 240: 332), and in a letter of 3
December 1533 concerning Jón Jónsson's donation of lands to Jón
Konráðsson, it is said that the letter was written "næsta dæginn
fyrir barbaarv Messo" (*DI* X 46: 69). Similarly, in his testimony to
the boundary marks of Bassastaðir, Snorri Gunnlaugsson says that
his letter of 29 November 1501 was written "mánudaginn næstañ
firir Barbárumessu" (*DI* XI 53: 58), and in a letter of 3 December
1449 concerning Hjalti Þorsteinsson's sale of half of the lands of
Steinnýjarstaðir to Þorsteinn Jónsson, it is stated that the sale took
place "miduikudaginn nęsta firir barbaru messu uirginis" (*DI* V 31:
31). A further reference to Saint Barbara's mass appears in the
instructions of Bishop Jón Stephánsson Krabbe of Skálholt (1462–
1465) for changes to the service in the Skálholt diocese in 1464; in

94. The main text of *Rím I* and *II* is based on AM 625 4to (fifteenth
century); that of *Rím III* is based on AM 624 4to (fifteenth century) and AM
727 4to (sixteenth century). Variants from other manuscripts are included.
95. Cf. *Bréfabók Gizurar biskups Einarssonar*: "Jolafasta skal jafnan hefiast
hinn næsta drottinz dag fyrir barbarumessu" (*DI* X 176: 437).

these it is specified: "Þa andress Messu ber aa midvikudag þa byriazt iolafasta sunnudag næsta fyrer festum barbare þat sem in secunda dominica skal færa aa manudagenn hafa commemoracionem af adventu" (*DI* V 363: 414).

Other references to Saint Barbara in Icelandic charters testify to a more personal devotion to the saint. Thus, in his will written in 1446, Þorvarður Loptsson of Möðruvellir commends his soul to the keeping of, among others, Saint Barbara ("Gef ec mic oc mina sal j valld oc vernnd skapara oc lausnara mins herra iesu christi oc j skiol oc myskunnar fadm heilagrar kirkiu oc arnadar ord jungfru sancte marie og ens blezada Martini erkibiskups oc sancte Nicvlaus erkibiskupz sancte Johannis holabiskups oc bartholomeus postula oc ennar blezudu barbaru oc allra gudz heilagra manna" [*DI* IV 720: 675]), as does Páll Brandsson of Möðruvellir in his will written in 1494 ("gef ec mig og mina sal j ualld og uernd skapara mins og lausnara herra ihesu christi og j skiol og myskunar fadm heilagrar kirkiu og arnadar orda jungfru sancte Marie og hins bleszada Martini erchibiskups sancte thome archiepiscopi sancte nichulai og sancte johannis holabiskups. Sancte petri og pauli og hinne blezudu barbaru. goda gudmundar biskups og allra guds heilagra manna og meya" [*DI* VII 292: 233]).

A further testimony to Saint Barbara's popularity is her patronage of two churches. Along with Saints Mary, Andrew, Martin, and Þorlákr, she is co-patron of the church of Haukadalr, which was consecrated 1323–1348 by Bishop Jón Halldórsson of Skálholt (1322–1339): "Kirkia j haukadal er vijgd af jone biskupi. helgud med gudi hanns sætustu modur. andree postula. martino biskupi. oc hinne helgu barbare" (*DI* II 408: 667).[96] Sigurveig Guðmundsdóttir (1981: 8) draws attention to the fact that Saint Barbara was a protectress against lightning and fire and observes that the Haukdælir

---

96. Cormack (1994: 190n31) notes that the church of Haukadalr was, however, one of the oldest church sites in Iceland and that the dedication to Saint Martin, the primary patron, is attested ca. 1285.

may have had in mind the geothermal dangers in their area when they chose Saint Barbara as one of the patrons of their church.

The other church with which Saint Barbara is associated is the church of Reykjaholt, of which, along with Saints Mary, Peter, and Denys, she is co-patron. The *Reykjaholtsmáldagi*, the oldest extant document of its kind,[97] specifies that "Kirkia su er stendr i reyækia hollti er helguð með guði MaRiv moðvr. drott*ins. oc* hinu*m* helga petro pos*tu*la. *oc* env*m* hælga dionisio b*y*sc*u*pi *oc* henni helgv Barbare meẏio" (Hreinn Benediktsson 1965: iii; *DI* I 120: 476–477).[98] An entry dated to 1204 or possibly a little later records a gift of two images ("Magn*us* oc hallfriþr gefa til kirkio roþo kross oc licneske þau es standa vfer altara" [Hreinn Benediktsson 1965: iii; *DI* I 120: 476]), which might be the images of Saints Peter and Barbara mentioned in an inventory dated 1392: "peturs likneski oc barbaru" (*DI* III 396: 482; cf. also the inventories dated 1394, 1503, 1518, and 1538 [*DI* III 413: 502, *DI* VII 623: 666, *DI* VIII 516: 675, *DI* X 154: 397]). That the church at Möðruvellir also boasted an image of Saint Barbara is known from the inventory which Bishop Ólafur Rögnvaldsson of Hólar (1460–1495) had made of the possessions of the churches in his bishopric; among the images owned by the church at Möðruvellir is mentioned a "barbare likneski" (*DI* V 233–314: 308). The inventory of the church at Holt in Saurbær also testifies to the existence of an image of Saint Barbara in 1523: "Jtem a kirkian fyrir jnnan sig brijk. oc er j marivskriftt. katerinar skrift. Barbarv skrift. magnus likneski. Thomas likneski" (*DI* IX 169: 195).

One such image of Saint Barbara (Þjms. 14293) has been preserved. In 1950, the upper part of a little figurine of Saint Barbara was found during excavations of what appears to have

---

97. The body of the text dates from the late twelfth century, possibly ca. 1185.

98. The dedication of the church is first mentioned in an addition to the original inventory written in the latter half of the thirteenth century (Hreinn Benediktsson 1965: ii; Cormack 1994: 83).

been a road-chapel in the late Middle Ages just south of Hafnarfjörður. The figurine, which is made of pipe-clay, now measures 3.3 cm.; in its original state it is believed to have measured 5.5 cm. Kristján Eldjárn (1956: 11–12) emphasizes the artistic quality of the work in his report on the excavation: Saint Barbara's rather stern facial features are framed by shoulder-length, curly locks of hair. She is wearing a long-sleeved, deep-cut dress with many pleats below the waistline. A cloak is draped over her shoulders and falls in deep, soft folds down her back. In her left hand, she is holding a tower. Vilhjálmur Örn Vilhjálmsson (1983: 172–174) draws attention to the fact that the production of such miniature images flourished from the mid-fifteenth century onwards in the Netherlands and Northern Germany and that in Springweg an identical figurine made in Utrecht, the best known location of such production, was discovered, which has been dated to the second half of the fifteenth century. Vilhjálmur Örn Vilhjálmsson considers it likely that the Icelandic figurine was manufactured in Utrecht or somewhere in the same region. To commemorate the find, members of the Catholic community in Iceland erected a bronze statue of Saint Barbara in the ruins in Kapelluhraun (Vilhjálmur Örn Vilhjálmsson 1983: 174; Anna Sigurðardóttir 1988: 327–331).

Another representation of Saint Barbara appears on the Hólar bishop Jón Arason's (1484–1550) cope (Þjms. 4401), which he procured for the cathedral from abroad. The cope is of red velvet with a richly decorated orphrey depicting saints (Kristján Eldjárn 1973: 35; Kristján Eldjárn and Hörður Ágústsson 1992: 16–17, fig. 11).[99] Three male saints, Thomas (the apostle), Jerome, and Anthony (the hermit), are depicted on the left-hand side of the orphrey, and three female saints, Anne, Barbara, and Catherine of Alexandria, on the right-hand side. Saint Barbara is portrayed with a tower with three windows in front of her and holding a chalice.

99. For a detailed description of the cope, see Matthías Þórðarson (1911: 43–59).

Saint Barbara also appears on the large altarpiece donated to the church of Hólar by Jón Arason. Here, too, Saint Barbara is depicted with the tower, her most common attribute (Kristján Eldjárn and Hörður Ágústsson 1992: 39, fig. 45). The altarpiece is still in the church at Hólar.

Finally, in his *Icelandic Journals* William Morris (1834–1896) relates that when he was visiting the physician Jósep Skaftason at Hnausar in Vatnsdalur in 1871, the physician introduced his daughter to him.[100] She was dressed "in gala clothes which included a really fine belt of silversmith's work ... not later than 1530 in date, for there was a St Barbara engraved on the smooth side of the tag in regular Hans Burgmair style: the openwork of the belt was very beautiful, the traditional northern Byzantinesque work all mixed up with the crisp sixteenth-century leafage" (74). The whereabouts of this fine belt remain unknown.

In Iceland, the name Barbara has been used at least since the fifteenth century. One of the abbesses, Þóra Finnsdóttir, of the Benedictine convent at Staður in Reynisnes, which was established in 1296, carried the name Barbara.[101] Abbess Barbara's seal is among those which are still preserved and is of interest in this context (Magnús Már Lárusson and Jónas Kristjánsson 1965–1967: 1: 223). In 1459, she sold land, and her seal followed the original document (Magnús Már Lárusson and Jónas Kristjánsson 1965–1967: 1: 222), but was separated from it when Árni Magnússon had it copied. The tongues and towers on the seal bear no relation to the Icelandic convent at Staður, however, and the seal is clearly an imported item (Guðrún P. Helgadóttir 1961–1963: 1: 95). The name Barbara also appears in a list of names from 1646 drawn up by Oddur, the minister at Reynivellir. A census taken in 1703 lists sixteen women by the name of Barbara. In 1845, six women car-

100. Sigurveig Guðmundsdóttir (1981: 21).
101. Cf. Anna Sigurðardóttir (1988: 8), who notes that although it is nowhere attested, Þóra adopted the name Barbara when she was consecrated abbess. In the annals, however, she is referred to as a Þóra.

ried the name, and in 1910 only one (Guðrún Kvaran and Sigurður Jónsson 1991: 138).

One must assume that it was primarily devotional interests that prompted the translation of the legend of Saint Barbara into Icelandic. Indeed, as Cormack (1994: 37) observes, there is on the whole a good correlation between the saints whose legends were translated and those known from other ecclesiastical sources. No doubt a demand for literary entertainment also played a significant role, however, for the legend of Saint Barbara appears in both prose and poetry and is found in a fair number of manuscripts.

The earliest literary treatment of the legend of Saint Barbara in Old Norse-Icelandic is the fourteenth-century *Heilagra meyja drápa* (ed. Finnur Jónsson 1908–1915: 2A: 526–529 and 2B: 582–597), where in stanza 52 her story is briefly summarized:

> Barbára gat frá blótum horfit
> blíðu-fyld ok skrýddiz fríðum,
> hennar faðir lét sælan svanna
> syrgiliga í húsi byrgja;
> kvíðu-fullu kvalara þjóðir
> knífum skáru brjóst af vífi;
> Ságu gulls með sverði vágu;
> seldiz hún enn í drottins veldi. (2B, 295)

The primary version of the legend of Saint Barbara is, however, the *Barbare saga*. This translation, which was undertaken sometime before 1425–1445, is extant in Stock. Perg. 2 fol. and AM 429 12mo. *Barbare saga* is the subject of chapter 3.

In addition, an epitome of her legend, the so-called *Um Barbáru mey*, is preserved in AM 672 4to. This epitome is edited and discussed in chapter 4.

Finally, there is a poetic version of the legend of Saint Barbara, the *Barbárudiktur* (ed. Jón Helgason 1936–1938: 2: 330–341),[102]

---

102. The first stanza of *A* was edited by Jón Þorkelsson (1888: 93).

which is found in two very different redactions designated A and B.[103] A is preserved in Addit. 4892,[104] Addit. 11179, JS 260 4to,[105] and Lbs 953 4to. According to Jón Helgason (1936–1938: 1: 250), Addit. 11179, JS 260 4to, and Lbs 953 4to all go back to the same copy (*Y); this copy (*Y) and Addit. 4892 are both derived from the same exemplar (*X), a copy of the original, which in Jón Helgason's opinion can hardly have been much later than ca. 1700. B is preserved in three manuscripts, all from the eastern part of Iceland: JS 201 4to, written by Jón Þorsteinsson á Kirkjubólsseli in Stöðvafjörður in 1849, Lbs 2222 8vo, written seventeen years later by Þórarinn Mattíasson á Kirkjubólsseli, and Lbs 2127 4to, written by Sigmundur Matthíasson (Long) á Hamragerði in 1873. According to Jón Helgason (1936–1938: 2: 33), the three manuscripts represent three independent recordings from oral tradition. JS 201 4to and Lbs 2222 8vo, which are quite similar, may have been recorded from the same informant; Lbs 2127 4to differs from the two in that attempts have been made to restore the rhyme and alliteration in the poem, which has suffered during its long oral transmission.

A contains 26 stanzas and B 31 (JS 201 4to and Lbs 2222 8vo have 29). Of these, 21 stanzas are common to both redactions. According to Jón Helgason (1936–1938: 2: 330), a comparison with

---

103. In the following discussion of *Barbárudiktur*, I rely on Jón Helgason (1936–1938: 2: 330–332, 335–336).

104. A copy of Addit. 4892 is found in JS 487 8vo (which again was copied in JS 494 8vo). The first stanza appears also in Lbs 754 8vo (which again was copied in Lbs 936 4to). Jón Helgason (1936–1938: 2: 331) notes that a very poor copy of Addit. 4892 is found also in Lbs 1326 4to by Jón Þorkelsson. Lbs 1326 4to was, in turn, used as the basis for another later copy also by Jón Þorkelsson in Lbs 2166 4to (ca. 1920), where also JS 260 4to is used.

105. There are two copies of JS 260 4to: JS 284 8vo and JS 514 8vo by Jón Árnason. A copy of JS 284 8vo was made by Páll Pálsson in Lbs 201 8vo. In this last-mentioned copy, Páll Pálsson later added variants from JS 514 8vo and JS 494 8vo; similarly he added variants from Lbs. 201 8vo in JS 514 8vo. Another copy of JS 284 8vo is found in JS 265 4to.

Barbare saga suggests that the majority of the preserved stanzas are original. However, the poem has suffered considerably in its oral transmission, making it impossible to restore it to its original form.

Following Jón Helgason's proposed reconstruction of the order of the stanzas, *Barbárudiktur* begins with a brief preface (1 = *B*1) followed by an introduction of the heathen Dioscorus (in *A* his name is not given and in *B* he is called Dyspöteus) and his daughter Barbara (2: *A*1 = *B*2). The poem then tells of Dioscorus's construction of a tower to protect Saint Barbara from suitors (3–5: *A*3 = *B*3–6), Saint Barbara's instructions to the workmen that a third window be added to the existing two (6–8: *A*4–5 = *B*7–9), her tracing of the sign of the cross on the precious stone (9: *A*9), and Dioscorus's questioning of her concerning the third window (10–12: *A*6 = *B*10–12). Stanzas 13–16 (*A*7–8 = *B*13–15) tell of his anger and Saint Barbara's miraculous escape through the wall: "Meyann út á mörkina rende / marga dírd Jesu kiendi / skógar epli oc hunáng hendi / hef eg þad friett hún fæddist á / h. m. B." (16: *A*8 = *B*15). Stanzas 17–21 (*A*10–13 = *B*27, 16–18) relate the miraculous transportation of Saint Barbara up onto a mountain (in *A*10 by "[h]imna gud," in *B*27 by "[e]inglar tveir"), Dioscorus's pursuit of her, her betrayal by the wicked shepherd, and the subsequent punishment of the shepherd (both *A*13 and *B*17 relate that he "i hörmung [*B*: hugsott] lagdist," but whereas in *A*13 his cattle are transformed into birds ["ad fuglum"], they are in *B*17 transformed into small flies ["ad flugum sma"]). Stanzas 22–29 (*A*14–21 = *B*19–26) then describe Dioscorus's capture of Saint Barbara, her refusal to sacrifice to the pagan gods, his torture of her, and, finally, her execution. In stanzas 30–31 (*A*24 = *B*28–29), Dioscorus's own death by lightning is described. The remaining part of the poem, stanzas 32–36 (*A*22–23, 25–26 = *B*30), consists of the poet's exhortations to his audience to venerate Saint Barbara.

In comparison with *Barbare saga*, the legend in *Barbárudiktur* is condensed, and many details have been omitted, although, obviously, the possibility cannot be excluded that in its original form *Barbárudiktur* contained some of these details. Thus, we are not told that the events took place during the reign of Maximianus, or of the earl and the holy man who buried Saint Barbara. There is no mention of Saint Barbara making the sign of the Cross in the anteroom, where she was subsequently baptized in the well by a holy man, or of the contempt she expressed on her way from the tower for her father's idols and the prayer she uttered for their destruction. Moreover, Saint Barbara's explanation of the significance of the third window is not included, and in the account of her tortures the poem only mentions that Dioscorus "hardlega hennar holdid kramde" (*A*17 = *B*20) and cut off her breasts. The miraculous healing of Saint Barbara and the appearance of the Savior are not mentioned. Finally, Saint Barbara's prayers are omitted as are many of the dialogues. Apart from these omissions, however, the legend as told in *Barbárudiktur* does not differ significantly from *Barbare saga*. The poem's description of the transformation of the wicked shepherd's cattle (turned into birds or flies and not grasshoppers) may well be attributed to textual corruption. Similarly, the poem's allusion to the "skógar epli oc hunang" on which Saint Barbara lived after her escape through the wall probably reflects a misplaced reference to the honey from the woods in *Barbare saga* on which the saint is said to have lived after her baptism.

The direct source for *Barbárudiktur* has not been established, but it appears that the poem goes back ultimately to the same Latin version of the legend as *Barbare saga*, that is, the version represented by *BHL* Suppl. 913a (see chapter 3.4). Both *Barbare saga* and *Barbárudiktur* share with *BHL* Suppl. 913a certain characteristics not found in other legend versions. As in *Barbare saga* and *BHL* Suppl. 913a, the treacherous shepherd's cattle are in the poem transformed into insects,[106] and as in *Barbare saga* and *BHL* Suppl. 913a, there is in the poem no mention of Juliana, who shared Saint Barbara's destiny. In one detail, however, *Barbare saga*

---

106. The *B* redaction of the poem appears to preserve the more original reading "ad flugum sma"; the reading in the *A* redaction, "ad fuglum," would seem to be a misreading or miswriting of "ad flugum."

and *Barbárudiktur* differ from *BHL* Suppl. 913a. According to *BHL* Suppl. 913a, Saint Barbara cursed the treacherous shepherd, and it seems implied that it was her curse that made the shepherd's cattle turn into grasshoppers. Both *Barbare saga* and *Barbárudiktur* remove from Saint Barbara her active role in the miraculous event by omitting any mention of the saint's curse and merely stating that the shepherd was punished in such a way that his cattle were transformed into grasshoppers (*Barbare saga*) or small flies (*Barbárudiktur*). Obviously, this detail is not sufficient evidence to propose a direct connection between *Barbárudiktur* and *Barbare saga*. On the other hand, nothing in *Barbárudiktur* other than a lack of verbal similarities between the poem and *Barbare saga* excludes the possibility that the poem may be based on the saga.

3   BARBARE SAGA

3.0 Transmission

The Old Norse-Icelandic legend of Saint Barbara is transmitted in Stockholm, Kungliga Biblioteket Perg. 2 fol. and Copenhagen, Det arnamagnæanske Institut AM 429 12mo. The legend was edited by Unger (1877: 1: 153–157), who used Stock. Perg. 2 fol. as his base text with variants from AM 429 12mo. A facsimile edition of Stock. Perg. 2 fol. was published in 1962 with an introduction by Foote.

3.1 Stockholm, Kungliga Biblioteket Perg. 2 fol.

Codex Stock. Perg. 2 fol. now contains 86 folios but is believed to have originally contained 110 or 112 folios.[107] Its double-columned leaves measure 30 × 23.5 cm. Foote (1962: 11) dates the codex to the period ca. 1425–1445 on the basis of the identification of hand II with Ormur Loptsson (1407 or before–ca. 1446).[108] On the

---

107. The following description of Stock. Perg. 2 fol. is based on Foote's (1962) introduction to the facsimile edition.

108. Cf. the marginalia "ERlighan*n* man*n ok* uelborin*n* orm*m* loptz son" (fol. 2r) and "Her byri*ar* benedict*us* soghu e*r* orm*ur* loptz son scrifuade" (fol. 53r). For biographical details about Ormur Loptsson, see Foote (1962: 11–12).

basis of early marginalia containing personal names, Foote (1962: 14) reckons that in the third or fourth decade of the fifteenth century the codex was at Staðarhóll, which was owned by Ormur Loptsson, although from around 1435/36 to 1445/6 his chief residence was Víðidalstunga, and that the codex passed from Solveig Þorleifsdóttir, Ormur's widow, or from Loptur Ormsson (d. ca. 1476), their son, to Guðni Jónsson (ca. 1435–1507) of Kirkjuból in Langadalur and Ögur. The history of the codex from about 1500 until Jón Eggertsson (ca. 1643–1689) acquired it in Iceland in 1682 and brought it to Stockholm in 1683 remains unknown. Foote (1962: 14) thinks that it may have stayed in the north-west, where Jón Eggertsson had many family connections and where (that is, Dalasýsla, Barðastrandarsýsla, and Ísafjarðarsýsla) he sent men and even went himself (that is, Dalasýsla and Barðastrandarsýsla).

Foote (1962: 14) observes that Stock. Perg. 2 fol. is written in three hands. Fols. 1–18, 19rb, 19vb, 20rb–23ra, 23rb19 (tekr)–27v, and 28va6–34 are written in Hand I. Fols. 19ra, 19va, 20ra, 23rb1–19, 28r–va5, 35–63va19, 63va29–64ra37, 64rb–74ra27, and 74rb–86 are the work of Hand II. Hand III characterizes fols. 63va19 (munu)–29 (lutv*m*), 64ra37 (ek hefi)–43, and 74ra27 (*ok þeir mæt-ti*)–43. There are 43 lines in each column throughout with only few exceptions.

The codex has been supplied throughout with illuminated initials except on fol. 57v and at the top of fol. 73ra. Saga- and chapter-titles have been supplied in red except on fols. 57v, 58r, 67r, and at the bottom of 79rb.[109] Very elaborate initials are found at the beginning of each new saga. The colors used are yellow, white, blue, light red, and reddish brown, but often only a single color is used, and, on the whole, the illuminations become more rudimentary as the work progresses. However, they are believed

---

109. Foote (1962: 8) notes that in the title "af pilato ia(rli)" (43va) "af" is in black touched with red. The title "H*er* hefr vp*p* sogv mavri abb*atis*" (60ra) is in black. Finally, the initial "H" in the saga-titles at the bottom of fols. 63vb and 66vb is in blue.

to be the work of a single illuminator. Many small capitals at the beginning of lines and a few larger ones as well are in ink; these capitals are the work of the scribes, who also make similar elaborate capitals within the line. Foote (1962: 8) notes that these capitals are somewhat more frequent in Hand I than in Hand II.

Stock. Perg. 2 fol. contains twenty-six texts, whole or fragmentary, making it the largest collection of saints' lives preserved from medieval Iceland. The texts comprise the legends of Saint Thomas Becket (ed. Unger 1877: 2: 315–320), Saint Martin (ed. Unger 1877: 1: 607–642), Saint Nicholas (ed. Unger 1877: 2: 21–41), Saint Ambrose (ed. Unger 1877: 1: 28–51), Saint Denys (ed. Unger 1877: 1: 312–322), Saint Silvester (ed. Unger 1877: 2: 245–280), Saint Gregory the Great (ed. Unger 1877: 1: 377–395), Saint Augustine,[110] Saint Blaise,[111] Saint Stephen (ed. Unger 1877: 2: 287–309), Saint Laurence of Rome (ed. Unger 1877: 1: 422–432), Saint Vincent (ed. Unger 1877: 2: 321–326), Saint Benedict (ed. Unger 1877: 1: 158–179), Saint Paul of Thebes (ed. Unger 1877: 2: 183–192), Saint Maurus (ed. Unger 1877: 1: 659–675), Saint Mary of Egypt (ed. Unger 1877: 1: 482–495), Saints Martha and Mary Magdalene,[112] Saint Catherine of Alexandria,[113] Saint Barbara (see above), Saint Lucy (ed. Unger 1877: 1: 433–436), Saint Cecilia (ed. Unger 1877: 1: 276–279^{20}, 289^{10}–297), Saint Agatha (ed. Unger 1877: 1: 1–6), Saint Agnes (ed. Unger 1877: 1: 15–19^{18}), Saints Fides, Spes, and Caritas (ed. Unger 1877: 1: 372^{23}–376), Flagellacio crucis in Berytho (ed. Unger 1877: 1: 308–311), and Saint Maurice.

110. Variants from this manuscript (called B) are given in Unger (1877: 1: 122–149). Stock. Perg. 2 fol. provides the base text for 142^{15}–143^4, 143^{22}–144^{14}, 146$^{5–28}$.

111. Variants from this manuscript (called B) are given in Unger (1877: 1: 256–269). Stock. Perg. 2 fol. provides the base text for 264^9–265^{29}.

112. Variants from this manuscript (called B) are given in Unger (1877: 1: 513–553). Stock. Perg. 2 fol. provides the base text for 550^{24}–553^{13}.

113. Variants from this manuscript (called B) are given in Unger (1877: 1: 400–421). Stock. Perg. 2 fol. provides the base text for 400–401^{24}.

The legend of Saint Barbara is thus placed in the middle of what appears originally to have been intended as a section on female saints (the arrangement is disrupted by the inclusion of the last two items).[114] The entire legend is by Hand II, which is found also on AM 238 fol. VIII.[115] At the beginning of *Barbare saga*, there is a decorated initial *A*, and at the beginning of chapter IV a decorated *Þ*. Smaller elaborate letters in black ink occur at 78va30 (*S*), 78vb26 (*E*), 79ra19 (*H*), and 79rb8 (*E*). At 79rb8, there is evidence of scribal guidance to the illuminator: a small *þ* to be inserted is visible between the columns (but has been correctly inserted as *E*). At 79rb (by chapter V), guidance to the chapter-title is found in the margin.

The following paleographic and orthographic description is limited to fols. 78rb–79rb (*Barbare saga*).

3.1.0 Paleography

Only the so-called two-storey *a* is found. The top storey is a closed loop as in, e.g., *maxímíani* (3). Occasionally, the back of the *a* may descend slightly below the line as in, e.g., *stauplínv*m (6).

b is always written with a loop as in, e.g., *barbara* (5).

Only insular or round *d* is in evidence. The ascender may be somewhat exaggerated as in, e.g., *hǫfdinghí* (3).

The *e* is always open.

---

114. Cf. Carlé (1985), who argues that the principle behind the composition was not primarily to keep male and female saints separate: "Den rækkefølge, som fortællingerne danner, afspejler derimod helgenhierarkiet, som igen har sin forklaring i den katolske kirkes sociale hierarki" (40). The hierarchy proposed is essentially the qualitative hierarchy of saints in, for example, the litany for Holy Saturday and the *Missale Romanum*. In these, the Virgin Mary and the *angeli et archangeli* occupy the highest seats, followed by *patriarchae et prophetae, apostoli et evangelistae, pontifices et confessores, doctores, sacerdotes et levitae, monachi et eremitae,* and, at the bottom, *virgines et viduae.*

115. Fol. 1r–1vb30 contains the ending of *Sebastianus saga*, 1vb31–42 the beginning of *Hallvarðs saga*, and fol. 2 contains a section of *Jóns saga baptista I*. For a discussion of this manuscript, see Foote (1962: 17–18).

Only insular *f* is in evidence. It consists of a vertical stroke with a figure 3 attached on the right. The lower loop of the 3 may end at the descender (e.g., *höfdinghí* [3]) or cross it (e.g., *fá* [12]).

The upper part of *g* is an *o*; its tail consists of a half-circle as in *god* (4) or a full circle as in *glugg* (23).

The right-hand vertical of *h* always extends well below the line (e.g., *heidín* [4]) ending sometimes with a curl as in *hafan* (6).

k appears both with and without a loop, e.g., *nöckurn* (11) and *ek* (11). The leg of the *k* sits on the line.

l is usually written with a loop.

Initially and medially, the right-hand minim of *m* and *n* does not extend below the line. In word-final position, the minim of *m* occasionally descends below the line, e.g., *monnum* (117).

Of *r*, there are three types: minuscule *r*, *r* rotunda, and small capital *r* (R). The minuscule *r* is often reminiscent of a *v* as in, e.g., *nockur* (3). The *r* rotunda is always tailed. It is used after *a*, *b*, *d*, *g*, *o* and *ö* and is in complementary distribution with minuscule *r*, except after *a*, where also minuscule *r* is found. In two instances, *r* rotunda appears after *v* (*hverrí* [82 see textual note] and *vrdv* [118]). Small capital *r* occurs three times: *grædaRín* (86–87), *þeiRe* (92), and *dyR* (101).

Of *s*, there are two types, round or small capital *s* (S) and long or cursive *s*. The former always sits on the line, whereas the latter extends well below the line. Small capital *s* is commonly used in *svo* (19, 67, 72, 119) and *sér* (34, 52, 99). In addition, round *s* is found in the following words: *keiSara* (3), *Sv(aradi)* (10), *Suörudu* (19), *Sidan*n (28, 81), *Sia* (33, 100), *S(varadi)* (49), *Sverdí* (51), *Sendi* (63), *hreSslíga* (110).

The vertical of *t* does not extend above the cross-bar except in the ligature of *s* and *t*.

The *þ* is often furnished with two loops as in, e.g., *þa* (5).

In word-initial position, *v* is often looped as in, e.g., *vænleik* (7).

The *x*, which occurs only in *maxímíani* (3), *gíafwaxín* (8), and in abbreviations of *Kristr* (xpc [87], xp̄c [126], xp̄o [71, 151]), extends below the line.

The *y* consists of a *u* with the descender extending from the second vertical of the *u* and veering to the left at the bottom (e.g., *byd* [22]).

The *z* sits on the line. Usually, it is not barred.

The *a* in *æ* is, as Foote (1962: 15) notes, "headless."

The Tironian nota has the shape of the figure 7 with the descender forming a small hook to the right at the bottom, making it similar to *z*. The stave never goes below the line, and it is always barred.

Of ligatures, only *a* + *a*, *a* + *u/v*, and *s* + *t* are in evidence; *a* + *u/v* occurs only once (*þau* [98]) and at the end of a line.

The following capital letters are found (excluding chapter headings, the ornamental *A* at the beginning of the legend [3], and the ornamental *Þ* at the beginning of chapter IV [85]): *E* (*Enn* [7, etc.]), *B* (*B(arbara)* [85]), *D* (*Drottín*n [114, etc.]), *F* (*Fadi*r [5, etc.]), *G* (*Giðr*it [20, etc.]), *J* (*J* [29, etc.]), *M* (*Mínztv* [135]), *S* (*Storgætinga*r [9, etc.]), *V* (*Vert* [87, etc.]). All these letters have the shape of Roman capitals, except for the two large capital *Es* (*Enn* [66, 123]), which have a rounded back. Five capitals appear in the margin: *Sia* (31), *Hvort* (69, which has the shape of a minuscule *h*), *Heilog* (96), and *Enn* (7, 140, 145).

An accent is commonly found over *i*, but appears to be no more than a graphic marker. In one instance, two accents are found over *ó* (*þő* [33]), and in two instances, two accents are found over *á* (*fá̋* [12] and *sár̋* [98]).

3.1.1 Abbreviations

Superscript *a* occurs once and stands for *afa* (*h*afa [56]).

Superscript *e* stands for *re* (*þreífa* [76]) and *anne* (*m*anne [30]).

The *er* abbreviation as in *hverso* (14) is used also for *r* (*er* [3]) and *ir* (*Fadi*r [5]). It is also used in abbreviations of *fyrir* (*fy*rir [44, etc.]), which is never written in full.

Superscript *i* stands for *il* (*til* [26]), *ri* (*fingri* [25]), *vi* (*þvi* [34]), and *igi* (*eigi* [56; cf. 7]).

Superscript *m* occurs once and stands for *um* (*vond*um [79]); the word is at the end of a line.

Superscript *n* occurs three times and stands for *an* (*heimanfôr* [43], *þiotandi* [129], *of*an [145]); the two former words are at the end of a line.

Superscript *o* is used for *ro* (*drottín* [125]), *ru* (eru [73]; cf. *eru* [90, etc.]), *oru* (voru [54]; cf. *vorv* [91]). Superscript *o* is used also in the abbreviation of *hon* (*h°* [8, etc.]), but is expanded *h*un in accordance with forms written in full (17, etc.). Finally, superscript *o* is used in the abbreviation of *messu* (*m°* [145]).

Superscript *r* is used for *ar* (*krossmark* [26]) and *adr* (*spam*adr [72]).

The *ra* abbreviation, which resembles a Greek pi as in *fram* (14), is also used for *ia* (*leggi*a [11]). In addition, it is used in the abbreviation of *svá* (e.g., 19), but is expanded *s*vo in accordance with the form written in full (6, etc.).

Superscript *t* stands for *it* (*Giôr*it [20]).

Superscript *u* occurs twice and stands for *ru* (*brunní* [34] and *truligh*a [136]).

The *ur*-abbreviation as in *dott*ur (6) resembles a superscript figure 2. In four instances, it is used for *r* (*y*dr [38], *fagnad*r [88], *apt*r [120], *fegrsta* [139]); the first two and the last of these words are at the end of a line.

The *us*-abbreviation as in *di < o > schori*us (4) resembles a super-script figure 9. It is also used for *ud* (*guds* [114]) and *uds* (guds [37]).

A tailed *r* rotunda is used for *ed* (*m*ed [25]).

The Tironian nota is used for *ok* (cf. 4).

The nasal stroke proper (which is often no more than a dot) is used for *m* (*dôgu*m [3]), *n* (*enn* [22]), *an* (*gang*a [76]), *ann* (*h*ann [14]), *en* (*m*enn [6]), *enn* (*m*enn [28]), *in* (*hím*in [71]), and *onnu* (*m*onnum [146]).

Abbreviation by suspension is fairly common. The following examples are in evidence: *Sv.* = *Sv(aradi)* (10), *sv.* = *sv(aradi)* (46, 70), *.s.* = *s(varadi)* (49), *.e.* = *e(da)* (69), *B* = *B(arbara)* (85), *.b.* = *b(arbara)* (124), *.s.* = *s(innar)* (125). At 10, 46, 49, 69, 70, and 124, it is, perhaps, doubtful, if the abbreviation should be classified as a suspension, since the respective letters are furnished with a superior curl.

A number of words are abbreviated in a somewhat more radical fashion with a raised horizontal stroke or a curl, e.g. *mællti* (9), *svðrudu* (20), *baptista* (31), *svaradi* (96), and *byskups* (145).

Jesús is abbreviated *ihc* (87, 126, 131), and in the dat. *ihu* (71, 151).

Kristr (103) is abbreviated *xpc* (87) or *xp̄c* (126) or *k^{i}str* (99, 131), in the acc. *k^{i}st* (34), in the dat. *xp̄o* (71, 151), and in the gen. *k^{i}stz* (70, 92, 144).

3.1.2 Orthography

Vowels

a is written *a*. The *æ* in *þeiræ* (12) is an isolated example. The word is at the end of a line, where *æ* no doubt serves as a line-filler (see Foote 1962: 17).

u-mutation is found in two- or three-syllable words with *u* in the second or third syllable.

The conjunction *eða/eðr* is written *eda* (73, etc.)

á is written *a* or *æ* In two instances, two accents are found over *á* (*fá́* [12] and *sá́r* [98]).

The preposition *á* is written *a* or *æ*; the latter is more common. The *æ* in *hæalsi* (76) is no doubt *á*.

Older *vá* has become *vo*: *svo* (6, etc.), *tvo* (17, etc.), *vor* (87, etc), *vorv* (91), and *vorvm* (151).

The noun *nátt/nótt* is written *nótt*: *not* (86), *nottvm* (144).

e is written *e*.

Diphthongization of *e* before *ng* is evident in *leíngi* (16, 80), *eíngi* (62), and *eingil* (118).

é is written *e*.

The spelling *ie* for *é* occurs once: *sied* (56).

Foote (1962: 15) notes that between *v* and *l* and between *v* and *r* original *é* has become *æ*. There are no examples of *é* between *v* and *l* in the text covered by *Barbare saga*. *é* between *v* and *r* is found in the 1st pers. plur. of the pronoun *vér*; however, the word is always abbreviated, but is transcribed *vær*.

There is no confusion between *i* and *y*.

Fyrir is always abbreviated. Foote (1962:15) observes that *fyrir* is written in full at 69vb15, 72vb40, 86va33, and not infrequently abbreviated *fyr*ir (e.g., 18ra44, 19vb16, 28ra32, 38va4, 57rb30, 61rb28); *firir* occurs once (65va22).

The noun *byskup* occurs only abbreviated (145). Foote (1962: 15) notes that *byskup* is written this way at, e.g., 39rb5 and 84ra8 and always by the hand that supplies the titles.

Of the forms –*liga/–lega*, –*ligr/–legr*, only the –*liga/–ligr* form is in evidence: *vandliga* (61), *hraustlíga* (105), *hofdínglígum* (109–110), *hresslíga* (110), *truligha* (136), *dyrlig*ri (142), and *leynilíga* (147).

The symbol *j* (without accent) is normally used for the preposition *í* and occurs also initially in the words *jarll* (66), *jlma* (75), *jallín*n (93), *jarllín*n (106), and finally in *sendj* (117).

o is normally written *o*, but in rare instances *ó* is used (*myrkvastófv* [85], *myrkvastófvn*ne [93–94]).

The fem. sing. pers. pronoun *hon* is written *hun* with one exception: *hon* (39).

ó is normally written *o*, rarely *ó* (*fórn* [71], *gróf* [148]). In one instance, two accents are found over *ó* (*þó* [33]).

The negative prefix is *ó*: *ouerdr* (100), *o arga* (101), *ostyrk*ir (137).

The preposition *ór* is always written *or* (12, etc.).

u and *ú* are written *u* or *v*. In word-initial position *w* for *u* occurs once: *wpp* (1 title).

The sounds conventionally represented by *ǫ* and *ø* have, of course, fallen together and are represented by *ó* (e.g., *dǫgu*m [3]) or *au/v* (e.g., *stauplínv*m [6], *nauktan* [116]) or, less commonly, by *o* (e.g., *vond*um [79]).

The verb *gjöra* is abbreviated with the *er* abbreviation sign (e.g., *ger*a [14]); when written in full it has –*ið*– (e.g., *giðrdi* [5]).

The *i*-umlaut of *á* and *ó* is written *æ*, e.g., *vænleik* (7) and *fæzlu* (31).

In unstressed, final syllables, *i* is more common than *e*, although *e* is by no means uncommon. *e* is particularly common in *henni* (*henne* [53, 55, 68, 93, 102, 120], *henne* [61, 86, 103]). It is found also in *hafde* (24), *manne* (30, 51), *hímne* (86), *hímens* (91, 107, 113), *þeiRe* (92), *myrkvastôfvnne* (93–94).

As for *u* and *o*, *u* is the more common. *o* is found in the following words: *hverso* (14, 98), *heilso* (29), *hôrdoztv* (70), and *þino* (131).

The svarabhakti vowel is not in evidence.

Consonants

Apart from geminate *k* (which is written *ck*), *c* occurs only in the names *Dioscorus* (*di<o>schori*us [4; cf., however, *dioskoru*s [42], *dioschoro* [41 chapter heading], *dioschoru*s [66], *dioscoro* [121]) and *Nikulás* (*nículas* [144]) and in the noun *locuste* (59).

Foote (1962: 16) notes that in weakly stressed endings (2nd pers. plur. of verbs, neut. of suffixed article, neut. of strong adjectives, and neut. of past participles), final –*t* is often written when the preceding syllable ends in -*ð* (*d*). He further comments that when the preceding syllable ends in other consonants, including *t*, both –*d* and –*t* are found finally. In words with the stem ending in a vowel, final –*d* is usual. The *Barbare saga* section fits this pattern, e.g., *gerdut* (18), *Giðrit* (20, 22), *settut* (44), *sied* (56), *husít* (62), *vítrad* (93), *ordit* (101), and *bedít* (143). It should be noted that there is ample evidence to show that in general final –*t* in weakly stressed words and syllables has become *ð*; the particle *at* is frequently written *ath* (e.g., 11).

The preposition *við* is written *vit* (occasionally *wit*) with only one exception: *vid* (44).

The noun *skurðgoð/skurgoð* is written with *ð* (*d*) (4, 35–36, 37, 39, 73).

f before *t* is usually written *p*, e.g., *eptír* (25), *aptr* (35), and *kraptí* (37).

The masc. acc. sing. of the adjective *hár* is written with *f*: *hafan* (6).

Note *f* in *algerfa* (43), but *v* (*u*) in *gerua* (18), *gervar* (90).

Indication of palatalization of *g* after a vowel before *i* is not in evidence. The palatalization of *g* after a vowel before *i* is shown by the "backward" spelling *flygía* (55).

Between vowels and between *n* and a vowel *g* is in two instances written *gh*: *hôfdinghí* (3), *truligha* (136).

The noun *jarteign/jartein* is written both with and without *g*: *iarteign*ar (59), *iartein*ir (130), *íarteín*ir (150).

The adjective *gnógr/nógr* is written with initial *g*: *gnogr* (88).

The dat. sing. of the noun *morginn/morgunn* is *morní* (93).

h is preserved before *l* (*hlut* [23], *hlut*ir [131], *hlyda* [131], etc.) and *r* (*hreínt* [27], *hrífa* [79]). The cluster *hn* is not in evidence.

k is written *k*. Geminate *k* is written *ck*.

There is no sign of *k* > *g*: *ek* (11, etc.), *mik* (100, etc.), *þik* (90, etc.).

The rule that *-lld* is written where the *d* is original and that *-ld* is written where the *d* is a late development from *ð* is followed, although not consistently: *willdi* (14), *margfallda* (28), *uilldi* (52), *villdí* (55, 68), *duldi* (56), *vardhalld* (62), *skylldi* (67), *selld* (70), *skyldi* (82), *hallda* (102), *dvalda* (105), *hlífskiolldr* (115), *huldi* (118), *milldi* (134), *huilld*ar (139), *elldr* (146), *alld*ir (152), *allda* (152).

ll is always written double before *t* and *z*: *gallt* (15), *fiallz* (61, 124), *iarllz* (67), *villtv* (69), *fylltiz* (78, 123), *skallt* (89), *Gíalltv* (109), *iarllzins* (119), *hellzt* (135).

The assimilation of *rl* is found once: *jallín*n (93).

m is represented either by *m* or by the nasal stroke, the determining factor being almost certainly graphic convenience.

m is retained in the 1st pers. plur. of verbs: *megu*m *vær* (21).

In *grimarí* (57), it may be that the nasal stroke was forgotten or has faded away.

n is represented either by *n* or by the nasal stroke. As with *m*, the determining factor seems to be graphic convenience. Length is shown by a horizontal stroke over the *n* or, less commonly, by doubling.

No distinction is made between the adverb *enn* and the conjunction *en*; both are written *enn*. Exceptions are *en* (the conjunction; 5, 9, 49, 110, 124) and *en* (the adverb; 112); in these cases it may be that the stroke (dot) was forgotten or has faded away. In general, however, there seems to be a lack of consistency with regard to *n* and *nn*, e.g., *heidín* (4; masc. nom. sing.), *sidann* [28, etc]; but *sidan* (15, etc.]), *en þridia glugg* (20; but *enn þridía glugg* [23]), *anar* (57; but *annar* [56]), *grædaRín* (86–87), *drottín* (91; but *drottínn* [86–87]), *groínn* (91; neut. nom. plur.), *bríostinn* (107), *hôggvínn* (143; fem. nom. sing.).

Long *p* is indicated by doubling (e.g., *vpp* [113]) or by a superscript dot (e.g., *vpp* [27]).

For forms of *r* and their distribution, see above. Long *r* is shown by a superscript dot as in *giðrr* (73) or by doubling as in *giðrr* (36). The R in *þeiRe* (92) may indicate long *r*. The dot over R in *grædaRín* (86–87) and *dyR* (101) would not seem to indicate doubling, and neither would R itself in these two instances.

For forms of *s* and their distribution, see above. Long *s* is shown by doubling (e.g., *oss* [19]). Note long *s* in *huss* (61) and *vítlauss* (neut. nom. plur.; 97).

In addition to the above-mentioned examples of gen. *s* written *z* (i.e., *fiallz* [61, 124], *iarllz* [67], *iarllzins* [119]), the following occurrences may be noted: *kristz* (70, 92, 144) and *kristz* (107).

Long *t* is indicated by doubling (e.g., *atti* [5]) or by a superscript dot (e.g., *spratt* [27]). In *drotníng* (20) and *not* (86), it may be that the dot was forgotten or has faded away.

Consonantal *u* (*v*) is written *v* or occasionally *w* in word-initial position (e.g., *war* [3], var [7]). Word-medially, *v* is written either *v* or *u* or, in one instance, *w* (*gíafwaxín* [8]). In word-final position both *u* and *v* are found.

The medio-passive ending is *z* or *zt*, e.g., *hrædvmzt* (20), *reidiz* (21), *standaz* (21), *liktizt* (32), and *liktiz* (34).

The superlative ending is usually –*zt*, sometimes –*z* or –*st*: *skiotaz* (13), *grandvar*<*a*>*zta* (24), *hôrdoztv* (70), *hellzt* (135), *fegrsta* (139), *glôduztv* (139), *helgvztv* (148).

Miscellaneous

The free definite article is, with only one exception (*hít o arga dyR* [101]), *enn* (not *inn* or *hinn*): *en þridia glugg* (20), *enn þridía glugg* (23), *enn* gran*dvar* < *a* > *zta mær* (24), *enni* lóngv heim*anför* (42–43), *enna* hórdoztv pisla (70), *enn fegrsta mær* (139), *ennar glóduztv huilld*ar (139), *ennar helgvztv mey*iar (148).

Barbara is declined as follows: acc.: *barbaram* (120); dat.: *barbare* (65 chapter heading; 84 chapter heading); gen.: *barbare* (1 title, 60, 122 chapter heading, 148).

Both the strong form *líkamr* and the weak form *líkami* are in evidence: *likama* (81, 95, 116), *likam*ir (138), *likam* (148).

As far as *–leikr*/*–leiki* forms are concerned, only the strong form occurs: *vænleik* (7).

Both *sær* and *sjór* are in evidence: *sæ* (72), *sia*var (127), *sía* (128).

The nom. form of *sonr* is *son* (99).

Ambátt is without *–u* in the dat.: *ambatt* (133). The same applies to *hǫll*: *hóllínní* (17, 25).

The acc. plur. of *smiðr* is *smídvna* (18) or *smidína* (44).

The masc. nom. plur. of *gǫfugr* is *gǫfgir* (*gaufgir* [8]).

Both *a* and *u* are found in the 1st pers. sing. pres. of *munu*: *ek mun* (22), *man ek* (89–90). In the 3rd pers. sing. pres., only *man* is in evidence (140).

The 1st. pers. sing. pres. of *vera* is *em*: *ek em* (89).

The imperative of *vera* is *vert*: *Vert þv* (87).

The 2nd pers. sing. pres. of *vilja* is *vill* (*þv will* [10]).

The 2nd pers. sing. pres. of *vita* is written *veitz* (103) and *veizt* (137).

The 2nd pers. sing. pret. of *bjóða* is *bauð*: *baud þv* (46).

The 2nd pers. sing. pret. of *biðja* is *batt* (140).

Both the *–a* and *–u* ending are found in the 3rd pers. plur. pres. of *mega*: *mega* (48, 49, 99), *megv* (98).

The 1st pers. sing. pret. ending is *–a*: *gerda ek* (47), *ek dvalda* (105).

The 3rd pers. sing. pret. of *þvá* (*þvó*) is *þó* (33).

The verb *fylla* takes the dat. or the gen.: *fadir hennar fylltíz mikilli reidi* (123), *fylltiz iarll mikillar reidí* (78). The negation is *eigi* (7, etc.). It is abbreviated *eī* (21) or *e^i* (56). The following forms of *engi* are found: masc. nom. sing.: *eíngi* (62); masc. acc. sing.: *óngan* (99).

The following forms of *nokkurr/nǫkkurr* are in evidence: masc. nom. sing.: *nockur* (3, 147); masc. acc. sing.: *nóckurn* (11); masc. dat. sing.: *nóckurv*m (30); fem. acc. sing.: *nockura* (30).

3.2 Copenhagen, Det arnamagnæanske Institut AM 429 12mo

AM 429 12mo consists of 84 leaves. Its single-columned leaves measure 11.5 × 8.8 cm. Kålund (1889–1894: 2: 480), Jón Þorkelsson (1888: 88), and Seip (1954: 137) date the manuscript to around 1500. Unger (1877: 1: XII) dates it to the middle of the fifteenth century. His view is shared by Konráð Gíslason (1860: XI), who maintains that it is from approximately the same time as AM 621 4to, which he dates to the mid-fifteenth century. Jón Helgason (1936–1938: 2: 341), however, comments that Konráð Gíslason's dating is "hardly correct."

The manuscript contains the legend of Saint Margaret of Antioch (fols. 2r–13r), a Latin prayer to Saint Margaret (fol. 13v), the legend of Saint Catherine of Alexandria (fols. 15r–27r),[116] the legend of Saint Cecilia (fols. 29r–45v),[117] a so-called "Cecilíudiktur" (fols. 46r–47v; ed. Konráð Gíslason 1860: 559–560),[118] the legend of Saint Dorothy (fols. 49–57r; ed. Unger 1877: 1: 322–328, Wolf 1998: 88–103), a so-called "Dórótheudiktur" (fols. 57r–59r; ed. Jón Helgason 1936–1938: 2: 359–363), a Latin verse about

---

116. Variants from this manuscript (called C) are given in Unger (1877: 1: 400–421).

117. Variants from this manuscript (called C) are given in Unger (1877: 1: 276–294).

118. The poem was edited by Jón Helgason (1936–1938: 2: 342–346) on the basis of AM 721 4to with variants and corrections from AM 429 12mo (called B). Stanzas 1 and 31 (based on AM 429 12mo) were printed in Jón Þorkelsson (1888: 88–89).

and prayer to Saint Dorothy (fol. 59v; ed. Wolf 1998: 62), the legend of Saint Agnes (fols. 61r–69r),[119] the legend of Saint Agatha (fols. 69r–76r), the legend of Saint Barbara (fols. 76r–80v; see above), and the legend of Saints Fides, Spes, and Caritas (fols. 81r–84v).[120] All texts are preserved in their entirety with the exception of the legend of Saint Catherine, of which a middle portion is missing, and the legend of Fides, Spes, and Caritas, the end of which is missing.

The upper half of fol. 81r was originally blank and may have been intended for an illumination of Saints Fides, Spes, and Caritas. Indeed, colored illuminations of Saints Margaret, Catherine, Cecilia, and Dorothy are found on fols. 1v, 14v, 28v, and 48v, respectively, and on fol. 60v, there is an illustration of Saint Agnes in black. Smaller illustrations of a similar kind appear in the text on fols. 7r, 8r, 10r, 12v, 57r, 69r (Saint Agatha, in black), and 76r (Saint Barbara, in black). Ornamental drawings appear at the bottom of fols. 35r, 52r, 52v, and 57r, and in the text of fol. 49r (the initial *J*). Many of the titles and initials are in red, and one initial is in blue. In some places, an open space has been left for the initials.

The illustration of Saint Barbara, which takes up well over a third of the Saint Barbara text on fol. 76r, is framed (except for the top). Above the left column is written "*Sancta barbara.*" Saint Barbara herself is depicted with shoulder-length wavy hair and wearing a crown. Her ankle-length dress is long-sleeved and with a low neckline. In her left hand, she is holding a sword, and in her right, a book with a clasp (presumably the Bible). What looks like a cactus, but what is probably meant to be a tower, is depicted in the background. The initial *A* (1) at the beginning of the saga is an illustration of an animal. Its tail (which extends into the right-hand frame of the illustration of Saint Barbara) and its right hind leg form the left-hand ascender of the *A*; its back forms the roof of the

119. Variants from this manuscript (called B) are given in Unger (1877: 1: 15–22).
120. Variants from this manuscript (called D) are given in Unger (1877: 1: 369–372).

A; its front legs form the right-hand ascender of the *A*; and its left hind leg, which is raised, forms the cross-bar.

On fols. 59v and 81r, some lines from Hallgrímur Pétursson's *Passíusálmar* are found. On fol. 27v it is written that "þetta er bok Gudrunar ad leika sier ad þui hun rifnar ei þo ostillt sie med fared," which suggests that the manuscript was, at least at one point, in private possession. On fols. 14r and 27v–28r, the alphabet is written in a seventeenth-century hand along with the formulaic prayer indicating the sign of the cross (in one instance referring only to the sign [of the cross]): "i nafne faudur og sonar og anda heilags amen" (27v), "Signinginn (28r), and "J nafne fødur og sonar og heilags Amen" (28r).

Little is known about the provenance and history of the manuscript. On a note accompanying the manuscript, Árni Magnússon gives the information that he received it from "Páll á Flókastöðum" ("Mitt, feinged af Paale ä Flokastödum") and lists the contents of the manuscript.[121] This Páll is most likely the Páll Ámundason (ca. 1645–1716), who was the administrator of the convent land of Kirkjubæjarklaustur from 1681 to around 1708, and who died at Flókastaðir in Fljótshlíð, where his son-in-law, Björn Thorlacius, served as a minister. Considering the fact that the manuscript contains legends of women saints exclusively, it is probable that the collection was intended for women and most likely nuns. Páll Ámundason's association with the volume makes it reasonable to suggest that it was written for and possibly by the nuns in the Benedictine convent at Kirkjubær in Síða, which was established in 1186.[122] If one accepts Kålund's dating of the manuscript (see above), the manuscript may have been written

---

121. The same information is found in Árni Magnússon's catalogue (AM 435a 4to): "Margretar Saga. de S. Catharinâ. de S. Cæciliâ, og þar i de Tiburtio et Valeriano. Carmen de S. Cæciliâ. de S. Dorotheâ. Carmen de S. Dorotheâ. de S. Agnete. de S. Agathâ. de S. Barbarâ. de S. Sophiâ, desunt nonnulla in calce. Er i 16 blade forme. feinged af Pale á Flokastödum" (*Håndskriftfortegnelser* 1909: 17).

122. For this convent, see Janus Jónsson (1887: 236–240), Guðrún P. Helgadóttir (1961–1963: 1: 81–88), and Anna Sigurðardóttir (1988: 17–84).

under the direction of Halldóra Sigvaldadóttir; Halldóra, who was the last abbess of Kirkjubær, was appointed around 1494 (Anna Sigurðardóttir 1988: 63).

The following paleographic and orthographic description is limited to fols. 76r–80v.

3.2.0 Paleography

Only the so-called two-storey *a* is found. The top storey is usually a closed loop as in, e.g., *daugu*m (1).

b is normally written with a loop as in *barbara* (3), except in conjunction with abbreviations (e.g., *barb*ara [8])

Only insular or round *d* is in evidence.

The *e* is always open.

Only insular *f* is in evidence. It consists of a vertical stroke with a figure 3 attached on the right. The lower loop of the 3 always ends at the descender.

The upper part of *g* is an *o*; its tail is usually triangular in shape as in, e.g., *daugu*m (1).

The right-hand vertical of *h* always descends below the line. The *h* is usually written with a loop, except in conjunction with abbreviations, e.g., *h*et (1).

The *j* is always barred; the bar does not cross the descender.

k is always written with a loop; exceptions are found only in conjunction with abbreviations (e.g., *k*onung*s* [1]).

l is usually written with a loop as in *stopul* (3) and *mikill* (2). In conjunction with abbreviations, however, it is normally without a loop (e.g., *męlk*ti [15]).

The right-hand minim of *m* and *n* does not extend below the line. (An exception is *sin*ar [126]). A small capital *n* (*N*) occurs three times: *þiN*ar (95, 101), *siN*ar (110); the minim of the *N* extends well below the line.

Of *r*, there are two types, minuscule *r* and *r* rotunda. *r* rotunda is used after *b, d, f, g, h, o, þ, u*, and *y* and is in complementary distribution with minuscule *r*, except after *f, þ, u*, and *y*, where also minuscule *r* is found, e.g., *sialfri* (60) / *silfrí* (64), *þria* (38) / *þridía* (17), *skurdgod* (29) / *murín*n (46), and *myrkír* (41) / *myrkkua* (71).

Of *s*, there are two types, round or small *s* and long or cursive *s*. The former always sits on the line, whereas the latter extends well below the line. Small capital *s* (*ѕ*) is used in abbreviations of *svo* (e.g., *ѕuo* [4]) and occurs also in *ѕ(uorudu)* (18, 37), *johanneѕ* (28), and *ѕ(uaradi)* (39, 44).

The vertical of *t* does not normally extend above the cross-bar except in the ligature of *s* + *t*.

x appears only in *Maxímaní* (1), *uaxín*n (5), and in abbreviations of *Kristr* (see below). The second cross-stroke goes well below the line, ending in a hook.

y is written with a dot. The upper part consists of a *u*; the descender veers to the left and may or may not end in a hook (e.g., *lysa* [40], *myrkír* [41]).

z is without a cross-bar. It is quite similar to *r* rotunda, except that it extends below the line.

The Tironian nota has the shape of a *z*. It is always barred.

Of ligatures, only *g* + *d* and *s* + *t* are in evidence.

Apart from the word *amen*, which is written in capital letters (*AMEN* [138]), the following capitals are found (excluding the ornamental *A* at the beginning of the legend): *E* (*En* [14, etc.]), *J* (*J* [26, etc.]), *M* (*Maxímaní* [1]), and *N* (*Nícholae* [129]). All appear as Roman capitals; it should be noted that *J* is furnished with a cross-bar, which, however, does not cross the upright, and that *N* is very similar to *H*.

An accent is commonly found over *i* and *j*, but appears to be no more than a graphic marker.

The deletion of a letter is indicated by a dot below the line: *brad* (45 see textual note). The deletion of a word is indicated by underlining (*þau* [82 see textual note]) or by crossing out (*bt* [53 see textual note], *kō* [57 see textual note], *þr* [60 see textual note]).

3.2.1 Abbreviations

Superscript *a* stands for *ar* (*fara* [11]) and *ara* (*fara* [45]). It also occurs in *manna* (64), written *ma* with a superscript *a* over the *m*.

Superscript *e* stands for *enn* (*menn* [6]).

The zigzag tittle is used for *er* (*gerdi* [3]), *ir* (*fadir* [3]), and *r* (*er* [1]). The use of the tittle in *mark* (23, 25) seems to represent erroneous use of the tittle.

Superscript *i* stands for *il* (*til* [6]), *it* (*husit* [55]), *ri* (*midri* [72]), *ui* (*þui* [46]), and *igi* (*eigi* [65], cf. *eígi* [8]). It is also used in abbreviations of *fyrir* (*fyrir* [16, etc.]), which is never written in full.

Superscript *n* stands for *an* (*sidan* [9]) and *ann* (*mann* [40]).

Superscript *o* stands for *or* (*giord* [10]), *oru* (*uoru* [15]), *uo* (*suo* [17]), and *ro* (*cross* [22]). It is also used in the abbreviation of *hon/hun* (*h°* [5, etc.]). The superscript *o* in *skurdgodum* (i.e., *skordgodum*, 31 see textual note) would seem to be an error.

Superscript *r* stands for *ar* (*uar* [4]) and *adr* (*madr* [2]).

The *ra* abbreviation as in *framar* (41) resembles a Greek pi. It is used also for *ua* (*myrkuastofu* [80]).

Superscript *t* is used for *at* (*þat* [10]), *et* (*het* [1]), and *it* (*uit* [7]).

Superscript *u* stands for *ru* (*rettruadir* [25]).

The superscript 2-like sign is used for *ur* (*dotur* [2], *fodurs* [18], *nockura* [27], etc.). Since no clear distinction is made between the endings *-r* and *-ur*, it is uncertain whether the sign, when it appears word-finally, should be expanded *-r* or *-ur*.

The *us* abbreviation occurs once: *hus* (24).

The *r* rotunda looking sign is used for *ed* (*med* [68]).

The Tironian nota is used for *ok/og*. The word is never written in full.

The nasal stroke proper stands for *m* (*daugum* [1]), *n* (*eina* [2]), *an* (*hana* [5]), *ann* (*hann* [4]), and *en* (*henar* [6]).

The following examples of abbreviation by suspension are in evidence: *.b.* = *b(arbara)* (17, etc.), *m.* = *m(ęllti)* (17, 19), *.s.* = *s(uorudu)* (18, 37), *.s.* = *s(uaradi)* (39, 44), *J.* = *J(arll)* (70), and *.J.* = *J(arlinn)* (92, 96).

A number of words are abbreviated in a somewhat more radical fashion with a raised horizontal stroke or a curl, e.g., *konungs* (1), *męllti* (7), *dioscorus* (9), *baptista* (28), and *þuiat* (74).

Jesús is in the nom. and dat. abbreviated *ihu* (62, 73, 111, 136).

Kristr (*Cristr*) is in the nom. abbreviated *c^{i}stí* (74, 111), in the dat. *xp̄e* (62, 136), and in the gen. *c^{i}stz* (93).

3.2.2 Orthography
Vowels
a is written *a*.

u-mutation is found in two- or three-syllable words with *u* in the second or third syllable with the exception of *logandu*m (88) and *gladustu* (124).

The conjunction *eða/eðr* is written *eda* (60, etc.).

á is written *a*.

Older *vá* has become *vo*: *S*uo (4, etc.), *tuo* (16), *uor* (82), *uorkynd* (121), *uorír* (122), and *uoru*m (136).

The noun *nátt/nótt* is written *nótt*: *nott* (72), *nottu*m (129).

e is written *e*. The *i* (for *e*) in *míssu dag* (129) may be an error.

Diphthongization of *e* before *ng* is evident in *eingi* (4, 131), *leingí* (13, 69), and *eingil* (103).

The verb *gera* (12) is abbreviated with both the zigzag tittle (e.g., *gerdi* [3]) and with a superscript *o* (e.g., *giordu* [16]).

Note *ei* in *heilgu*m (30) and *heilgustu* (133).

The *e* in *kuelu*m (70 see textual note) is no doubt an error.

é is written *e*.

There is no confusion between *i* and *y*. *Fyrir* is always abbreviated *f^i*. *Yfir* is written *yfir* (73). The noun *byskup* occurs only abbreviated (129). The preposition *í* is written *j*.

The endings *–liga/–lega*, *–ligr/–legr* have *e*: *uanlega* (54), *hraustlega* (92), *hofdínglegu*m (95–96), *trulega* (121), *dyrlegr*i (126).

o and *ó* are written *o*.

The fem. sing. pers. pronoun *hon* is always abbreviated *h^o*.

The negative prefix is *ó*: *oarga* (88), *ostyrkír* (122).

The preposition *ór* is always written *or* (30, etc.).

The *i*-umlaut of *á* and *ó* is written *ę* (e.g., *męttí* [4], *uęnleik* [4], *fęzlu* [28]).

The *u*-umlaut of *a* is written *o* (e.g., *hofdínge* [1]), less frequently *au* (e.g., *auskuna* [132]) and, in two instances, *uo* (*huollína* [12] and *huogua* [44]). The *oo* in *heiloog* (8) may be an error.

In unstressed, final syllables, *i* is more common than *e*. *e* is especially common in *henni* (*henne* [36, 45, 53, etc.]). In addition, *e* is found in the following words: *hofdínge* (1), *steíne* (25), *manne* (27), *hollune* (39), *heimenn* (40), *manne* (43), *kẹme* (56), *husenu* (57), *skyllde* (58), *huere* (71), *hímne* (73), *grẹdare* (73), *himne* (75, 123), *þínne* (75), *greníiade* (88 see textual note), *híalpare* (100), *uerde* (102), and *syne* (136). Note also *criste* (62, 136).

As for *u* and *o*, *o* is uncommon, occurring only in *þino* (94, 116), *bylgíor* (113), *fíallíno* (130), and *loptíno* (131).

The svarabhakti vowel is not in evidence.

Consonants

Apart from geminate *k* (which is written *ck* with the exception of *gecc* [113] and *myrkkua* [71]), *c* occurs only in the names *Dioscorus* (*díoscorus* [9, 34, 57], cf., however, *díoskorus* [1], *dioskoro* [107]), *Nikulás* (*Nícholae* [129]), *Cristr* (*cristí* [74, 111], *cristz* [93]) and in the nouns *kross* (*cross* [22, 25], *crossínum* [114]) and *locuste* (51).

Note double *d* in *stundd* (27) and single *d* in *leidi* (108).

There is limited evidence that final *-t* in weakly stressed syllables has become *ð*, e.g., *þangad* (38, 47), *sed* (49), and *annad* (132). The particle *at* is always written *at*.

The preposition *við* is written *vit* (*uit* [7, 15, etc.]) or, in one instance, *viðr* (*uídr* [118]).

The noun *skurðgoð/skurgoð* is written with *ð* (*d*) (29, 31, 33, 63).

f before *t* is written *p*, e. g., *þarptu* (8), *eptir* (10), and *aptr* (29).

The masc. acc. sing. of the adjective *hár* is written with *f*: *hafann* (3).

Note *f* in *giorfuir* (15), but *v* (*u*) in *algíorua* (35) and *gíoruar* (77).

g is written *g*. Length is shown by doubling.

The adjective *gnógr/nógr* is written without initial *g*: *nogr* (74).

Note single *g* in *gluga* (36, 39), which is elsewhere written double, and in *huogua* (44). Of note is also the *giœ-* (not *gœ-*) spelling in *storgíẹdíngar* (7).

The noun *jarteign/jartein* is written with *g* (51, 115, 135).

The dat. sing. of the noun *morginn/morgunn* is *morni* (79).

h is preserved before *l* and *r* (e.g., *hlut* [20], *hreint* [24]). The cluster *hn-* is not in evidence.

k is written *k*. Geminate *k* is written *ck* or in one instance *kk* (*myrkkua* [71]) and *cc* (*gecc* [113]).

k > *g* is found in *míg* (84, 86, 91, 95, 121), *þig* (76, 82), and *míog* (81). *Ek* is throughout written *ek* (9, 19, etc.). *Ok* is always abbreviated.

l is written double before *d* (and *ð*): *uilldí* (12, 44, 47, 59), *margfallda* (25), *dulldí* (48), *halld* (55), *skyllde* (58), *fylldíz* (67, 107), *skylldi* (72), *hallda* (88), *dualldí* (92), *helldr* (95, 132), *hlif skylldr* (100), *skíolld<r>* (117), *mílldí* (118), *huilldar* (124), *elldr* (131), *allar* (137), *alldír* (137), and *allda* (137). There is only one exception: *huldu* (104 see textual note).

l is also written double before *t* and *z*: *uillt* (8), *skalltu* (75), *męllti* (82, 89), *gíallt* (95), *allz* (98), *fíallz* (108), and *hellz* (119). Note also double *l* in *hellgum* (136).

m is represented either by *m* or by the nasal stroke, the determining factor being almost certainly graphic convenience. In *grimari* (49), the nasal stroke was possibly forgotten.

n is represented either by *n* or by the nasal stroke. As with *m*, the determining factor appears to be graphic convenience. Length is shown by a nasal stroke over the *n* or by doubling or, in three instances, by small capital *n*: *þiNar* (95, 101) and *siNar* (110).

Distinction is made between the adverb *enn* and the conjunction *en* (with the exception of *en* [24]). In general, however, there is some inconsistency in the use of *n* and *nn*, e.g., *uaxínn* (fem. sing. nom.; 5), *enndílangrí* (21), *bruní* (26), *hollune* (39), *sannann* (43), *henar* (53), *allann* (70), and *helgann* (94).

Long *p* is shown by a superscript stroke as in, e.g., *upp* (24).

For forms of *r* and their distribution, see above.

rs > *s* is found in *fegusta* (123).

For forms of *s* and their distribution, see above. Long *s* is shown by doubling. Note double *s* in *huerssu* (41; cf. *huersu* [12, 84, 85]) and gen. *s* written *z* in *fíallz* (108; cf. *fíals* [54]), *cristz* (93), and *allz* (98).

Long *t* is shown by doubling or by a superscript dot. There appears to be some inconsistency in the use of short and long *t*, e.g., *blott* (2), *dot*ur (2, 3, 38, 56, 57), *spytí* (31), *dot*ir (37, 38), *stretti* (97), and *portt* (98).

Consonantal *u* (*v*) is written *u*.

The medio-passive ending is −*z*.

The superlative ending is −*st* (*hordustu*m [61], *fegusta* [123], *gladustu* [124], *heilgustu* [133]) or −*z* (*skíotaz* [11], *hellz* [119]).

Miscellaneous

The free definite article is written with initial *h*-.

Both the strong form *líkamr* and the weak form *líkami* are in evidence: *likama* (70, 101), *líkam*ir (122), *líkam* (133).

As far as −*leikr*/−*leiki* forms are concerned, only the strong form is in evidence: *uenleik* (4).

The gen. of *faðir* is *fod*urs (18) or *fod*ur (20, 30, 124).

Both *sær* and *sjór* are in evidence: *se* (62, 113), *siaf*ar (112).

The nom. form of the noun *sonr* is *sonr* (86).

Holl is written with and without −*u* in the dat. sing.: *hollínní* (15, 22, 36), *hollunní* (16), *hollune* (39). The same applies to *ambátt*: *ambatt* (115), *ambattu* (117–118).

The acc. plur. of *smiðr* is *smíduna* (16) or *smidína* (36).

The masc. nom. plur. of *gofugr* is *gau*<*f*>*gu*ir (6).

Myrkr is declined according to the ā-/ō-stem declension: *myrkír* (41).

Only *u* is found in the 1st and 3rd pers. sing. pres. of *munu*. The 2nd pers. sing. pres. is not in evidence.

The 1st pers. sing. pres. of *vera* is *er*: *ek er* (76).

The 2nd pers. sing. pres. of *vilja* is *vilt*: *þu uillt* (8).

The 2nd pers. sing. pres. of *vita* is written *ueítz* (90) and *ueíz* (122).

The 3rd pers. plur. pres. of *mega* is *mega* (41, etc.).

The 2nd pers. sing. pret. of *bjóða* is *bauð*: *baud þu* (38).

The 2nd pers. sing. pret. of *biðja* is *batt* (124).

Both the −*a* and −*i* endings are found in the 1st pers. sing. pret.: *gerda ek* (39), *ek dualldí* (91).

The verb *líkja* takes the dative: *liktí hun fẹzlu sínní* ok *lífí* (28). The verb *fylla* takes the gen.: *fylldíz iarll mikillar reídí* (67), *fad*ir *hen*ar *fylldíz míkillar reidí* (107).

The negation is *eigi* (8, etc.) or *ei* (49, etc.).

Only the masc. nom. sing. form of *engi* is in evidence: *eingi* (4), *eingi* (132).

Only the masc. nom. sing. and the fem. acc. sing. forms of *nokkur/nọkkur* are in evidence: *nockur* (132), *nock*ura (27).

3.3 The Filiation of the Manuscripts

Of the two manuscripts of *Barbare saga*, Stock. Perg. 2 fol. and AM 429 12mo, Stock. Perg. 2 fol. preserves the better text. AM 429 12mo is characterized by a number of stylistic problems, many of which are due to omissions caused by what appears to be sloppy copying:

Stock. 2: A dọgu*m* maxímíani kei*S*ara w*ar* nockur hǫfdinghí (3)
AM 429: A daugu*m* Maxímaní konu*n*gs at sa hofdínge uar (1)

Stock. 2: þa geck en*n* grandvar < a > zta mær barbara eptír hǫllín*n*í (24–25)
AM 429: þa geck hín b(arbara) ept*ir* en*n*dílangrí hollín*n*í (21–22)

Stock. 2: en*n* þeir svor*u*du. dott*ir* þín baud oss svo (44–45)
AM 429: e*n* þeir s(uorudu) dot*ir* ydr at g*er*a s*u*o (36–37)

Stock. 2: þa reiddízt fad*ir* hen*n*ar *ok* bra *S*verdí *ok* uilldi þeg*ar* hǫggua dottur sína (51–52)
AM 429: þa s(uaradi) fadír hen*ar* u*it* h*an*a *ok* bra suerdi uílldí huogua h*an*a (43–44)

AM 429 12mo also has factual errors not found in Stock. Perg. 2 fol.; again, these are no doubt due to misreadings of the exemplar:

Latin: q*ua*liter p*er* pẹnas consumer*et* ea*m* (89–90)
Stock. 2: m*ed* hverrí písl h*an*n skyldi luka yf*ir* h*an*a (82–83)
AM 429: m*ed* huere pisl e*r* h*an*n skylldi *eigi* fa yf*ir* h*an*a lok*it* (71–72)

Latin: exaudi me famula*m* tua*m* (139)
Stock. 2: heyrdv mik ambatt þína (130)
AM 429: hialptu m*er* ambatt þin*n*i (115)

On several occasions, Stock. Perg. 2 fol. preserves material in the Latin text not found in AM 429 12mo, as demonstrated in the following examples:

Latin: Hoc lauachru*m* similabat*ur* fonti syloe, in q*uo* a natiuitate cecus lauans lumen recepit. Hoc lauachru*m* similabat*ur* probatic*ę* piscin*ę*, in q*ua* paraliticus u*er*bo curatus est. H*ę*c est natatoria, *et* fons incorruptibilis. Hec *est* natatoria et aqua uiua, q*ua*m samaritana ad fonte*m* a *christ*o petiuit (34–38)

Stock. 2: Sia brun*n*r. e*r* barb*ar*a v*ar* skírd j liktizt þ*eim* brun*n*i er gudspiðll segía ath sa þ*ő* andlít sítt j e*r* blíndr v*ar* borín*n* *ok* tok syn sína. Sia brun*n*r liktiz þ*ui* lífanda watní er syndug kona bad k*ri*st gefa S*er* at br*u*nní (31–34)

AM 429: -

Latin: Finito autem op*ere* atq*ue* p*er*fecto, reu*er*sus est pater ei*us* de peregrinatione (49–50)

Stock. 2: En*n* e*r* dioskor*us* kom heím aptr fad*ir* henn*ar* or en*n*i lðngv heim*ar*nfðr þa leít h*ar*nn *æ* holl sína alg*er*fa (42–43)

AM 429: En e*r* díoscor*us* fad*ir* henar ko*m* aptr þa leit h*ann* holl sína algíorua (34–35)

Latin: Q*ua*re tres fenestras instituistis? (51)

Stock. 2: fyr*ir* hui settut þer þr*ia* glugga (44)

AM 429: fyr*ir* hui g*er*du þer gluga ahollin*n*i (36)

Latin: Similes illis fiant q*ui* faciunt ea, *et* om*n*es qui confidunt in eis (84–85)

Stock. 2: v*er*di þ*eim* lik*ir* þ*eir* er þav giðra *ok* allír þ*eir* er treystaz þ*eim* (77–78)

AM 429: -

Latin: Cum aute*m* *et* hanc plaga*m* supra memorata*m* fortiter sp*iritu* s*ancto* roborata sustinuisset (117–119)

Stock. 2: en er hvn hafdi þetta m*æ*l*t* *ok* stodz hr*e*sslíga þessar píslír allar af styrk heilags anda (110–111)

AM 429: -

Latin: D*omi*ne ih*es*u *christ*e p*ro*tector meus á juuentute mea (140)

Stock. 2: Drottin ih*es*us k*ri*str hlif*ar*i mín*n* j æskv mín*n*i (131–132)

AM 429: drottin*n* mín*n* u*er*tu hlíf skíolld<r> mín*n* (116)

AM 429 12mo cannot be derived from Stock. Perg. 2 fol., however, because in a few instances the text of AM 429 12mo is closer to the Latin than that of Stock. Perg. 2 fol.:

> Latin: dioscor*us* (2–3)
> AM 429: díoskorus (1)
> Stock. 2: di < o > schori*us* (4)

> Latin: Et erant duo pastores pascentes oues in eode*m* monte (62–63)
> AM 429: en a þ*ui* fíallí uor*u* fehird*ar* (46–47)
> Stock. 2: En*n* j þ*eim* stad vor*u* hírdar tveír (54)

> Latin: T*unc* quoq*ue* p*r*eses confusus (128–129)
> AM 429: þa hręddíz j < arll > ín*n* (106)
> Stock. 2: þa reiddíz íarllín*n* (120)

Moreover, AM 429 12mo preserves material in the Latin not found in Stock. Perg. 2 fol., as demonstrated by the following examples:

> Latin: qu*ę* p*er*mane < n > t ad sepulchru*m* eius us*que* in hodiernu*m* diem (67–68)
> AM 429: ok min*n*íng þ*ess*arar i*a*rteígn*ar* er m*or*kut yf*ir* leídí heilagr*ar* b(arbare) S*uo* at sia ma allt t*il* þessa dags (51–53)
> Stock. 2: ok er minni*n*g þ*ess*arar i*a*rteignar m*ò*rkud yf*ir* leidi heilagr*ar* barbara (59–60)

> Latin: Quomo*do* rep*r*opi*t*iati sunt t*ibi* dí*j* et diligunt te barbara, q*ui*a plagas tuas sanauerunt? (101–102)
> AM 429: huí gegn*ir* þ*at* b(arbara) at god uor elska þig S*uo* at þau miskun*n*a þer S*uo* at sar þ*in* eru groín*n* (81–83)
> Stock. 2: hvi gegn*ir* þ*at* b*a*rbara er gud vor elska þ*ik* o*k* mískun*n*a þer (95–96)

> Latin: iussit adhuc insan*us* p*r*eses nuda*m* eam circuire omne*m* regione*m* illa*m*, *et* plagas á ministris inferentib*us*, ubiq*ue* ea*m* flagellari (119–121)
> AM 429: þa baud J(arlinn) þíonu*m* sinu*m* at þ*eir* fęrdí h*a*na en*n* or klędu*m* o*k* beria h*a*na o*k* draga nakta u*m* aull stręttí o*k* portt fyr*ir* auglítí allz lyds (96–98)
> Stock. 2: þa bavd iarlín þionv*m* sinv*m* at þeir færdi h*a*na en or fòtum o*k* dręgi naukta vm h*er*at alþydu man*n*a (111–113)

Latin: Et hęc orante ea, uenit do*minus* in adiutoriu*m* ei*us*, mittens*que* angel*u*m suu*m* coope*r*uit ea*m* stola candida (125–127)
AM 429: En e*r* hun bad a þessa lund þa ko*m* d*r*ottin*n* at híalpa he*nn*e *ok* sendí ei*n*gil sín*n* þa*nn* e*r* ha*n*a huldi huítu klędí (102–104)
Stock. 2: En*n* e*r* hun bad æ þessa lund þa sendj drottín eingil sín þa*nn* e*r* hana huldi huítv skrudi (117–118)

Latin: *et* da m*ihi* famulę tuę grat*i*am hanc, ut si q*ui* in toto corde memoria*m* mei fecerunt in necessitatib*us* suis, facias mise*r*ico*r*diam tua*m* cum eis (142–144)
AM 429: *ok* gef þu ambattu þi*nní* þessa miskun*n* at þu ge*r*i*r* mílldí þi*n*a uídr þa men*n* e*r* af ollu hi*a*rta gera mi*n*a mí*nn*íng j sínu*m* naudsyníu*m* (117–119)
Stock. 2: *ok* gef þv ambatt þí*nn*i drottín þa miskun at þu ge*rí*r milldi þína. e*r* af öllu híarta ge*r*a mína mí*nn*íng j sínvm navdsyníum (133–135)

In one instance, both manuscripts have omissions, although they are different, which suggests that the original translatation was not abridged:

Latin: Dicit eis famula d*ei* barbara (23)
Stock. 2: Guds ambatt m*æ*l*l*ti (22)
AM 429: b(arbara) m(ęllti) (17)

The above evidence reveals that AM 429 12mo is not a copy of Stock. Perg. 2 fol., but that both manuscripts seem to be independently derived from the same exemplar, AM 429 12mo probably at several removes. The date of this exemplar cannot be determined, although, obviously, the date of Stock. Perg. 2 fol. (ca. 1425–1445) serves as a *terminus ante quem*, nor can its provenance. It is worth noting, however, that the inventory of the convent of Kirkjubær for 1397 lists among other things "xx latinv bækur og norrænu" (*DI* IV 17–300 [*Vilchinsmáldagi*]: 238).[123] Although no further information is provided about these books, it is reason-

___

123. The other books mentioned are: "songbækur tuennar j huorn kor per anni circulum. jtem iiij gradvalia. Liber Evangeliorum oc Epistolarum. hin þridia ferivbok. fernar sequenciubækur. jtem tuennar songbækur fornar. capitularij tuenner. lesbækur per anni circulum. jtem ordobok. processionale. ymnabækur xiiij" (238).

able to assume that they were saints' lives. It is not unlikely that a legend of Saint Barbara, in Latin or Icelandic, was included among them, and the possibility that it had been copied from an existing Icelandic translation or even been translated from Latin into Icelandic by nuns at Kirkjubær cannot be excluded.[124] Of the twenty Latin and Icelandic books, Anna Sigurðardóttir (1988: 52) comments that the nuns without doubt copied them themselves from books which they borrowed. She considers it likely that the nuns at Kirkjubær exchanged books with the monks at Þykkvabær and that Arnbjörg Ögmundardóttir, who was a nun at Kirkjubær around 1250, borrowed books from her uncle, Abbot (later Bishop) Brandr Jónsson, who is known to have translated *Alexanders saga* and *Gyðinga saga* into Old Norse-Icelandic.

The only mention of a legend of Saint Barbara in medieval Icelandic sources is, however, in the inventory which Bishop Ólafur Rögnvaldsson of Hólar had made of the possessions of the churches in his bishopric (see above). The legend of Saint Barbara – entitled "barbare," which is presumably an abbreviation of "Barbare saga" (Olmer 1902: 8) – is included among a number of legends all "a einne bok" listed under the heading "Þessar norrænv bækur" among the books belonging to the monastery of Möðruvellir in 1461 (*DI* V 233–314: 289; Eiríkur Þormóðsson 1968: 19).

3.4 The Latin Source

Of the two main versions of the passion of Saint Barbara (see pp. 16–20), the Old Norse-Icelandic text is, as Carlé (1985: 103) points out, closer to the version represented by *BHL* 914 than to that rep-

---

124. It is known that the church did offer a few women opportunities to study. The *Jóns saga helga* (ed. Jón Sigurðsson and Guðbrandur Vigfússon 1858–1878) says about a certain Ingunn who studied ("var ... í fræðinæmi" [1: 241]) at the cathedral school in Hólar: "Öngum þessum var hon lægri í sögðum bóklistum, kenndi hon mörgum *grammaticam* ok fræddi hvern er nema vildi; urðu því margir val mentir undir hennar hendi. Hon rétti mjök látínubækr, svá at hon lét lesa fyrir sér, en hon sjálf saumaði, tefldi, eða vann aðrar hannyrðir með heilagra manna sögum" (1: 241).

resented by *BHL* 916.[125] Nonetheless, there are a number of significant divergences between the two texts. In *BHL* 914, for example, the treacherous shepherd and his cattle are turned into a marble statue ("et conuersi sunt statim in statuam marmoris" [139]); in the Old Norse-Icelandic, his cattle are transformed into locusts ("sauðir hans allir urðu at kvikendum þeim er *locustae* heita" [58–59]), while he remains unscathed. Furthermore, Juliana, who shared Saint Barbara's destiny, does not figure in the Old Norse-Icelandic text, and the name of the holy man, Valentinus, who took care of Saint Barbara's burial, is not mentioned. Finally, Saint Barbara's last confrontation with the judge is also related differently in the two texts. According to *BHL* 914, she was led naked through the region, whereafter the judge commanded that she and Juliana be executed; "[t]unc cum furore et ira Dioscorus pater eius accepit eam a Martiano principe: et ascendit in montem cum beatissima Barbara" (140). According to the Old Norse-Icelandic version, however, in answer to Saint Barbara's prayer, the Lord sent an angel who covered her with a white shroud, so that her naked body would not be seen by wicked men. The shroud blinded the earl's men, and the earl became afraid and returned her to Dioscorus.[126] In the Old Norse-Icelandic, the handing over of Saint Barbara to Dioscorus is thus motivated by the judge Martianus's fear at the blinding of his men, while in *BHL* 914 there is no real motivation for Saint Barbara's being turned over to her father.

---

125. "Det er ... uden for al tvivl, at *Legenda aurea*'s version af Barbara-fortællingen ikke har dannet forlæg for den version der foreligger i *Stock. 2*" (104).

126. "Þá hóf heilǫg Barbara enn upp augu sín til himins ok kallaði til Guðs ok mælti: Dróttinn Guð er hylr himin með skýjum, vertu nú hlífskjǫldr minn ok hjálpari á þessi stundu, ok hyl nøktan líkama minn með þaki miskunnar þinnar, at hann verði eigi sénn af vondum mǫnnum. En er hon bað á þessa lund, þá kom Dróttinn at hjálpa henni ok sendi engil sinn þann er hana huldi hvítu skrúði. Þá urðu riddarar jarlsins blindir, svá at þeir máttu eigi Guðs mey sjá fyrir ljósi því er henni fylgði. Þá hræddiz jarllinn ok lét aptr leiða hana til handa fǫður hennar Díóskoro" (114–123).

Concerning the source of *Barbare saga* Carlé (1985) argues: "Sammenfattende kan det konstateres, at der ikke hos Mombritius [*BHL* 914] foreligger noget væsentligt handlingselement, der ikke genfindes i teksten i *Stock. 2*. Omvendt er heller ikke noget væsentligt handlingsmoment tilføjet i *Stock. 2*" (103). However, the differences between *BHL* 914 and *Barbare saga* seem significant enough to exclude *BHL* 914 as the direct source for the Old Norse-Icelandic translation, which must have been a text closely related to *BHL* 914. Indeed, in his discussion of *Barbare saga*, Foote (1962) argues that "[t]he source followed is the version of the Passio noted under BHL Suppl. 913a" (26).

BHL Suppl. 913a is represented by Codex 838 now housed in the Bibliothèque Municipale in Douai in France. The life of Saint Barbara, which is found on fols. 143r–144r, is edited on pp. 156–160.

The text of the legend of Saint Barbara as represented by *BHL* Suppl. 913a shares the characteristics of *Barbare saga* as opposed to those of *BHL* 914 (e.g., the transformation of the shepherd's cattle into grasshoppers, the lack of mention of Saint Juliana, the omission of the name of the man who buried Saint Barbara), and, as demonstrated below, *Barbare saga* is a faithful rendering of this version of the legend.

3.5 The Translation

Barbare saga must be considered a close rendering of the Latin source text as represented by *BHL* Suppl. 913a. The very opening of the story of Saint Barbara's *passio* serves as an example of the translation style used:

> Temporibvs Maximiani imp*er*atoris, erat quidam satrapa dioscor*us* nomine, diues ualde, pagan*us* u*er*o existens *et* colens ydola. Hic habebat filia*m* unica*m*, nomine barbara*m* (2–4) > Á dǫgum Maximíani keisara var nǫkkurr hǫfðingi sá er Díóskorus hét, auðigr harðla ok heiðinn ok trúði á skurðgoð, en hann átti eina dóttur þá er Barbara hét (3–5)

On only two occasions does the Old Norse-Icelandic text differ significantly from its Latin source. One concerns Saint Barbara's defamation of her father's idols. After having spat in the face of the idols and uttered the curse based on Psalm 113:8 ("Simulachra gentium argentum et aurum, opera manuum hominum. Similes uestri fiant qui faciunt uos, et omnes qui confidunt in uobis" [46–48] > "Verði yðr líkir þeir er yðr gerðu ok allir þeir er yðr treystaz" [38–39]), the Latin says that she went to a prominent place and there prayed to the Lord ("Et ascendens in eminentiorem locum, erat ibidem deprecans deum" [48–49]); the Old Norse-Icelandic text, however, relates that she prayed that God's might would destroy the idols and that her prayer was answered ("En er hon hafði þetta mælt, þá bað hon Guðs krapt fella skurðgoðin, ok varð sem hon bað" [39–40]).[127] The other concerns the shepherd who revealed to Dioscorus his daughter's hiding place. The Latin suggests that it was Saint Barbara's curse that made the shepherd's cattle turn into grasshoppers: "Et maledixit eum beata barbara. Statimque factę sunt oues eius locustę" (66–67); the Old Norse-Icelandic text suppresses Saint Barbara's active role in the miraculous event by omitting the phrase and simply stating that the shepherd was punished in such a way that his cattle turned into grasshoppers: "Sá tók þegar þat víti, at sauðir hans allir urðu at kvikendum þeim er *locustae* heita" (58–59).

In comparison with the Latin source, *Barbare saga* shows signs of abridgement. Some of the omissions may, however, have accidentally occurred in the transmission of the text. This is almost certainly the case in the typological presentation of the well in which Saint Barbara was baptized. The Old Norse-Icelandic retains the New Testament references to the blind man who washed in

---

127. Günter (1949: 143–144) observes that the destruction of idols as a hagiographical *topos* of the victory over demonic powers is found in many legends. It is possible, that the translator knew of such miracles from other legends and that this constitutes his own addition.

the pool of Siloe and received sight (John 9:7)[128] and to the Samaritan woman who requested water from Jacob's well (John 4:7-26),[129] but omits mention of the pond at Jerusalem (Bethsaida) in which a paralyzed man was healed (John 5:2-9).[130] Other omissions may be original. Thus, proper names are almost as a rule left out; the names of only the saint herself (Barbara), her father (Dioscorus), the emperor (Maximianus), and the burial place of Saint Barbara ("in loco solis dicto" [159] > "í þeim stað er kallaðr er Sólarstaðr" [151]) are mentioned; the translator seems to have considered the names of the earl (Minas [93]), the executioner (Claudius [113, 129]), the guard (Gerontius [73]), and the place in which the earl's men were blinded (Dalasium [128]) irrelevant. Perhaps for similar reasons the translator also omitted the phrase stating that Saint Barbara's martyrdom took place during the reign of Maximianus Augustus and the rule of Martianus ("Passa est autem beatissima uirgo et martyr christi barbara imperante Maximiano augusto, et presidente Martiano" [161-162]). In a similar vein, unnecessarily detailed passages are simplified, as demonstrated in the following examples:

> Et suscipiens spiritum sanctum multifarie, bene mobilem, incontaminatum, disertum, luculentum, benignum, acutissimum, beneficum, certum, diligentissimum, securum, cuncta superinspicientem. Circuiuit uapor dei uirtutis eam, et affluentis omnipotentis gloriȩ ac sinceritatis (40-44) > ok tók traust af Helgum Anda ok mátt af Guðs krapti (36-37)

---

128. Hoc lauachrum similabatur fonti syloe, in quo a natiuitate cecus lauans lumen recepit" (34-35) > "Sjá brunnr, er Barbara var skírð í, líktiz þeim brunni, er guðspjǫll segja, at sá þó andlit sitt í er blindr var borinn ok tók sýn sína" (32-34).

129. "Hec est natatoria et aqua uiua, quam samaritana ad fontem a christo petiuit" (37-38) > "Sjá brunnr líktiz því lifanda vatni, er syndug kona bað Krist gefa sér at brunni" (34-35).

130. "Hoc lauachrum similabatur probaticȩ piscinȩ, in qua paraliticus uerbo curatus est" (35-37).

... et reclusit ea*m* in cellula*m* paup*er*c*u*lam, *et* muniuit claue, instituit*que* cathenas ut no*n* ap*er*iret ei q*ui*squam, constituens *et* custodes (69–71) > ... ok læsti vandliga hús þat er hann lauk hana inni ok setti varðhald fyrir húsit, at engi mætti hana þaðan leysa (62–63)

Repetitive statements or statements that seem obvious from the context are also often omitted:

Descendens aute*m* famula d*ei* barbara de turri, ut uider*et* opus q*u*od factu*m* est (16–18) > En ambátt Guðs Barbara kom at sjá verk smiða (16–17)

Adueniens ita*que* p*re*ses, iussit ea*m* sibi p*re*sentari. Jta*que* ingressus pater ei*us* una cu*m* gerontio co*m*mentariense eiecit ea*m* de cella, *et* tradidit eam p*re*sidi, adiurans eu*m* p*er* potentiam deo*rum*, quatin*us* atrocib*us* torme*n*tis consumeret ea*m* (72–76) > En er jarl kom, þá leiddi Díoskorus dóttur sína út ór húsinu fyrir dómstól jarls ok mælti svá fyrir, at jarl skyldi láta bana henni ef hon vildi eigi blóta (67–69)

Tunc iub*et* iniquissim*us* pr*e*ses claudio carnifici, abscidi mamillas eius. Amputans u*er*o ut iussit uberib*us* (113–114) > Þá reiddiz jarlinn ok lét skera af henni brjóstin (107–108)

Q*ue* cum ad crudelia iussa denudata fuisset, denuo eleuatis ocu*l*is in celos ad de*u*m dixit (121–122) > Þá hóf heilǫg Barbara enn upp augu sín til himins ok kallaði til Guðs ok mælti (114–115)

Finally, it seems that doublet renderings are avoided: "inquerelosa *et* immaculosa" (26) > "grandvarasta" (24) and "l*e*tissima*m* et suauissima*m*" (148–149) > "glǫðustu" (42).

Consonant with the translator's efforts at verbal economy, the instances of amplification of and addition to the source text are few. Those that do occur are mostly of an explanatory nature. Thus, the Old Norse-Icelandic explains that Dioscorus locked his daughter in the tower so that men would not be able to see her and her beauty "þvíat hann var vandlátr" (7) and that noble men asked for her hand in marriage when she was "gjafvaxin" (7–8); none of these details has any equivalent in the Latin. Of the idols her father worshipped, we are also told they were made of metal ("ór málmi ger" [36]); of the grasshoppers, that they are creatures ("kvikendum þeim er *locustae* heita" [59]); and about the earl, it is added that he marvelled ("undraðiz hann" [96]) when he saw all Saint Barbara's wounds healed. Moreover, in referring to the figure of the blind man who washed and received sight from John 9:7, the Old Norse-Icelandic version adds that this is related in the Gospels ("guðspjǫll segja" [33]), and in the extensive quotation from Psalm 113:5–8, the translation includes also the text of Psalm 113:4: "De demoni*bus* na*m*q*ue* tuis, *prophe*ta ait" (80–81) > "En spámaðr hans mælti svá um skurðgoð þau sem manna hǫndum eru ger ór gulli eða silfri" (73–74).

In accordance with what seems to be an effort to clarify and explain, the translator often renders pronouns with proper names and nouns, e.g., "Jpse" (8) > "Faðir hennar" (8), "Jpsa" (10) > "Heilǫg Barbara" (10), "Jpsi" (24) > "smiðirnir" (23), and "eos" (64) > "hirðana" (56).

The translation is virtually devoid of literary embellishment. Alliteration, however, is found now and then and may, in part, explain some of the additions mentioned above, e.g., "... svá at menn máttu eigi sjá hana ok vænleik hennar, þvíat hann var vandlátr" (6–7) and "En er hon var gjafvaxin, þá báðu hennar gǫfugir menn" (7–8). Generally, this stylistic device is limited to the prayers ("Dróttinn Guð er hylr himin með skýjum, vertu nú hlífskjǫldr minn ok hjálpari á þessi stundu, ok hyl nøktan líkama minn með þaki miskunnar þinnar, at hann verði eigi sénn af vondum mǫnnum" [116–119]) and the descriptions of the tortures of Saint Barbara ("Þá fylldiz jarl mikillar reiði ok lét Guðs mey føra ór fǫtum ok berja hana með sinvǫndum ok hrífa snǫrpum hárklæðum um hǫrund hennar" [79–81]). Stylistic elegance seems not to have been a priority in the adaptation of the Latin into Old

Norse-Icelandic; the translator's primary concern appears to have been to produce a clear and coherent text as close to the Latin original as possible.

4   *UM BARBÁRU MEY*

4.0 Transmission

An epitome of the legend of Saint Barbara is preserved in Copenhagen, Det arnamagnæanske Institut AM 672 4to. The epitome covers the first nineteen lines of text on fol. 56r. It ends with the comment "amen. jllt er blek*it* en*n* ve*ra* skr*i*fit b*a*rbara." The epitome does not carry a title. The designation "Um Barbáru mey" seems to be Kålund's (1889–1894: 2: 89) translation of Árni Magnússon's "De S. Barbarâ" (see n133).

4.1 Copenhagen, Det arnamagnæanske Institut AM 672 4to

AM 672 4to now consists of 88 leaves, measuring 18 × 12.5 cm. The manuscript has not been preserved in its entirety; both the beginning and end are missing, and there are lacunae after fol. 86 and 87. Fol. 83 has been cut to such an extent that only a small strip of vellum close to the spine is left. Red headings and red and blue initials are found regularly throughout the manuscript. On the bottom of fol. 86v, there is an illumination of a human head.

Folios 1–55r of the manuscript are occupied by *Parva pars oculi dextri sacerdotis* ("parua pars ocu*li*. dext*ri* sacerdotes" [55r18–19]), a collection of devotional and didactic texts in translation for use by those in charge of delivering the message of the Gospels. It begins defectively in a treatise on the Ten Commandments with the words "hin fi*r*sta ef m*a*d*r* lyg*ur*" (that is, the Eighth Commandment; 1r1). Fols. 1v–10r treat the sevenfold virtues of the Holy Spirit ("víj. fallda gipt hín*s* helga anda" [1v14–15]), and fols. 10v–20v the seven mortal sins. On fols. 21r–41v, the seven sacraments are expounded. Fols. 41r–47r consist of a brief penitential for the confessor. Fols. 47r–49v are on *casus reservati* and fols. 49v–54v on *casus majores*, which are followed by a number of somewhat more special *casus*. Fols. 55r–56r contain epitomes of the legends of Saint Bartholomew (55r–v) and Saint Barbara (56r). Fol. 56r to the middle of fol. 56v concerns the observance of the Lenten fast. The rest of fol. 56v is taken up by the story of the sower (Luke 8:5–15; ed. Þorvaldur Bjarnarson 1878: 188).[131] Fols. 57r–61r contain *Messuskýring* (ed. Kolsrud 1952: 57–64), and fols. 61r–62v epitomes of the legends of Saint Agatha (61r–v), Saint Blaise (61v–62r), Saint Nicholas (62r–v), and Saint Thomas (62v). The rest of the manuscript is taken up by theological treatises (63r–88v; see Widding 1960: 347–348).

Widding (1960: 345) observes that the last section (fols. 63r–88v) forms an independent section of the manuscript and is not a continuation of the devotional and didactic texts on fols. 1–55r, as suggested by Kålund (1889–1894: 2: 90). The comment at the end of the epitome of the legend of Saint Thomas, "latu koma sel skínit gamall *ok* nyr *prettari ok* lat *eigi* frægd þína þiona *prettum*" (62v33–34), suggests that the scribe considered the manuscript completed and ready for binding, in which case fols. 63r–88v should be regarded as a separate manuscript. Louis-Jensen (1977) notes that the more original portion of the manuscript (fols. 1–62v) is by two scribes: the *Parva pars oculi dextri sacerdotis* is the work of one scribe, while fols. 55r–62v is the work of the other. (The last 25 leaves are in a third hand.) On the basis of an identification of the Hallfríður mentioned in a comment at the end of the epitome of the legend of Saint Bartholomew ("les bet*ur* en*n* skrifat *er* kiærí fad*ir* ok seg halfridi goda notth" [55v28–29]) with Hallfríður Þórðardóttir, cousin and *próventukona* of the farmer Gísli Filipusson at Hagi in Barðaströnd, she hypothesizes that fols. 55r–62v were written by Gísli Filipusson's son for his father after 1479, the year in which Hallfríður Þórðardóttir and her husband Jón Ólafsson passed on the farm Botn in Patreksfjörður to Gísli Filipusson in return for "æfinligt framfæri ok profentv hia ... gisla filipvssyne

---

131. Widding (1960: 344–345) argues that this part, which is written in a very small handwriting, is a later addition by a different hand.

ok ingibiorgv eyolfs dottvr konv hans. ok þeira órfvm" (AM Fasc. XXIV, 22).[132]

Little is known about the provenance and origin of the manuscript. In his catalogue (AM 435a 4to), Árni Magnússon specifies that "Bokin hefur fyrrum verid eign Skalholltskirkiu, þo alldri stadid i neinu registre þar" (*Håndskriftfortegnelser*: 17) and gives a list of the contents of the manuscript.[133] A similar list by Árni Magnússon appears on a note accompanying the manuscript. Carlé (1985) argues that "[d]en private karakter af skriverens noter, det enspaltede håndskrifts lidet ambitiøse ydre og indholdets praktiskdidaktiske art sandsynliggør, at det drejer sig om et håndskrift, hvis primære opgave har været at støtte en islandsk kirkeejer og hans præst under arbejdet med at varetage de liturgiske opgaver i forbindelse med den nye tro" (42–43).[134]

Kålund (1889–1894: 2: 89) dates the manuscript to the fifteenth century, and his dating was adopted by Widding (1960: 344). Þorvaldur Bjarnarson (1878: XIII) claims that it was written around the middle of the fifteenth century. In the light of Louis-Jensen's observations concerning the scribe of fols. 55r–62v, it would seem reasonable to assign the manuscript to the last two or three decades of the fifteenth century.

132. Louis-Jensen (1977: 150) points out that in 1473 Hallfríður's father, Þórður Sigurðarson, had sold half of Hagi in Barðaströnd to his brother's son Gísli Filippusson for Botn in Patreksfjörður (*DI* V 632).

133. "De x. Præceptis. xxx ... De VII. Criminibus Capitalibus. De VII. Sacramentis. De Casibus Reservatis. De Bartholomæo Apostolo nonnulla. De. S. Barbarå. De Celebratione Jejunii qvadragesimalis. De officio Missæ. De Agatha virgine. De S. Blasio. De S. Nicolao. De S. Thomå. Et nonnulla istiusmodi plura. omnia Islandicè. 4to minori" (*Håndskriftfortegnelser*: 16).

134. Cf. Louis-Jensen (1977): "Man kan måske spørge hvilken glæde bonden på Hagi kunne have af en håndbog for præster, men man må betænke at Hagi var kirkested, og kirkebonden kan have anskaffet bøger der i virkeligheden først og fremmest kom præsten til nytte. For øvrigt indeholder den del af 672 der iflg. hypotesen er skrevet for Gísli Filippusson, tekster af mere almen interesse end håndskriftets hoveddel" (151). She also notes that one of Gísli Filipusson's sons, Jón, became a minister and appears to have served for some time as a minister at Hagi.

4.2 Um Barbáru mey

< B > ARbara v*ar* dott*ir* blotm*annz* þess er discori*us* het. h*on* var væn at a̋ líte. en*n* wæne at sidu*m*. godu*m* monnu*m* þek enn g*u*di þe*k*are. j br*u*ne þeim ed b*ar*bara v*ar* skird j <voru> giord*ar* m*ar*gar j*ar*teign*ir ok* feíngu siuk*ir* þ*ar* heilssu. fad*ir*
5 hen*ar* r`e´idiz`t´ er h*on* hafdi t*ru* te*k*ith *ok* b*ar*di h*ana* akaf- liga. en*n* h*on* hellth þ*ui* ath fast*ar* t*ru* sin*n*e *ok* *braut h*on* skurgod faudur síns. er v*oru* af gullí *ok* silf*re ok* gaf þ*ur*fa monnu*m*. þa selldi disko*r*íus h*ana* heidn*um* jallí t*il* pisla. en*n* hann lett *ber*ia h*ana* suip*um ok* dr*a*ga *nagtta vm strætt*í*. En*n*
10 gud *skryddí h*ana* mi*k*lu liose. so ath eíngín m`a´tte *litta t*il* hennar. en*n* er h*on* v*ar* *sett j myrkua stofu. þa vítradizth hen*n*e drottín sialf*r*. *ok* mæltte widh h*ana*. We*r*ttu styrk *ok* stadfóst barb*ar*a. þ*ui* ath fagnad*r* mu*n* verda a̋ hím*n*e *ok* jordu yf*ir* pisl þín*n*e. en*n* er drottín leid t*il* *hímens f*ra* auglite
15 hennar þa̋ v*oru* groín oll sar*r* hen*ar*. jallín let*t* an*n*an dag leida h*ana* or myrk<u>a stofu *ok* let*t* skera br*i*ost af hen*n*e. þa er h*on* *lastadi sk*u*rgod hans *ok* jatte g<u>dí. en*n* er jallín sa ath barb*ar*a mundí æigi blott*a*. ne pissl*ir* hrædaz. þa selldi h*ann* h*ana* diskorio faud*ur* hennar. en*n* h*ann* leidi h*ana* a̋ fíall f*ra*
20 bæ sínu*m*. *ok* hio h*ana*. sialfr. en*n* h*ann* v*ar* lostín elldíngu. adr en*n*. h*ann* kiæmí heím or þeirí for. en*n* kristn*ir* men. g*ra*fu likam barb*ar*u m*ed* dyrd mi*k*ilí

6 braut] b^{u}aut.   9 b*er*ia] be*rr*ia.   nagtta] nagt*t*a.   10 skryddí] sk^{i}yddí. litta] litt*t*a.   11 sett] sett*t*.   14 hímens] *with nasal stroke between* m *and* e.   17 lastadi] lasteadi.   18 hrædaz] az *abbreviation uncertain.*

4.3 Relation to *Barbare saga*
The source for *Um Barbáru mey* has not been established, but cer- tain verbal similarities between *Um Barbáru mey* and *Barbare saga* indicate a connection between the two texts:

Barbare saga: ok vitraðiz henni sjálfr grœðarinn várr Dróttinn Jesús Kristr ok mælti: Vertu styrk ok staðfǫst, Barbara, þvíat nógr fagnaðr verðr á himni ok á jǫrðu yfir písl þinni (87–90)

Um Barbáru mey: þa vítradizth he*nn*e drottín sialf*r. ok* mæltte widh ha*n*a. Werttu styrk *ok* stadfóst barb*a*ra. þ*u*i ath fagnad*r* mu*n* verda áŕ hím*n*e *ok* jordu yf*ir* pisl þí*nn*e (11–14)

Barbare saga: váru þá gróin sár hennar ǫll (92)
Um Barbáru mey: þáŕ voru groín oll sar*r* hen*a*r (15)

On a few points, however, *Um Barbáru mey* differs from *Barbare saga*. Thus, it is nowhere said in *Barbare saga* that Saint Barbara gave to needy people ("gaf þurfa mo*nnum*" [7–8]) her father's gold and silver idols which she had destroyed. (Interestingly, in the legend of Saint Christina [*BHL* 4 Epitomae], with which the legend of Saint Barbara shows affinities [see p. 4], it is said that Saint Christina smashed her father's idols and distributed the gold and silver to the poor.) Moreover, according to *Barbare saga*, Saint Barbara's body was buried by a holy man ("nǫkkurr heilagr maðr" [149]), whereas in *Um Barbáru mey* it was buried by Christian men ("kristn*ir* men" [21]). Finally, in *Barbare saga* the order of the earl's torture of Saint Barbara is different from that of *Um Barbáru mey*, according to which the earl first had her flogged and led naked through the streets, then had her imprisoned, and finally ordered her breasts to be cut off; in *Barbare saga*, the cutting off of her breasts precedes her being led naked through the streets. These deviations could possibly be accounted for by a composer's reliance upon memory or notes. The epitomes listed in *BHL* can be excluded as sources for *Um Barbáru mey*.

5 EXCURSUS: THE SEVERED BREAST

The central part of the legend of Saint Barbara is the account of her *passio*.[135] She was stripped of her clothes, flogged, scratched with sharp combs, and imprisoned. She then had burning torches held to her sides and was hit on her head with a hammer. Finally, she had her breasts cut off and was again stripped of her clothes,

---

135. This section is a revised version of my 1997 article.

beaten, and led naked through the city before being executed by her father. A number of critics have commented on the excessiveness of her suffering in the various adaptations of her legend. Frank (1960), for example, finds her torments "peculiarly sadistic" (200) and Ljunggren (1864) claims that the author "seems to have made efforts to outdo himself in trying to come up with the wildest and most repulsive kinds of tortures." (70).

While the physical sufferings of Saint Barbara may seem exceptionally spectacular, they are by no means unique. Indeed, most sufferings, if not all, resemble accounts of sadomasochistic tortures by pagan tormentors, full of gore and eloquence, in the lives of other female saints, who repulse the spiritual assaults – the attempts at conversion – of a male antagonist, as well as, in a number of legends, his sexual advances.[136] Saint Agatha (*BHL* 4 Epitomae), for example, was first sent to a bordello; she was then slapped in the face, after which she was imprisoned; she was stretched on the rack and imprisoned again; her breasts were twisted and cut off, after which she was starved in prison; and finally, she was rolled naked over potsherds and live coals strewn on the ground and imprisoned again. Saint Christina (*BHL* 4 Epito-

---

136. As Delehaye (1927) notes, borrowings from other legends are common: "Les Vies de saints remplies d'extraits d'autres. Vies de saints sont très nombreuses, et il en est qui ne sont guère autre chose qu'un centon hagiographique" (95). Often a compiler of a saint's life had only scanty information about the saint in question, and, in order to satisfy the devout curiosity of pilgrims and others and supply edifying reading matter from such inadequate data, he would take the only course open to him and make liberal use of the method of development used in the schools or else fall back on borrowings from other writers: "Avec plus ou moins d'imagination et de faconde, d'innombrables hagiographes se sont résignés à suppléer au silence des sources, en racontant, sur la matière, ce qui leur paraissait vraisemblable .... Il s'agit, par exemple, d'un martyr. Le cadre de la narration est nettement dessiné. D'abord, une description plus ou moins détailée de la persécution. Les chrétiens sont partout recherchés; un grand nombre tombent aux mains des soldats, et parmi eux le héros du récit; il est arrêté et jeté en prison. Mené devant le juge, il confesse sa foi et endure d'affreux supplices. Il meurt, et son tombeau devient le théâtre d'une foule de prodiges" (86–87).

mae) was first stripped and beaten, after which she was bound in chains and thrown into prison; her flesh was then torn off with hooks and her limbs broken; she was stretched on a wheel with an oil-fed fire under her and then thrown into the sea with a large stone around her neck; she was thrown into a cradle fired with oil, pitch, and resin, whereupon her head was shaved and she was led naked through the city, and then into a furnace with asps, vipers, and cobras; and finally, her breasts were cut off and her tongue was cut out. Saint Dorothy (*BHL* 2324) was cast into a vessel of burning oil, starved in prison, and lacerated with hooks; then her breasts were burnt with torches, and her face and body were bludgeoned. Saint Juliana (*BHL* 3 Epitomae) was first stripped and beaten; secondly, she was hung up by the hair and had molten lead poured on her head; later she was bound in chains and shut up in prison; next she was stretched on a wheel until all her bones were broken and the marrow spurted out; and finally, she was put in a tub filled with molten lead. Saint Margaret of Antioch (*BHL* 5309) was hung upon a rack, beaten with rods, lacerated with iron rakes, and imprisoned, then stripped of her clothes and burned with torches, and finally bound and put in a tub full of water. Fides (*BHL* 5 Epitomae), one of Saint Sophia's three daughters, was punished by being beaten, by having her breasts torn off, by being thrown on a red-hot gridiron, and by being put in a cauldron full of boiling wax. Spes (*BHL* 5 Epitomae), the second daughter, was first beaten with ropes, then thrown into a fiery furnace, and finally placed in a cauldron full of boiling wax. And Caritas (*BHL* 5 Epitomae), the third daughter, was stretched on the rack and then thrown into a fiery furnace. None of these measures succeed in wounding the virgins in any significant way, however: angels fly to their aid and smash the heathen idols and torture devices to pieces, earthquakes set them free, and their mutilated bodies are invariably restored in a miraculous fashion. And throughout these lengthy, but fruitless physical assaults, the virgin's spiritual resolve remains undaunted. She succumbs neither to torments nor to sexual advances, but perseveres in the aggressive defense of her chastity, because she enjoys a spiritual bond with Jesus Christ, her immortal bridegroom.[137] The blow that eventually kills her seems a fortuitous stroke that is allowed to produce its natural effect only because the saint – and God – have decided it should.

Most scholars who have studied the legends of female virgin martyr saints have been struck by the extraordinary emphasis on the saints' physical sufferings and the writers' lingering over these episodes. As Gad (1961) observes:

> The legends of female martyrs occupy a special place among the legends of the martyrs, because of the many amplifications in the account of their passions. There is much emphasis on the way faith turns weak young girls into [as it were] heroes and enables them to defy their persecutors with male courage. 'Viriliter age' also applies to female martyrs, and the effect of the martyr's courage is that much greater when it turns out that the weak female nature can endure the same [onslaught] as male soldiers of the faith. (31; my translation)

A number of scholars have commented on the apparently sexual orientation of the tortures. Atkinson (1983: 189) draws attention to the fact that while both men and women were beaten and burned, women saints were also sexually humiliated and assaulted, stripped naked, taken to brothels, and subjected to torture such as the severing of their breasts. Although the accounts of the sufferings of male saints often seem equally incredibile and without consideration for the limitations of human endurance, it

---

137. Cf. Cazelles (1991), who, commenting on the topics of sacrifice and suffering, points out that "[m]ost noteworthy is the often mentioned relation between physical suffering and female sanctity. Indeed, if the history of sainthood originated with that of the martyrs of early Christianity, it seems that martyrdom was gradually to become a predominant if not the sole mode of female characterization. The fact that women – martyrs and non-martyrs alike – tended to be portrayed in a sacrificial context and were sanctified to the extent that they castigated their bodies is certainly a remarkable element in the discourse proffered by medieval hagiographers" (16).

is clear that male saints were spared sexually humiliating tortures.[138] Saint Blaise (*BHL* 7 Epitomae), for example, was beaten with cudgels, imprisoned, hung from a rafter and torn with iron spikes, and imprisoned again. Saint Theodore (*BHL* 2 Epitomae) was starved in prison, hung from a limb and torn with iron hooks so as to expose his bones, and burnt on the stake. Saint Vincent (*BHL* 8640) was stretched on the rack, burnt by red-hot embers, torn with iron hooks, seared, singed, and roasted on a gridiron, and thrown into a prison the floor of which was covered with sharp pebbles. And Saint Vitus (*BHL* 6 Epitomae) was beaten, imprisoned, placed in a fiery furnace into which was poured boiling wax, oil, and lead, thrown before a lion, and stretched on the rack.

The *passio* of Saint James the Dismembered may serve as another example and one that is of interest in this context. Saint James, a native of Persia, was sentenced to die by being dismembered piecemeal. First his fingers were cut off one by one, next his toes, then his feet, hands, arms, and legs. Each time a member was cut off, Saint James had a suitable comment, altogether twenty-eight times, until finally his head was cut off as the twenty-ninth and last member. What is noteworthy about the sufferings of Saint James the Dismembered in comparison with those of female virgin martyrs, so many of whom have their breasts, the most visible signs of their female identity, severed, is not so much what is cut off as what is not cut off: the insignia of his maleness. In fact, not a single male martyr is described as being castrated in the legends.

The different treatment of male and female martyrs allows Atkinson (1983: 189) to claim that it is difficult to avoid the conclusion that the description of the sufferings of female virgin martyrs were experienced as erotic. Heffernan (1988), in a similar

138. The masterpiece as far as accounts of torments are concerned is unquestionably the martyrdom of Saints Clement of Ancyra and Agathangelus, which goes on for no less than twenty-eight years. For a summary of their torments, see Delehaye (1927: 89–91).

vein, argues that "[t]he dominant image of the female invariably turned sacred biography into something akin to a sexual melodrama, replete with anguish and physical cruelty depicted in an unabashedly erotic manner" (281–282). Gad (1961: 58) comments on the apparent sadism, which does not conceal the instincts to which the genre also appeals. Carlé (1980) goes so far as to assert that the legends of female virgin martyr saints may have served as a kind of pornography:

> The pornographical details are especially numerous, though extremely unvaried in details, in the last part of each legend, when the woman is tortured and humiliated in various ways in order to break her down and make her sacrifice to the Roman gods. Keeping in mind that the story began with a conflict concerning the sexual integrity of the woman, the writers of the legends could gain some pornographic value from these situations as well. The most common examples will be about women who are raped in prison, or undressed in court; the amputation of the woman's breasts is also rather common. On the whole, the legends could be described as 'yellow' literature, sadistic scenes, staged on the great theater of society. (82)

A similar assertion is made by Atkinson (1983): "On the highest level they [the legends] inspired faith and courage, perhaps especially in women, for whom these were the only models of active and heroic femininity. ... But on the lowest level, their indulgence – perhaps even delight – in the details of sexual abuse can only be described as pornographic" (190).[139]

---

139. Unlike Heffernan (1988) and Gad (1971), Atkinson (1983: 190n51) distinguishes between erotic writings, which "are designed to arouse sexual feelings," and pornographic writings, which "arouse such feelings through suggestion of violence, abuse, or degradation of the sexual 'object'." The distinction is an important one often overlooked in studies of saints' legends, although the labeling of writings as "pornographic" presumes at once a uniform and a male audience. The issue is one of reception, for a female audi-

The possibility that the legends are a by-product of some libidinal restraint that generates vivid sensual fantasizing under the guise of anti-sensual polemics cannot be excluded. Nor can the possibility be denied that the legends served as models of female piety and courage; indeed, as demonstrated by Goodich (1982: 178), the legend of Saint Catherine of Alexandria (*BHL* 1667), whose intellectual superiority and eloquence so confounded the pagan philosophers that she convinced them to convert, thus condemning them to martyrdom, enjoyed great popularity, especially in the thirteenth century, and she often appears in contemporary saints' lives as patroness and advisor to holy women. (It is worth noting, however, that in the legend of Saint Catherine, the issue of her womanhood is subordinate to her intelligence and eloquence and, accordingly, she is spared sexually humiliating tortures.[140])

This excursus seeks to demonstrate that the legends of female virgin martyr saints and the description of their sufferings in particular could, and perhaps should, be viewed and interpreted not only as inspiring religious narratives and/or pornographic writings, as argued by Atkinson, but as a reflection of the medieval theology of womanhood and the patristic views of the female body. After all, the saints, whether male or female, martyrs or confessors, were intended to serve as vehicles for the transmission of religious images, and most of the legends of the saints are

---

ence would not, one can generally presume, become sexually aroused by such displays of violence against women. A related issue concerns the reception of iconographic images of the saints, for which the term "pornographic" stands as starkly inadequate. The application of the term "pornographic" here betrays an insufficiently nuanced perspective of iconography, its cultural function, and its multiple audiences.

140. By contrast, the queen, who in the legend is converted to Christianity by Saint Catherine, has both her breasts cut off. In some respects, Saint Catherine is comparable to Saint Christina. In the legend of Saint Christina, both the issue of her womanhood and the matter of her eloquence are stressed; accordingly, the tormentor cuts off not only her breasts, but also cuts out her tongue so as to silence her.

designed simply, if not exclusively, to bring out some religious truth or moral principle. The reason for the legends' apparent simplicity, their lack of inspiration and originality, is obvious. The audiences were primarily illiterate, and the context for most of these texts was an oral one. They were read to an assembly, and the demands of orality required texts that were lexically familiar, easily remembered, didactically pointed, and relatively short (Heffernan 1988: 266). Accordingly, complexity yields to simplicity: the number of characters is usually very limited, and the plot generally simple. Idealized figures take the place of historical portraits and often become no more than personifications of abstract virtue; instead of an individual, only a type is presented. Whether the female saint is called Barbara, Agatha, or Dorothy, she is, generally speaking, endowed with the same qualities (aristocratic background, irresistible beauty, firmness of religious conviction, and, of course, virginity); she voices the same thoughts (the refusal to apostatize and the defense of her chastity) and undergoes the same ordeals (psychological and physical tortures and death by the sword). All personal and indidual elements have been removed. In the narratives, the senses – what can be touched, seen, or heard – govern the understanding: ideas are replaced by pictures, and the supernatural – the soul's mysterious commerce with God – is blended with the marvellous and made concrete; hence the miracles. As Delehaye (1927) observes:

> Le cerveau de la multitude est ... étroit, incapable de porter l'empreinte d'un grand nombre d'idées, même de n'importe quelle idée complexe, incapable aussi de se livrer à des raisonnements subtils ou suivis, tout préparé, au contraire, à recevoir les impressions des sens. Le concept s'efface aisément, l'image est durable; c'est le côté matériel des choses qui attire le peuple, et c'est aux objets sensibles qu'il attache toutes ses pensées et ses sentiments. (38)

This process of "simplification" was, in part, accomplished through the rhetorical structure of the legends, through the use of linguistic figurative devices, such as metaphor, metonymy, hyperbole, and synecdoche. And since the comprehension of the legends is mediated primarily through language, the identification of these tropes and the proper interpretation of their meaning are essential for the understanding of the narratives themselves, their symbolism, and their didactic purposes (Heffernan 1988: 25–26).

The tortures, taken as a whole, in the legends of male and female martyr saints are naturally to be viewed as a ritualized reenactment of the *imitatio Christi*; as such, their sufferings serve the same purpose. What distinguishes the female martyrs from their male counterparts is, as Atkinson points out, the nature of their tortures. In a great number of scenes of physical mutilation in the legends of female virgin saints, the focus of torture is on the saint's breasts. The statement that the virgin's breasts were battered, burned, pierced, cut, or severed entirely occurs so frequently in the legends that it is nearly formulaic.

Why this obsession with breasts? Anson (1974), arguing that "the cutting off of her [the saint's] breasts and the whipping ... bring to the surface a latent sexual sadism of great psychological interest" (27), notes that the severing of breasts may represent "a 'euphemism' for the pre-execution defloration of virgins practiced to meet the Roman law that forbade their execution." Yet he adds that "[e]ven if this explanation is correct, it does not preclude a psychological interest in such sadism as well" (27n69).

While it is possible that this particular element in the sufferings of the female saints echoes ancient Roman legislation, Anson's observation – coupled with what seems almost a preoccupation with the saints' breasts – more importantly suggests that "the severed breast" should be taken not at face value, as an example simply of male sexual aggression, but as a synecdoche that has become nearly a hagiographical cliché, and that the sexually humiliating tortures should not be summarily dismissed as mere fantasy or hagiographical exaggeration, but be viewed as allegorical. As Heffernan (1988) stresses, "[t]hese *vitae sanctarum* are elaborate tales whose meanings are far more complex than one which praised misanthropy or feminine heroics" (267).

The legends of the female virgin martyr saints were composed at a time when the virginal religious life was extolled by the Church Fathers as a way that promised a perfect form of eternal bliss.[141] Saints Cyprian, Ambrose, Jerome, Augustine, and Anselm all devoted lengthy treatises to the topic, some using legends of virgin saints to demonstrate to their readers that virginity entailed struggle, aggressive defense, but ultimately great apocalyptic and eschatological reward. Kinship with the corporeal life, with the distractions of sexual activity, personal attachments, and notions of domesticity, redirects, according to these writers, the gaze away from the proper love that is to be channeled toward God. Further, sexual activity erodes both consciousness and rational control. Virginity thus draws the individual away from the corporeal and relocates a core of being within the spiritual while promoting intensified love of God and, as a consequence, approximates a recovery of the purer prelapsarian state (see McLaughlin 1974: 233). It is this view that Saint Cecilia (*BHL* 4 Epitomae) attempts in very simplistic terms to convey to Valerian, her husband, on their wedding night:

> ... angelum Dei habeo amatorem, qui nimio zelo custodit corpus meum. Hic si vel leviter senserit, quod tu me polluto amore contingas, statim feriet te et amittes florem tuae gratissimae juventutis, si autem cognoverit, quod me sincero amore diligas, ita quoque diliget te sicut me et ostendit tibi gloriam suam. (772)

Obviously, virginity is predicable of both sexes; it involves complete sexual abstinence, which can also apply to celibacy on the part of the male. Although the Church extolled the virtues of the chaste life for both men and women, female virginity received disproportionate emphasis and exaggerated admiration, becoming,

---

141. For a thourough study of the tradition of virginity, see Bugge (1975).

in large measure, a defining characteristic of the female saint, while for men virginity was neither emphasized in the same way nor became a prevalent or mandatory emblem of male sanctity in the lives. As Newman (1995) remarks, while the path of the male religious was marked by the continual struggle to acquire virtues, the virgin "already *has* the exalted virtue that defines her state, and must apply herself only to preserving it" (29).

The Church's view of virginity is ambiguous and by no means consistent throughout the Middle Ages, but the basis for the unequal definition of virginity as it is applied to the female was, of course, the association of the soul-flesh dualism with the male-female bipolarity in patristic theology. While it was believed that men's and women's souls were equal,[142] their bodies were not; women had a conflict of body and soul that men did not, and as the flesh was inferior to the soul, so were women subordinate to men. The transcendence of the body and the means of severing the ties with Eve, whose transgression bound women to the pains of childbirth (cf. Genesis 3:16: "Multiplicabo aerumnas tuas, et conceptus tuos: in dolore paries filios, et sub viri potestate eris, et ipse dominabitur tui"), was achieved through the struggle for sexless perfection, through virginity. It was thus through virginity that woman came closest to resembling man and adopting his attributes. As McLaughlin (1974) points out: "For the female, virginity is not an affirmation of her being as a woman but an assumption of the nature of the male which is identified with the truly human: rationality, strength, courage, steadfastness, loyalty" (234). Only as a virgin, as a sexless being, could a woman rise to equality with the male; but in order to achieve this equality, she had to transcend

---

142. Saint Paul in his statement, "[n]on est Iudaeus, neque Graecus: non est servus, neque liber: non est masculus, neque femina. Omnes enim vos unum estis in Christo Iesu" (Galatians 3:28), specified what would become the Christian position of spiritual egalitarianism. Thus, as Schulenburg (1978) observes, "theoretically in sainthood, where the sexual barriers were to be non-existent, there should have been an equality in membership" (119).

not just her body (as did men who chose celibacy) and all earthly desires, but also her entire female nature. For the female, virginity is thus not an affirmation of her being as a woman; her salvation involves a complete repudiation of her sexuality, a negation of her nature, both physically and mentally, and an assumption of the nature of the male. As Bullough (1974: 1383) notes, this is implied as early as the fourth century by Saint Jerome, who in his *Commentarius in Epistolam ad Ephesios* wrote that "quandiu mulier partui servit et liberis, hanc habet ad virum differentiam, quam corpus ad animam. Sin autem Christo magis voluerit servire quam sæculo, mulier esse cessabit, et dicetur vir" (567). Similar views are expressed by Saint Ambrose and others.

The "equality" of which the Church Fathers write is, of course, a celestial condition and not a temporal one. Nonetheless, the transformation from female to male is given literal expression in the legend of Saint Perpetua (*BHL* 6633; McNamara 1976: 154). The night before being condemned to the beasts, Saint Perpetua has a vision of herself being led by the deacon to the arena:

> Et tenuit mihi manum, & cœpimus ire per aspera loca & flexuosa. Vix tandem peruenimus anhelantes ad amphitheatrum, & induxit me in mediâ arenâ ... Et adspicio populum ingentem attonitum: & quia sciebans me ad bestias datam esse, mirabar quòd non mitterentur mihi bestiæ. Et exiuit quidam contra me Ægyptius, fœdus specie, cum adiutoribus suis, pugnaturus mecum. Veniunt & ad me adolescentes decori, adiutores & fauitores mei: & expoliata sum, & facta sum masculus. (*Acta Sanctorum Martii* 1: 635)

A number of other saints' lives corroborate this idea by describing female saints of heroic chastity and spirituality, who shed all affinity with the female sex by literally donning a masculine disguise. The best known of these female transvestite saints is no doubt Saint Pelagia (*BHL* 4 Epitomae), a wealthy and beautiful woman of Antioch, who was converted to Christianity by Bishop Nonus. She gave all her possessions to the poor, and, without letting anyone know, left by night for Mount Olivet, where she donned the robe of a hermit, moved into a small cell, and served God in strict abstinence for the rest of her life. She was held in high esteem and was called Brother Pelagius. Her sex was not revealed until her death: "cumque de cella corpus ejus extraxissent, repererunt, quod mulier esset" (676).

A similar tale is told of Saint Marina (*BHL* 4 Epitomae). When her father was widowed and entered a monastery, he dressed his daughter as a male and asked the abbot to admit his son. He agreed, and Marina was received as a monk and was called Brother Marinus. One of her duties in the monastery was to fetch supplies. Now and then she stopped at the house of a farmer, whose daughter conceived a child by a soldier. She accused Marinus of having seduced her, and Marinus was banished from the monastery. The woman's son was sent to the abbot and entrusted to Marinus to be raised. After three years, Marinus was readmitted into the monastery, where she died within a short time. When the monks came to prepare her body for burial, they discovered her true sex:

... cum autem corpus ejus lavarent, et in vili loco sepelire disponerent, respicientes mulierem ipsum esse viderunt. Stupefacti sunt omnes et perterriti, se in Dei famulam plurimum deliquisse fatentur: currunt omnes ad tam grande spectaculum et veniam postulant ignorantiae et delicti. Corpus igitur ejus in ecclesia honorifice posuerunt, illa autem, quae famulam Dei infamaverat, a daemone arripitur et scelus suum confitens et ad sepulchrum virginis veniens liberatur. (353)

As Bullough (1974: 1382–1383) points out, Christianity has been hostile to transvestism (cf. Deuteronomy 22:5), but more so to men wearing women's clothes than to women wearing men's clothes. The reasons for this are obvious: the female transvestite imitates the superior sex, attempting to become rational, while the male transvestite imitates the inferior sex, becoming less rational, and so losing status. In fact, Bullough argues that there are reasons to believe that "the Christian church to a certain extent encouraged women to adopt the guise of men and live like men in order to attain the higher level of spirituality normally reserved to males" (1383). Bullough further draws attention to the fact that in folk belief transvestism among women was generally admired and not usually punished and makes the interesting observation that there are no male transvestite saints. However, as McLaughlin (1974) observes: "[E]ven the masculinized female saint never wholly escapes her female dependence and weakness, for in the idealized portrait she is often the bride of Christ, her weakness by nature overcome by the strength of Christ" (235).[143]

With the characteristics of the saints' legends as a literary genre, the medieval theology of womanhood, and the patristic view of the female body in mind, we can now return to the legend of Saint Barbara and those of other female virgin martyrs. It is in the light of these considerations that the sufferings typical of female virgin saints, such as the severing of their breasts, must be seen. It may seem paradoxical that a literary genre that seeks to extol matters of the soul and negate those of the body should dwell on the corporeality of its protagonist, the female virgin martyr saint. But paradox stands at the center of the virgin martyr as she navigates the movement from the corporeal to the spiritual, for in having had stripped from her the outward mark of her identity, the virgin martyr fulfills Saint Jerome's pronouncement in both literal and symbolic fashion: in the violent (and sexual) mutilation of the body, in suffering the torments that negate her perceived function as sexual and procreative, the virgin martyr redefines herself as *sponsa Christi* within the celestial state. The process

---

143. See also Bynum (1987), who sees cross-dressing as "primarily a practical device" for women: "Women sometimes put on male clothes in order to escape their families, to avoid the dangers of rape and pillage, or to take on male roles such as soldier, pilgrim, or hermit." Men, in contrast, "gained nothing socially by it [cross-dressing] except opprobrium," and to them it was "primarily a religious symbol" (291).

that began with self-denial of her own sexuality, moves through the mutilation of the outward signs of the sexual presence to achieve, paradoxically, authentication of the sexual self realized in spiritual union with God, as demonstrated very clearly in the legend of Saint Agnes (*BHL* 9 Epitomae), where Saint Agnes says to her suitor:

> ... illum amo, qui longe te nobilior est et genere dignior, cujus mater virgo est, cujus pater feminam nescit, cui angeli serviunt, cujus pulchritudinem sol et luna mirantur, cujus opes nunquam deficiunt, cujus nunquam divitiae decrescunt, cujus odore reviviscunt mortui, cujus tactu confortantur infirmi, cujus amor castitas est, tactus sanctitas, unio virginitas. ... qui annulo suo subarravit dextram meam et collum meum cinxit lapidibus pretiosis, induit me ciclade auro texta et immensis monilibus ornavit me, posuit signum in faciem meam, ut nullum praeter eum amatorem assumam, et sanguis ejus ornavit genas meas; jam amplexibus ejus castis adstricta sum; jam corpus ejus corpori meo sociatum est; ostendit mihi thesauros incomparabiles, quos mihi se daturum, si in eo perseveravero, repromisit. (114)

As Robertson (1991: 272) observes, physicality, then, is not only a woman's problem, it is also her solution, and it is for this reason that the legends of female saints tend to make issues of the body of primary importance in their descriptions of the saint's trials. Within this context, the symbolic significance of the severing of the saint's breasts seems obvious. The breasts are the most visual aspect of the saint's womanliness, and their amputation presents in a dramatic and concrete manner the defeminization which, according to medieval theology, is essential for her salvation. Only by negating her female nature can she transcend the weaknesses and limitations of her sex, and only as a sexless being is she viewed as nearly spiritual equal to the male.

Heffernan (1988), one of the few critics to call specific attention to the topos of the mutilation of the breasts, explains the paradoxical transformation as follows:

[T]he virgin becomes the bride of God, and finally the mother of the God, while retaining her virginity. Her breasts as the symbol of her maternity are mutilated and finally severed, to underscore the miraculous metamorphosis of the virgin into a nurturing mother, virtually a deity in her own right. (283)

The notion that such scenes of mutilation are attended by eroticism or must be understood as pornographic reduces the vital complexity of the topos. If, in the male gaze, scenes of sexual mutilation are construed as erotic, the final transformation of the virgin – the ungendering of the body that paradoxically reengenders it as bride and nurturing mother – refocuses the narrative away from male discourse and appropriation, reclaiming it within a specifically female locus distinct from male experience.

The Texts

THE PRESENT EDITION

The Old Norse-Icelandic legend of Saint Barbara is preserved in only two manuscripts, both of which appear to be independently derived from the same exemplar. The reconstruction of a *textus optimus*, or *Urtext*, in this case stands as a methodological practice unsuited to the particular demands of the texts and would lead directly to the creation of a fabricated text without authority and possibly misrepresentative of the hypothetical uncorrupted archetype. Accordingly, *Barbare saga* seems an excellent candidate for the editorial approach that has been labelled the "new philology."[1]

By presenting the two texts *in extenso* on facing pages, a linear rather than a hierarchical model is offered where both texts are accorded an equal voice as discrete units. This format of presentation is not intended to release the editor from the task of editing (a misdirection taken by some under the banner of "new philology" [see Wolf 1993]), but to permit an unobstructed view of texts from two periods in the transmission of a single exemplar that offer certain substantive differences in copying and that, by virtue of the decades that elapsed between the time each text was written, show different practices in orthography, syntactical structure, and the like. The construction of a *textus optimus* risks obscuring many features of interest for the philologist, textual historian, and stylist.

In accordance with the "new philology," editorial interventions and emendations are kept to a minimum. Both the punctuation and the distribution of upper and lower case letters in the manu-

---

1. See *Speculum* 65.1 (1990): 1–180. The entire issue is devoted to the subject of the "new philology."

scripts are retained. Abbreviations are expanded in accordance with the normal spelling of the scribe. The expansion of abbreviations by means of a supralinear symbol or letter are given in italics, as are instances of abbreviation by contraction. In cases of abbreviation by suspension, the expansion is placed in parentheses. Obvious misspellings are corrected and marked with an asterisk, the original being given in the footnotes. Letters or words assumed to have been accidentally omitted by the scribe are added in diagonal brackets. Words or letters added above or below the line are presented in ` ' and ' ` respectively.

Given that *Barbare saga* is a relatively brief text, and in view of the fact that the presentation of diplomatic texts is directed toward the needs of a specialized readership, a normalized text of *Barbare saga* has been supplied to accommodate the more general reader.[2] This text is based on Stock. Perg. 2 fol., which preserves the better text. Where in comparison with the Latin source text, *BHL* Suppl. 913a, AM 429 12mo can be proven to preserve more accurate and, presumably, more original readings, these readings have been incorporated into the main text, while those of Stock. Perg. 2 fol. have been relegated to the footnotes. This normalized text serves as the basis for the appended English translation of *Barbare saga* on facing pages.

The Latin text itself draws on Codex 838 in the Bibliothèque Municipale in Douai, France, from the thirteenth century. It consists of 222 leaves. Its double-columned leaves measure approximately 44 × 29 cm. The manuscript contains the lives of about five dozen saints, including a number of female saints. (For a detailed description of the contents of the manuscript, see *Analecta Bollandiana* 20 [1901]: 389–393.) The legend of Saint Barbara is found on fols. 143r–144r.

---

2. Cf. Jorgensen (1993): "The only benefits to the optimal edition ... are (1) that the user of the edition would no doubt save some time in the decipherment of the texts thanks to the work expended initially by the editor, and (2) that the user will be spared the task of finding and visiting all the extant manuscripts" (331).

Barbare saga
On facing pages:

1 Stockholm, Kungliga Biblioteket Perg. 2 fol., fols. 78rb–79rb; and Copenhagen, Det arnamagnæanske Institut AM 429 12mo, fols. 76r–80v.

2 Normalized text; and English translation.

Passio Sancte Barbare
Douai, Bibliothèque Municipale Codex 838, fols. 143ra–144ra.

Her byri*ar* wpp sǒgv heilag*rar* barbare meyiar *ok* seg*ir* hve*r*su hun
endi sitt lif m*ed* storv*m* þrautv*m* *ok* pislum
    A dǒgu*m* maxímíani keiSara w*ar* nockur hǒfdinghí sa e*r*
di<o>schori*us* het audigr hardla ok heidín *ok* trudi a skurd god
5 en h*ann* atti dottur þa e*r* barbara he`t´ Fad*ir* h*enn*ar giǒrdi stǒpul
hafan *ok* lukti dott*ur* sína j stauplínv*m* svo at m*enn* mattu **[78va]**
eigí sía hana *ok* vænleik h*enn*ar þvi*a*t h*ann* var vandlatr. En*n* e*r*
h*un* var gíafwaxín þa badu h*enn*ar gaufg*ir* m*enn* fad*ir* h*enn*ar geck
j stǒpulín *ok* m*æll*ti wit h*a*na. Storgæting*ar* bidia þín dott*ir* en þu
10 seg síalf hve*r*n þv will kiosa heilaug barbara Sv(aradi) m*ed* reídi *ok*
m*æll*ti. eígi þarftv þat at ætla fad*ir* ath ek legg*ia* þocka a nǒckurn
þeir*a* þa geck fad*ir* h*enn*ar brott or stǒplínv*m* *ok* let fá at hallar
gerd *ok* safnadí mǒrgum smidu*m* at þetta verk mættí sem skiotaz
fram fara *ok* syndi h*ann* smídu*m* hverso h*ann* willdi ge*r*a lata
15 haullína. *ok* gallt h*ann* þeim j hond allt ve*r*kkaup *ok* for sidan j
fíarlægt herad *ok* var leíngi heímann. En*n* ambatt gvds barbara
kom at sia verk smida *ok* sa hun tvo glugga nordan a hǒllínní
ge*r*ua *ok* m*æll*ti wít smídvna *fyrir* hui ge*r*dut þer tvo at eíns glugga.
Smídír*ni*r Suǒr*udu*. Fad*ir* þín*n* baud oss Svo. barbara m*æll*ti vit þa.
20 Giǒr*it* mer en þridia glugg. þeir svǒr*udu* hrædvmzt vær drotníng
ath fadir þín*n* reidiz oss *ok* megu*m* vær eigi standaz reidi h*ann*s.
Guds ambatt m*æll*ti. Giǒrít þer sem ek byd en*n* ek mun stǒdva
reidi fǒd*ur* míns vm þenna hlut þa ge*r*du smid*ir*nír en*n* þridía glugg
sem h*un* hafde m*æll*t. þa geck en*n* grandvar<a>zta mær barbara
25 eptír hǒllínní. en*n* er hun kom j austratt þa reist h*un* m*ed* fing*ri*
sínv*m* krossm*ar*k a steíní *ok* ma þat sia allt t*il* þessa dags. þa geck
barbara ín*n* i afhus þat er vpp spra*t*t hreínt vatn *ok* ge*r*di hun þ*ar*
en*n* kross m*ar*k a steíní *ok* taka truad*ir* m*enn* Sidan*n* m*ar*gfallda
hialp *ok* heilso J þeim stad. J þessum brvn*ní* tok barbara skirn af
30 nǒckurv*m* helgv*m* m*anne* *ok* lífdi hun þ*ar* nockura tid vít skog*ar*
hvnang *ok* likti fæzlu sína *ok* líf ept*ir* Joh*ann*í bapt*ist*a. Sia brun*n*r.

4 skurd god] *between* skurd *and* god *there is a hole in the vellum.* 6 mattu]
only the top part of ttu *is visible.* 7 En*n*] E *in margin.* 31 Sia] S *in*
margin.

A daugum Maxímaní *konungs sa hofdínge uar er díoskorus het
audígr at fe ok heídingí mikill blott madr en hann atti eina dotur
er het barbara fadir henar gerdi stopul hafann ok lauk dotur sína j
stoplinum Suo at eingi madr mętti sía henar uęnleik þuiat hann uar
5 *uanlatr um hana en er hun uar gíaf uaxínn þa [76v] badu
gau < f > guir menn henar fadir henar geck a stopulínn til henar ok
męllti uit hana storgíędíngar bídia þin dottir en þu síalf seg huern
þu uillt eíga heiloog barbara suaradi med míkilli reídí eígí þarptu
at ętla at ek felli hug mínn til eins þeira ok sidan geck díoscorus a
10 *braut ok eptir þat let hann fa at hallar giord ok safnadi morgum
smídum Suo at hans uerk mętti sem skíotaz fram fara ok sagdi
hann smídunum huersu hann uilldí lata gera huollína ok feck þeim
allt *uerkkaup sidan for hann j fiarlęg herud ok uar leingí heím-
an. En er ambatt guds kom til at sía uerk smídanna ok sa *hun
15 at tueír gluggar uoru giorfuir nordan a hollínní ok męllti uit
smíduna fyrir huí giordu þer tuo glugga a hollunní fadir þinn baud
oss at gera Suo. b(arbara) m(ęllti) gerit hinn þridía mer gluggínn.
þeir S(uorudu) hrędumz uer reidí fodurs þins þuiat uer megum eígí
standaz reidi hans b(arbara) m(ęllti) gerit sem ek beídí en ek mun
20 stodua reidi fodur mins um þenna hlut þa gerdu þeir [77r] hínn
þridía glugg sem hun męllti. þa geck hín b(arbara) eptir enndílangrí
hollínní en er hun kom j austr ętt þa reist hun med fingri ser cross
mark a steíninum ok ma hann þar sia til þessa dags þa geck b(arbara) j af hus þat er upp *spratt hreint uatn ok gerdi hun þar en
25 cross mark a steíne ok taka rettruadir menn þar margfallda híalp
af ok heilsu j þeim stad. J þessum bruní tok barbara skírn af
eínum heilogum manne ok lifdí hun þar nockura stundd uit skogar
hunang ok liktí hun fęzlu sínní ok lífí eptir johanneS baptista en er

---

1 konungs] + at.   3 henar] *written in margin with an insertion mark in the*
text.   5 uanlatr] + at.   10 braut] baurt.   13 uerkkaup] uerttkaup.   14
hun] hann.   24 spratt] sprap.

er barbara var skírd j liktizt þeim brunni er gudspiöll segía ath sa
þő andlít sítt j er blíndr var borínn ok tok syn sína. Sia brunnr
liktiz þvi lífanda watní er syndug kona bad krist gefa Ser at brunní
35 enn er heilőg barbara kom aptr j stőpul sínn þa leít hvn þar skurdgod fodur síns or malmí giőrr ok tok traust af helgvm anda ok
mátt af guds kraptí ok spytti hun j andlit skurdgodunvm ok mællti
verdi ydr likír þeir er ydr gerdv ok allír þeir er ydr treystaz enn er
hon hafdi þetta mællt þa bad hun guds krapt fella skurdgodínn ok
40 vard sem hun bad.

fra dioschoro
  Enn er dioskorus kom heím aptr fadir hennar or enni lőngv
heimanfőr þa leít hann á holl sína algerfa ok sá [78vb] þria glugga
ok mællti vid smidína. fyrir hui settut þer þria glugga. enn þeir
45 svorudu. dottir þín baud oss svo þa kalladí hann þangat dottur sína
ok mællti baud þv dottir at gera þriá glugga. hun sv(aradi) þat
gerda ek ok vel gerda ek. þviat þrir lysa hvern mann er kemr j
heím enn tveír gluggar mega myrkvir vera. fadir hennar mællti
hversv mega þrír framar lysa en tveír. barbara S(varadi) þrir merkia
50 fődur ok son ok helgan anda eínn sannann gvd þann er hveríum
manne byriar at gőfga. þa reiddízt fadir hennar ok bra Sverdí ok
uilldi þegar hőggua dottur sína enn hun bad drottín Ser hialpar ok
gafzt henne rum ath fara j gegnum steínveggin ok var hun vti því
næst á fiallí. Enn j þeim stad voru hírdar tveír þeir er hana sa
55 flygía. fadir hennar kom eptir henne ok villdí taka hana ok spurdi
hírdana ef þeir sæi hana annar duldi ok kvedz eigi hana hafa sied
enn anar sa er grimarí var retti fíngr sínn ok visadi til hennar. Sa
tok þegar þat vítí at savdir hans allír urdu at kuikendum þeim er
locuste heíta. ok er minning þessarar iarteignar mőrkud yfir leidi
60 heilagrar barbare. enn fadir hennar fann hana ok bardi ok tok j
hár henne ok dro hana til fiallz ok læstí vandliga huss þat er hann

---

38–39 er hon] *between* er *and* hon *there is a hole in the vellum.*   39 krapt fella]
between krapt *and* fella *there is a hole in the vellum.*   55 spurdi] i *corrected*
possibly from u.   56 duldi] l *corrected from* d.   59 minning] *superior curl over* n[1].

b(arbara) ko*m* apt*r* t*il* stopul < s > síns. þa leít h*un* þ*ar* skurdgod
30 fod*ur* síns or malmí gío*r* o*k* tok h*un* traust af heilgu*m* anda o*k*
matt af guds kraptí o*k* spytí h*un* j andlít *skur*dgodu*m* o*k* m*e*llti
ue*r*di ydr liki*r* þeir e*r* ydr ge*r*a o*k* allír þeir e*r* ydr treystaz e*n* e*r*
h*un* hafdí þe*tt*a m*e*llt. þa bad h*un* krapt guds fella skurdgodi*n* nídr
o*k* u*a*rd þeg*ar* sem h*un* bad. En e*r* díosco*rus* fadi*r* henar ko*m* apt*r*
35 þa leit h*ann* holl sína algío*r*ua o*k* þa þria glug[77v]ga e*r* þ*ar* uo*ru*
a henne o*k* m*e*llti u*it* smidína fy*r*ir hui ge*r*du þer gluga aholli*nn*i e*n*
þeir S(uorudu) doti*r* ydr < baud oss > at ge*r*a S*uo* þa *kalladi h*ann*
a dot*ur* sina þangad o*k* m*e*llti u*it* h*a*na baud þu doti*r* at ge*r*a þría
gluga a hollune h*un* S(uaradi) þ*at* ge*r*da ek o*k* uel ge*r*da ek þ*at* þ*ui*at
40 *þrir glugg*ar* lysa hue*r*n m*a*nn e*r* *kemr j heim*e*nn e*n* tueír mega
myrkír ue*r*da fadi*r* henar m*e*llti u*it* h*a*na hue*r*ssu mega *þrir f*r*amar
lysa e*n* tueír b(arbara) m*e*llti þrír m*e*rkia fod*ur* o*k* son o*k* helga*nn*
a*n*da eí*nn* sa*nn*a*nn* gud þa*nn* e*r* hue*r*íum m*a*nne byri*ar* at gaufga þa
S(uaradi) fadír henar u*it* h*a*na o*k* b*r*a suerdi uíllldí huogua h*a*na e*n*
45 h*un* bad d*r*otti*nn* ser hialp*ar* o*k* gafz henne rum at f*a*ra ut u*m* stein
murí*nn* o*k* u*a*r h*un* utí þ*uí* n*e*st o*k* afíallí en a þ*ui* fíallí uo*ru*
fehird*ar* þeir e*r* h*a*na sa flyía e*n* fadi*r* henar ko*m* þangad o*k* uilldi
taka h*a*na o*k* spurdi hirdana ef þeir s*e*i h*a*na a*nn*ar dulldí o*k* kuez
eí sed hafa h*a*na e*n* a*nn*ar sa e*r* g*r*imari u*a*r o*k* rettí fing*r* si*nn* o*k*
50 uísadi t*il* henar sa tok þeg*ar* uiti o*k* saudi*r* h*a*ns alli*r* [78r] urdu at
*kuikendum þei*m* e*r* locuste heíta o*k* mi*nn*íng þess*ar*ar *ia*r*teígn*ar*
e*r* m*o*rkut yfi*r* leídí heilag*r*ar b(arbare) S*uo* at sia ma allt t*il* þessa
dags en fadir hen*ar* fa*nn* h*a*na o*k* bardi h*a*na o*k* tok j h*a*r henne o*k*
leiddi h*a*na t*il* fials o*k* l*e*sti h*a*na uanlega j husi o*k* setti h*ann* u*a*rd

---

31 skur*dgodu*m] skordgodu*m*.   37 kalladi] kallat.   40 þrir] þrid.   kemr]
koma.   41 þrir] þridr.   44 fadír] d *corrected from* f.   45 bad] brad *with*
deletion mark under r.   51 kuikendum] kuikendi.   ok] + j *which is partly*
erased.   ia*r*teignar] ia*r*teingn*ar*.   53 henar] + bt *which is crossed out.*

lauk hana inni ok setti vardhalld fyrir husít at eíngi mætti hana
þadan leysa Sidan Sendi hann ord iarllí ath hann kæmí ok neyddi
dottvr hans til blota.

65 Fra iarlli ok barbare meyiu
   Enn er jarll kom þa leiddi dioschorus dottur sina vt or husínv
fyrir domstol iarllz ok mællti Svo fyrir ath iarll skylldi lata bana
henne ef hun villdi eigi blota. enn er iarll sa fegrd hennar þa mællti
hann vit hana Hvort villtv vægia þer sialfrí ok blota godum e(da)
70 vera selld til enna hórdoztv pisla. kristz mær barbara sv(aradi) ek
aa fórn at færa drottní mínvm ihesu kristo þeim er gerdi hímin ok
iórd ok sæ ok allt þat er þeim fylgir. enn spamadr hans mællti Svo
vm skvrdgod þav sem manna hóndvm eru giórr or gvlli eda silfri.
mvnn hafa þav ok mæla eigi. augv hafa þav ok sia eigi. Eyru hafa
75 þau ok heyra eigí. nasir hafa þau ok jlma eigi. hendr hafa þav ok
þreífa eigi. fætr hafa þau ok ganga eigi ok eigi er ravdd i haalsi þeim
ne andi j munní þeím verdi þeim likir þeir er þav giðra ok allír þeir
er treystaz þeim. þa fylltiz iarll mikillar reidí ok let gvds mey færa
or fótum ok beria hana med sín vondum ok hrífa snórpum har-
80 klædvm vm hórvnd hennar [79ra] Enn er hun var leíngi þíad j
þessi kuðl þa rann blod vm allann hennar likama. Sidann let hann
setia hana j myrkuastofv ok hvgsadi med *hverrí písl hann skyldi
luka yfir hana

fra barbare meyiu
85   Þa er heilog mær B(arbara) var í myrkvastófv sett skeín yfir
hana lios af hímne aa sialfri not midrí ok vítradizt henne sialfr grædaRín vor drottínn ihesus kristr ok mællti. Vert þv styrk ok
stadfóst barbara þviat gnogr fagnadr verdr aa hímní ok aa iordv yfir
pisl þínní. Eigi skallt þv hrædazt íarll. þviat ek em med þer ok man
90 ek leysa þik or ollvm pislum þeim er þer eru gervar. þa blezadí

69 Hvort] H in margin. 73 giórr] the curl over o resembles an abbreviation
sign. 76 ok] o in margin. 82 hverrí] written hvrrí with er abbreviation sign
over v. 85 í myrkvastófv] ímyrkvastófv. 89 ek em] ekem with k corrected
possibly from e.

55 halld fyrir hus*it* S*u*o at e*igi* m*ę*ttí h*a*na þad*an* leida sid*an* sendí h*ann*
ord iarlin*um* at h*ann* k*ę*me *ok* neyddí h*ann* dot*ur* h*a*ns t*i*l blota *en*
er ia*r*ll ko*m* þa leiddí diosc*orus* dot*ur* sína or husenu fyrir do*m*stol
iarlsíns *ok* m*ę*l*t*i S*u*o fyrir ia*r*llin*num* at h*ann* skyllde lata drepa h*a*na
ef h*un* uilldí e*igi* blota *en* er íarll sa h*a*na *ok* *fegurd he*n*ar þa m*ę*lti
60 h*ann* u*it* h*a*na u*ę*gía sialfri þer *ok* blota god*um* eda u*er*a pínd hínu*m*
hordustu*m* pislu*m* guds m*ę*r b(arbara) m*ę*lti ek a for*n* at f*ę*ra
drottní mínu*m* ihesu *criste* þei*m* er gr*ę*ddi hímín*n* *ok* íord *ok* s*ę* *ok*
allt þ*at* er þei*m* fylgdí en spam*a*dr h*a*ns m*ę*lti S*u*o u*m* skurd god
þau er m*a*nna hondu*m* e*ru* gior or gullí eda silfrí þau hafa mun*n*
65 *ok* m*ę*la eígí augu hafa þau *ok* sia e*igi* eyru hafa þau *ok* heyra eí *ok*
nasír *ok* ken*n*a e*igi* ilm hendr *ok* þreífa eí f*ę*t*ur* *ok* ganga e*igi* *ok* e*igi*
er rodd j barka þei*m* þa fylldíz iarll mikillar reídí *ok* let guds mey
b(arbara) f*ę*ra or **[78v]** fotu*m* bería h*a*na *med* límuondu*m* *ok* hrífa
h*a*na *med* snorpu*m* har kl*ę*du*m* *ok* er h*un* u*a*r leíngi hofd j þessu*m*
70 *kuolu*m* þa ran*n* blod u*m* allan*n* likama he*n*ar. sid*an* let J(arll)
setia h*a*na j myrkkua stofu en h*ann* feck *hug satt *med* hu*er*e *pisl
er h*ann* skylldi e*igi* fa yf*ir* h*a*na lok*it* En at midr*i* nott skein lios
yfír h*a*na af hímne *ok* uítradíz he*n*ne sialfr gr*ę*dare drottin*n* ihesu
cristí *ok* m*ę*lti u*er*tu styrk *ok* stadfost b(arbara) þ*ui*at nogr fagnadr
75 uerdr a himne *ok* íordu yf*ir* *písl þín*n*e eígí skalltu hr*ę*daz iarl
þ*ui*at ek er *med* þer *ok* mun ek leysa þig or ollu*m* píslu*m* þei*m* er
þer e*ru* gíoru*ar* sid*an* blezadi drottín*n* h*a*na *ok* ste sid*an* t*i*l him*n*a

---

57 þa] + ko*m* *which is crossed out.* 59 fegurd] fegudr. 60 godu*m*] + þeir
which is crossed out. 70 kuolu*m*] kuelu*m*. 71 hug satt] hug sott. pisl]
pils. 73 he*n*ne] *written* h*a*na *with* a *corrected to* e. 75 písl] píls.

drottín hana *ok* ste t*il* hímens *ok* vorv þæ groín*n* sar he*nn*a*r* oll
en*n* k*r*istz mær fagnadí af ollu híarta þei*R*e vit*r*an e*r* gud hafdí
he*nn*e vítrad. En*n* at morní let jallín*n* leida hana or myrkvastófvn*n*e *ok* fyri*r* domstol sín. En*n* e*r* ha*nn* sa ha*n*a grædda. af
95 ollu*m* sarum likama. þa undradíz ha*nn* *ok* m*æ*/*l*ti hvi gegni*r* þat
barbara e*r* gud vor elska þik *ok* mískun*n*a þer Heilog mær svar*adi*
ok m*æ*/*l*ti vít íarlín*n* þer lik erv gvd þín blínd *ok* dauf *ok* vítlauss
hve*r*so mattv þaɪ græda sá*r* mín. eda hve*r*su megv þav ódrv*m* biarga
e*r* þav mega óngan dugnat veíta síalfv*m* S*er*. En*n* k*r*istr son guds
100 lífanda græddi mik sa e*r* þv e*r*t ouerdr at Sia þv*ia*t híarta þítt e*r*
ha*r*t ord*it* af diófli. þa reiddízt iarll *ok* greníadí sem hít o arga dy*R*
ok let hallda bren*n*ondu*m* logu*m* at sidv*m* he*nn*e *ok* liosta hamrí j
hófvt he*nn*e en*n* hu*n* leit til himíns *ok* m*æ*/*l*ti þv veítz kristr ath ek
tek lystandi þe*ss*ar pislir fyri*r* ast heilags nafns af þvi fyri*r* lat þv
105 mík eigí allt til enda ʿþviʾ at ek dvalda e*igi* ath be*r*a hraustlíga
pislí*r* fyri*r* þín*n*í ast. þæ reiddiz jarllín*n* *ok* let skera af he*nn*i
bríostin*n*. en*n* kristz mæʿrʾ leít þa en*n* til hímens *ok* m*æ*/*l*ti. ve*r*p þv
e*igi* me*r* f*r*a auglíti þínv drottín*n* *ok* tak eígi fra me*r* helgan anda
þín*n*. Gíalltv me*r* gledí þrifsemí þínnar *ok* styrkíumz me*d* hofdíng-
110 lígum anda. en e*r* hvn hafdi þetta m*æ*/*t* *ok* stodz hre*ss*líga þe*ss*ar
píslír allar af styrk heilags anda. þa bavd iarlín þionv*m* sinv*m* at
þeir færdi ha*n*a en or fótum *ok* drægi naukta vm *herat alþydu
man*n*a þa hof heilóg B*a*rba*r*[a] en*n* vpp augu sin til hímens *ok*
kalladi t*il* gu*d*s *ok* m*æ*/*l*ti. Drottín*n* gud e*r* hylr hímín me*d* skyíu*m*
115 ver þv nv hlífskiolldr mín *ok* hialpa*r*í a þe*ss*i stvndv [79rb] *ok* hyl
nauktan likama med þaki mískunna*r* þin*n*ar at ha*nn* ve*r*di e*igi*
sen*n* af vondv*m* mon*n*u*m*. En*n* e*r* hun bad æ þe*ss*a lund þa sendj
drottín eingil sín þa*nn* e*r* hana huldi huítv skrudi þa vrdv riddara*r*
iarllzins blindi*r*. Svo at þeir mattv e*igi* gvds mey sía fyri*r* liosi þvi
120 e*r* he*nn*e fylgdi. þa reiddíz íarllín*n* *ok* let apt*r* leida barbaram t*il*
handa fódur he*nn*ar dioscoró.

92 vit*r*an] *with superior curl over* v. 93 jallín*n*] j *corrected from* þ. 94 sa
hana] *written* ha*n*a sa *with transposition marks.* 96 Heilog] H *in margin.*
102 liosta hamrí] *between* liosta *and* hamrí *two letters appear to have been
erased; it seems that the scribe wrote* med, *then tried to correct* m *to* h, *and
finally erased it.* 112 he*r*at] + j. 113 B*a*rba*r*[a]] a³ *invisible due to a hole
in the vellum.* 116 med] e *reminiscent of* u *and furnished with an accent.*

ok uoru þa groínn oll sar henar en guds mer fagnadí af ollu hiarta
af þeirí uitran er gud hafdi henne fyrir sagt at morní let iarl leida
80 b(arbara) or myrkuastofu fyrir dom stol sínn en er hann sa hana
gredda af ollum sarum þa undradíz hann míog *ok* mellti. huí
*gegnir þat b(arbara) at god uor elska þig Suo at þau miskunna þer
Suo at sar þin eru groínn heilog b(arbara) mellti þer lik eru [79r]
god þin blind *ok* dauf *ok* uít laus huersu mattu þau greda míg eda
85 huersu mega þau bíarga audrum er þau mega eigi biarga ser sialfum
En sonr guds lífandí greddí míg sa er þu ert eigi uerdr at sía þuiat
hiarta þítt er hartt ordít af díoflí þa reiddíz íarlínn *ok* *greníade
sem hít oarga dyr *ok* let hallda logandum brondum at sidum henne
ok líosta *hamrí j hofud henne en hun leít til hímíns *ok* mellti þu
90 ueítz drottínn mínn at ek tok uílíandí þessa písl fyrir ast heilags
nafns þins af þui fyrir lattu míg eígí at ek dualldí eigi at bera
hraustlega píslír fyrir ast þinni. þa reiddíz J(arlinn) *ok* let skera
briost af henne en cristz mer leit til hímíns *ok* mellti uerptu eigi
mer fra auglíti þino drottínn *ok* tak eigi fra mer helgann anda þínn
95 gíallt mer helldr þrifsemi gledí þiNar *ok* styrk míg helldr med hof-
dínglegum anda þa baud J(arlinn) þionum sinum at þeir ferdí hana
enn or kledum *ok* beria hana *ok* draga nakta um aull strettí *ok*
portt fyrir auglíti allz lyds. þa hof heilog b(arbara) [79v] upp augu
sínn til hímíns *ok* kalladí til guds *ok* mellti drottínn gud mínn er
100 hylr himna skyíum uertu hlif skylldr mínn *ok* híalpare a þessí
stundu *ok* hyl naktann likama mínn med þaki myskunar þiNar Suo
at hann uerde eigi lítínn af uondum monnum En er hun bad a
þessa lund þa kom drottinn at híalpa henne *ok* sendí eingil sínn
þann er hana *huldi huítu kledí þa urdu ríddarar íarlsíns blindir
105 Suo at þeir mattu guds m`e´y eígí sia fyrir liosi þui er henne fylgdí
þa hreddíz j < arll > ínn. *ok* let hana leida aptr til handa faudur
sinum dioskoro En fadir henar fylldíz míkillar reidí er hann tok

---

82 gegnir] gengnir.   elska] + þau *which is underlined presumably to indicate
deletion.*   83 lik] likír *with the last two letters partly erased.*   87 greníade]
greníiade.   89 hamrí] harmrí.   104 huldi] huldu.

Vm píníng barbare

Enn fadir hennar fylltíz mikilli reidi. ok leiddi hana enn til
fíallz. en heilog b(arbara) skyndi fagnandi til algiorrar avmbvnar
125 sígrs síns. ok bad hvn drottín at hun tæki lok pislar s(innar) j
þessvm stad ok mællti drottínn ihesus kristr er himna skopt ok iörd
smidadír ok byrgdir vndir díup ok settir endi mörk siavar þu er
bydr skyíum at rigna yfir goda ok illa þu geckt yfir sía ok stod-
vadir þiotandi bylgiur hans. þv er rettir helgar hendr þínar a krossi
130 ok gerdir margar adrar iarteinir heyrdv mik ambatt þína þviat allir
hlutir hlyda þino bodí. Drottin ihesus kristr hlifari mínn j æskv
mínní. Veíttv mer þa bæn at ek luka nu þegar þraut mínní med
godum lokum ok gef þv ambatt þínni drottín þa miskun at þu gerír
milldi þína. <vid þa menn> er af öllu híarta gera mína mínníng
135 j sínvm navdsyníum allra hellzt æ degi pislar mínnar Mínztv eigi
drottín synda þeira a doms degi er truligha kalla a mik ok veíttv
þeim likn j syndvm þviat þv veízt at vær erum ostyrkir likamir.
Enn er hun lauk bæn sínní þa kom rödd af hímní ok mællti kom
þv enn fegrsta mær mín til ennar glöduztv huilldar fódur míns er
140 a hímnvm er enn allt þat er þv batt man þer veítt vera. Enn er
guds mær heyrdi þetta af drottní med fagnadí þa kom hun til
stadar pislar sínnar ok lauk þar dyrligri þravt svo sem hun hafdi
bedít af gvdí. þviat hun var j þeim stad höggvínn af fódvr sínvm
ok endi hun líf sítt j iatníngu kristz tveím nottvm fyrir nículas
145 messu byskups Enn er fadir hennar ste ofan af fiallí med sínvm
monnum þæ kom elldr or loptí ok brendi hann svo at þatki var at
aska hans fyndíz enn nockur heilagr madr kom leynilíga ok tok a
bravt likam ennar helgvztv meyiar barbare ok gróf j þeim stad er
kalladr er solar stadr ok let hann þar gíóra bæna hus j mínníng
150 hennar ok verda þar margar íarteínir til lofs ok dyrdar drottní
vorvm ihesu kristo þeim er med fedr ok helgvm anda lifir ok rikir
<einn> gud vm allar alldir allda. amen.

125 drottín at hun] written in margin with an insertion mark in the text. 136
a mik] amik. 140 a hímnvm] ahímnvm. Enn] E in margin. 141 af
drottní] afdrottní. 145 Enn] E in margin.

u*it* h*ana* ok leidi h*ann* h*ana* t*il* fíallz en*n*. En heilog m*ę*r b(arbara)
skyndí *fagna*ndi t*il* ambun*ar* síns sígr<s> ok bad h*un* drottin*n*
110 at hialpa s*er* ok at h*un* tęki lok píslar siɴ*ar* j þessu*m* stad ok mę*l*lti
drottin*n* ihe*s*u crí*s*tí er skopt hímín*n* ok íord ok by<r>gd*ir* und*ir*
*díup ok sett*ir* endí m*or*k siaf*ar* þu er byd*r* skyíum at rígna yf*ir*
goda ok illa þu er gecc yf*ir* sę ok stoduadír þíotandí bylgíor h*an*s
þu er rett*ir* þi*n*[80r]ar hendr helg*ar* a crossínum ok gerd*ir* m*ar*gar
115 adr*ar* íarteíg<n>ír hialptu m*er* ambatt þin*n*i þ*uia*t allir hlut*ir*
hlyda þi*n*o bodí drottin*n* mín*n* u*er*tu hlíf skíolld<r> mín*n* ok ueít
m*er* at ek líukí nu mín*n*í þraut m*ed* godu*m* luktu*m* ok gef þu ambattu þin*n*í þe*ss*a miskun*n* at þu ger*ir* mílldí þi*n*a uídr þa men*n* er
af ollu hi*ar*ta gera mi*n*a mín*n*íng j sínu*m* naudsyníu*m* allra hellz a
120 degí píslar *mínar mín*n*ztu eí *synda þeira a doms degí *drottín*n*
er trulega kalla a mig ok ueit þeim uorkynd j syndu*m* þ*uia*t þu
ueíz at ostyrkír *er*u likam*ir* uorír e*n* er h*un* lauk bęn sín*n*í þa ko*m*
rodd af hi*m*ne ok mę*l*lti uít h*ana* ko*m* þu hín fegusta mę*r* t*il* hin*ar*
gladustu huilldar fodur mi*n*s er j himnum er en allt þ*at* er þu batt
125 mu*n* þer ueit u*er*da e*n* er guds mę*r* heyrdí þe*tt*a af *drottni m*ed*
fagnadí þa ko*m* h*un* t*il* stadar píslar sin*ar* ok lauk þ*ar* dyrlegr*i*
þraut h*enar* sᴜo sem h*un* hafdí þeg*it* af gudi þ*uia*t h*un* uar j þeim
stad *hoggín*n* af fod*ur* sínu*m* ok endí [80v] h*un* líf sítt j íat-
<n>íngu drottíns tueí*m* nottu*m* fyr*ir* míssu dag Nícholae b*yskups
130 en er fad*ir* h*enar* ste ofan af fíallíno m*ed* sínu*m* mon*n*um þa ko*m*
elldr or loptíno ok brendi h*ann* sᴜo at eingi aurmul sa ok eígi
auskuna ept*ir* helldr en an*n*ad. nockur heilagr m*adr* ko*m* til ok tok
likam sęllug<ra>r *barba*re hin*ar* heilgustu meyi*ar* guds ok grof
j þeim stad er solar stadr er kalladr ok let h*ann* þar gera bęna hus
135 j h*enar* mín*n*íng ok u*er*da þ*ar* margar *íarteígnir t*il* lofs ok dyrdar
drottní uoru*m* ihe*s*u crí*s*te þeim er m*ed* syne ok hellgum anda lifir
ok rikír eín*n* gud j *þrenningu um allar alldír allda AMEN

---

109 fagna*n*di t*il*] til fagna*n*di. 112 díup] díups. 120 mínar] *it appears that the scribe began to write* mínz *(as in* mín*n*ztu*), but forgot the minim of the* n. synda] + sin*n*a. drottín*n*] *superscript* o *placed after* tt. 124 hin*ar*] *after which two letters have been erased.* 125 drottni] drottin*n*. 128 hoggín*n*] hofgín*n*. 133 barba*re] barbaro. 135 íarteígnír] íarteíngír. 137 þrenningu] þreínnigu.

Normalized text

[I] Hér byrjar upp sǫgu heilagrar Barbare meyjar ok segir hversu hon endi sitt líf með stórum þrautum ok píslum.

Á dǫgum Maximíani keisara var nǫkkurr hǫfðingi sá er Díó-skorus hét, auðigr harðla ok heiðinn ok trúði á skurðgoð, en hann
5 átti eina dóttur þá er Barbara hét. Faðir hennar gerði stǫpul hávan ok lukti dóttur sína í stǫplinum, svá at menn máttu eigi sjá hana ok vænleik hennar, þvíat hann var vandlátr. En er hon var gjaf-vaxin, þá báðu hennar gǫfugir menn. Faðir hennar gekk í stǫpul-inn ok mælti við hana: Stórgætingar biðja þín, dóttir, en þú seg
10 sjálf hvern þú vill kjósa. Heilǫg Barbara svaraði með reiði ok mælti: Eigi þarftu þat at ætla, faðir, at ek leggja þokka á nǫkkurn þeira. Þá gekk faðir hennar brott ór stǫplinum ok lét fá at hallar-gerð ok safnaði mǫrgum smiðum, at þetta verk mætti sem skjótast fram fara, ok sýndi hann smiðum, hversu hann vildi gera láta
15 hǫllina, ok galt hann þeim í hǫnd allt verkkaup ok fór síðan í fjarlægt herað ok var lengi heiman. En ambátt Guðs Barbara kom at sjá verk smiða, ok sá hon tvá glugga norðan á hǫllinni gerva ok mælti við smiðuna: Fyrir hví gerðu þér tvá at eins glugga? Smiðir-nir svǫruðu: Faðir þinn bauð oss svá. Barbara mælti við þá: Gerið
20 mér inn þriðja glugg. Þeir svǫruðu: Hræðumz vér, dróttning, at faðir þinn reiðiz oss, ok megum vér eigi standaz reiði hans. Guðs ambátt Barbara mælti: Gerið þér sem ek býð, en ek mun stǫðva reiði fǫður míns um þenna hlut. Þá gerðu smiðirnir inn þriðja glugg sem hon hafði mælt. Þá gekk in grandvarasta mær Barbara
25 eptir hǫllinni, en er hon kom í austrátt, þá reist hon með fingri sínum krossmark á steininum, ok má þat sjá allt til þessa dags. Þá gekk Barbara inn í afhús þat er upp spratt hreint vatn, ok gerði hon þar enn krossmark á steini, ok taka trúaðir menn síðan marg-falda hjálp ok heilsu í þeim stað. Í þessum brunni tók Barbara
30 skírn af nǫkkurum helgum manni, ok lifði hon þar nǫkkura tíð við skógarhunang ok líkti fœzlu sína ok líf eptir Jóhannesi bap-

---

3–4 Díóskorus] AM 429 12mo; Dí<ó>schorius Stock. 2.   5 eina] AM 429 12mo; –Stock. 2.   22 Barbara] AM 429 12mo; –Stock. 2.   31 Jóhannesi] AM 429 12mo; Jóhanni Stock. 2.

English translation

[I] Here begins the legend of the holy virgin Barbara and relates
how she ended her life with great struggles and torments.

In the days of Emperor Maximian, there was a chieftain named
Dioscorus. He was very wealthy and a pagan and believed in idols;
5   and he had one daughter named Barbara. Her father made a high
tower and locked his daughter in the tower, so that men would
not be able to see her and her beauty, because he was jealous. But
when she was of marriageable age, noble men asked for her hand
in marriage. Her father went to the tower and said to her: Great
10 chiefs ask for your hand in marriage, daughter, but you yourself
say whom you want to choose. Saint Barbara answered in anger
and said: Do not think, father, that I like any of them. Then her
father left the tower and obtained materials to build a hall and
gathered many craftsmen, so that the work could be accomplished
15 as soon as possible, and he showed the craftsmen how he wanted
the hall built, and he paid them in advance for all the work, and
then he went to a distant district and was away from home for a
long time. But God's handmaid Barbara came to see the craftsmen's work and saw two windows on the northern side of the hall
20 and said to the craftsmen: Why did you make only two windows?
The craftsmen answered: Your father told us so. Barbara said to
them: Make me a third window. They answered: We fear, mistress,
that your father will become angry with us, and we cannot bear
his anger. God's handmaid Barbara said: Do as I request, and I
25 shall put an end to my father's anger in this matter. Then the
craftsmen built the third window as she had asked. Then the guile-
less virgin Barbara went along the hall, and when she came to the
eastern part, she scratched with her finger the sign of the cross on
the stone, and that can be seen to this day. Then Barbara went
30 into the anteroom in which a pure spring gushed forth, and there
she once again made the sign of the cross, and since then believers
have received help and healing in many ways in that place. In this
spring, Barbara was baptized by a holy man, and she lived there
for some time on honey from the woods and ate and lived like

tista. Sjá brunnr, er Barbara var skírð í, líktiz þeim brunni, er
guðspjǫll segja, at sá þó andlit sitt í er blindr var borinn ok tók
sýn sína. Sjá brunnr líktiz því lifanda vatni, er syndug kona bað
35 Krist gefa sér at brunni. En er heilǫg Barbara kom aptr í stǫpul
sinn, þá leit hon þar skurðgoð fǫður síns ór málmi ger ok tók
traust af Helgum Anda ok mátt af Guðs krapti, ok spýtti hon í
andlit skurðgoðunum ok mælti: Verði yðr líkir þeir er yðr gerðu
ok allir þeir er yðr treystaz. En er hon hafði þetta mælt, þá bað
40 hon Guðs krapt fella skurðgoðin, ok varð sem hon bað.

[II] Frá Díóskoro

En er Díóskorus kom heim aptr, faðir hennar, ór inni lǫngu
heimanfǫr, þá leit hann á hǫll sína algerva ok sá þrjá glugga ok
mælti við smiðuna: Fyrir hví settu þér þrjá glugga? En þeir svǫ-
45 ruðu: Dóttir þín bauð oss svá. Þá kallaði hann þangat dóttur sína
ok mælti við hana: Bautt þú, dóttir, at gera þrjá glugga? Hon svaraði: Þat gerða ek ok vel gerða ek, þvíat þrír gluggar lýsa hvern
mann er kemr í heim, en tveir gluggar megu myrkvir vera. Faðir
hennar mælti við hana: Hversu megu þrír framar lýsa en tveir?
50 Barbara mælti: Þrír merkja Fǫður ok Son ok Helgan Anda, einn
sannan Guð þann er hverjum manni byrjar at gǫfga. Þá reiddiz
faðir hennar ok brá sverði ok vildi þegar hǫggva hana, en hon bað
Dróttin sér hjálpar ok gafz henni rúm at fara í gegnum stein-
vegginn, ok var hon úti því næst á fjalli. En á því fjalli váru hirðar
55 tveir þeir er hana sá flýja. Faðir hennar kom þangat ok vildi taka
hana ok spurði hirðana ef þeir sæi hana. Annarr duldi ok kveðz
eigi hana hafa séð, en annarr, sá er grimmari var, rétti fingr sinn
ok vísaði til hennar. Sá tók þegar þat víti, at sauðir hans allir
urðu at kvikendum þeim er *locustae* heita, ok er minning þessarar

46 við hana] AM 429 12mo; –Stock. 2.   47 gluggar] AM 429 12mo; –Stock. 2.
49 við hana] AM 429 12mo; –Stock. 2.   50 mælti] AM 429 12mo; svaraði Stock.
2.   52 hana] AM 429 12mo; dóttur sína Stock. 2.   54 á því fjalli] AM 429
12mo; í þeim stað Stock. 2.   55 þangat] AM 429 12mo; eptir henni Stock 2.

35 John the Baptist. This spring in which Barbara was baptized resembled the well about which the Gospels say that a man who was
born blind washed his face in it and received sight. This spring
resembled the living water, which a sinful woman asked Christ to
give her at the well. And when Saint Barbara came back to her
40 tower, she saw there her father's idols made of metal and received
confidence from the Holy Spirit and strength from God's might
and spat in the face of the idols and said: May those who made
you and all who believe in you become like you. And when she
had said this, she prayed that God's might would destroy the idols,
45 and what she prayed for happened.

[II] About Dioscorus

But when her father Dioscorus came home again from the long
journey, he looked at his finished hall and saw three windows and
said to the craftsmen: Why did you put in three windows? And
50 they answered: Your daughter requested us to do so. Then he
summoned his daughter and said to her: Did you, daughter,
request to have three windows made? She answered: That I did,
and it is well that I did, because three windows give light to each
person who is born, but two windows may be dark. Her father
55 said to her: How may three light more than two? Barbara said:
Three signify the Father and the Son and the Holy Ghost, one
true God whom it behooves each person to worship. Then her
father became angry and drew his sword and wanted to kill her
right away, but she asked the Lord to help her, and the stone wall
60 opened for her to pass through, and next she was out on the mountain. But on that mountain there were two shepherds who saw her
fleeing. Her father came there and wanted to catch her and asked
the shepherds if they had seen her. One concealed the fact and said
he had not seen her, but the other, who was crueler, pointed his
65 finger and showed where she was. He immediately received the
punishment that all his cattle turned into the creatures that are
called *locustae* [grasshoppers], and this miracle is commemorated at

60 jarteignar mǫrkuð yfir leiði heilagrar Barbare, svá at sjá má allt til
þessa dags. En faðir hennar fann hana ok barði ok tók í hár henni
ok dró hana til fjalls ok læsti vandliga hús þat er hann lauk hana
inni ok setti varðhald fyrir húsit, at engi mætti hana þaðan leysa.
Síðan sendi hann orð jarli, at hann kœmi ok neyddi dóttur hans
65 til blóta.

[III] Frá jarli ok Barbare meyju
En er jarl kom, þá leiddi Díóskorus dóttur sína út ór húsinu
fyrir dómstól jarls ok mælti svá fyrir, at jarl skyldi láta bana henni
ef hon vildi eigi blóta. En er jarl sá fegrð hennar, þá mælti hann
70 við hana: Hvort viltu vægja þér sjálfri ok blóta goðum eða vera
seld til inna hǫrðustu písla? Krists mær Barbara svaraði: Ek á fórn
at fœra Dróttni mínum Jesú Kristi, þeim er gerði himin ok jǫrð ok
sæ ok allt þat er þeim fylgir. En spámaðr hans mælti svá um skurðgoð þau sem manna hǫndum eru ger ór gulli eða silfri: Munn hafa
75 þau ok mæla eigi. Augu hafa þau ok sjá eigi. Eyru hafa þau ok
heyra eigi. Nasir hafa þau ok ilma eigi. Hendr hafa þau ok þreifa
eigi. Fœtr hafa þau ok ganga eigi. Ok eigi er rǫdd í hálsi þeim né
andi í munni þeim. Verði þeim líkir þeir er þau gera ok allir þeir
er treystaz þeim. Þá fylldiz jarl mikillar reiði ok lét Guðs mey
80 fœra ór fǫtum ok berja hana með sinvǫndum ok hrífa snǫrpum
hárklæðum um hǫrund hennar. En er hon var lengi þjáð í þessum
kvǫlum, þá rann blóð um allan hennar líkama. Síðan lét hann setja
hana í myrkvastofu ok hugsaði með hverri písl hann skyldi lúka
yfir hana.

85 [IV] Frá Barbare meyju
Þá er heilǫg mær Barbara var í myrkvastofu sett, skein yfir
hana ljós af himni á sjálfri nátt miðri ok vitraðiz henni sjálfr
grœðarinn várr Dróttinn Jesús Kristr ok mælti: Vertu styrk ok
staðfǫst, Barbara, þvíat nógr fagnaðr verðr á himni ok á jǫrðu yfir

---

60-1 svá at sjá má allt til þessa dags] AM 429 12mo; –Stock. 2.   81-2 þessum
kvǫlum] AM 429 12mo; þessi kvǫl Stock. 2.

Saint Barbara's grave, so that it can be seen until this day. But her
father found her and hit her and took her by her hair and dragged
70 her to the mountain and carefully locked the house in which he
shut her and set guards at the house, so that no one could release
her. Then he sent word to the earl that he should come and force
his daughter to sacrifice.

[III] About the earl and the virgin Barbara
75 And when the earl came, Dioscorus led his daughter out of the
house and before the earl's judgment seat and requested that the
earl have her executed if she would not sacrifice. But when the earl
saw her beauty, he said to her: Which do you want, to spare yourself and sacrifice to the gods or to be delivered to the harshest
80 tortures? Christ's virgin Barbara answered: I have an offering to
bring to my Lord Jesus Christ, who made heaven and earth and
sea and everything that follows them. And his prophet said thus
about idols made by human hands out of gold or silver: They have
mouths and speak not. They have eyes and see not. They have ears
85 and hear not. They have noses and smell not. They have hands
and feel not. They have feet and walk not. And there is no voice
in their throats nor breath in their mouths. May those who make
them and all who believe in them become like them. Then the earl
became very angry and had God's virgin stripped of her clothes
90 and flogged with a whip made out of sinews and her flesh scratched
with sharp combs. And when she had suffered these torments for
a long time, blood ran all over her body. Then he had her put in
prison and pondered with what torment he could overcome her.

[IV] About the virgin Barbara
95 When the holy virgin Barbara had been put in prison, a light
shone over her from heaven at midnight, and the Savior Himself
our Lord Jesus Christ appeared to her and said: Be strong and
firm, Barbara, because there will be much joy in heaven and on

90 písl þinni. Eigi skaltu hræðaz jarl, þvíat ek em með þér, ok mun
ek leysa þik ór ǫllum píslum þeim er þér eru gervar. Þá blezaði
Dróttinn hana ok sté til himins, ok váru þá gróin sár hennar ǫll.
En Krists mær fagnaði af ǫllu hjarta þeiri vitran er Guð hafði
henni vitrað. En at morni lét jarlinn leiða hana ór myrkvastofunni
95 ok fyrir dómstól sinn. En er hann sá hana grœdda af ǫllum sárum
líkama, þá undraðiz hann ok mælti: Hví gegnir þat, Barbara, er
goð vár elska þik ok miskunna þér svá at sár þín eru gróin? Heilǫg
mær Barbara svaraði ok mælti við jarlinn: Þér lík eru goð þín,
blind ok dauf ok vitlaus. Hversu máttu þau grœða sár mín, eða
100 hversu megu þau ǫðrum bjarga er þau megu engan dugnað veita
sjálfum sér? En Kristr sonr Guðs lifanda grœddi mik, sá er þú ert
óverðr at sjá, þvíat hjarta þitt er hart orðit af djǫfli. Þá reiddiz jarl
ok grenjaði sem it óarga dýr ok lét halda brennǫndum logum at
síðum henni ok ljósta hamri í hǫfuð henni. En hon leit til himins
105 ok mælti: Þú veizt Kristr, at ek tek lystandi þessar píslir fyrir ást
heilags nafns þíns. Af því fyrirláttu mik eigi allt til enda, þvíat ek
dvalða eigi at bera hraustliga píslir fyrir þinni ást. Þá reiddiz jarlinn
ok lét skera af henni brjóstin. En Krists mær leit þá enn til himins
ok mælti. Verptu eigi mér frá augliti þínu, Dróttinn, ok tak eigi
110 frá mér Helgan Anda þinn. Gjaltu mér gleði þrifsemi þinnar ok
styrkjumz með hǫfðingligum anda. En er hon hafði þetta mælt ok
stóðz hressliga þessar píslir allar af styrk Heilags Anda, þá bauð
jarlinn þjónum sínum, at þeir fœrði hana enn ór fǫtum ok berja
hana ok drægi nøkta um herað alþýðu manna. Þá hóf heilǫg Bar-
115 bara enn upp augu sín til himins ok kallaði til Guðs ok mælti:
Dróttinn Guð er hylr himin með skýjum, vertu nú hlífskjǫldr
minn ok hjálpari á þessi stundu, ok hyl nøktan líkama minn með
þaki miskunnar þinnar, at hann verði eigi sénn af vondum mǫn-

97 goð] AM 429 12mo; Guð Stock. 2. svá at sár þín eru gróin] AM 429
12mo; –Stock. 2. 98 Barbara] AM 429 12mo; –Stock. 2. goð] AM 429
12mo; Guð Stock. 2. 106 þíns] AM 429 12mo; –Stock. 2. 113–114 ok
berja hana] AM 429 12mo; –Stock. 2. 117 minn] AM 429 12mo; –Stock. 2.

earth over your torment. Do not fear the earl, because I am with
100 you, and I shall release you from all the torments that are inflicted
upon you. Then the Lord blessed her and ascended to heaven, and
then all her wounds were healed. And Christ's virgin rejoiced with
all her heart at the revelation God had revealed to her. But in the
morning, the earl had her led out of the prison and before his
105 judgment seat. And when he saw her healed from all the wounds
on her body, he marvelled and said: How can it be, Barbara, that
our gods love you and have mercy on you, so that your wounds
are healed? The holy virgin Barbara answered and said to the earl:
Your gods are like you, blind and deaf and senseless. How could
110 they heal my wounds, or how can they help others, when they cannot help themselves? But Christ, the son of the living God, healed
me, He whom you are unworthy to see, because your heart has been
made hard by the devil. Then the earl became angry and roared like
a lion and had burning torches held to her sides and her head hit
115 with a hammer, but she looked toward heaven and said: You
know, Christ, that I gladly suffer these torments out of love for
your holy name. Therefore, do not ever forsake me, because I did
not desist from courageously enduring torments for the sake of
your love. Then the earl became angry and had her breasts cut off,
120 but Christ's virgin again looked toward heaven and said: Do not
let me out of your sight, Lord, and do not take away from me
your Holy Spirit. Give me the joy of your salvation, and let me
be strengthened by a noble spirit. But when she had said this and
bravely endured all these torments with the help of the strength
125 of the Holy Spirit, the earl commanded his men to strip her of her
clothes once again and beat her and lead her naked throughout the
region. Then Saint Barbara again lifted her eyes to heaven and
prayed to God and said: Lord God, who covers the sky with clouds,
be now my safe shield and helper at this time and cover my naked
130 body with the cloak of your mercy, so that it will not be seen by

num. En er hon bað á þessa lund, þá kom Dróttinn at hjálpa henni
120 ok sendi engil sinn þann er hana hulði hvítu skrúði. Þá urðu
riddarar jarlsins blindir, svá at þeir máttu eigi Guðs mey sjá fyrir
ljósi því er henni fylgði. Þá hræddiz jarlinn ok lét aptr leiða hana
til handa fǫður hennar Dióskoro.

[V] Um píning Barbare

125   En faðir hennar fylldiz mikilli reiði er hann tók við hana ok
leiddi hana enn til fjalls. En heilǫg Barbara skyndi fagnandi til
algerrar ǫmbunar sigrs síns, ok bað hon Dróttin, at hon tæki lok
píslar sinnar í þessum stað ok mælti: Dróttinn Jesús Kristr, er
himna skópt ok jǫrð smíðaðir ok byrgðir undirdjúp ok settir endi-
130 mǫrk sjávar, þú er býðr skýjum at rigna yfir góða ok illa, þú er
gekk yfir sjá ok stǫðvaðir þjótandi bylgjur hans, þú er réttir helgar
hendr þínar á krossi ok gerðir margar aðrar jarteignir, heyrðu mik
ambátt þína, þvíat allir hlutir hlýða þínu boði. Dróttinn Jesús
Kristr, hlífari minn í æsku minni, veittu mér þá bœn, at ek lúka
135 nú þegar þraut minni með góðum lokum, ok gefðu ambátt þinni
þá miskunn, at þú gerir mildi þína við þá menn, er af ǫllu hjarta
gera mína minning í sínum nauðsynjum allra helzt á degi píslar
minnar. Minnztu eigi, Dróttinn, synda þeira á dómsdegi er trúliga
kalla á mik, ok veittu þeim líkn í syndum, þvíat þú veizt at vér
140 erum óstyrkir líkamir. En er hon lauk bœn sinni, þá kom rǫdd af
himni ok mælti við hana: Komdu, in fegrsta mær mín, til innar
glǫðustu hvíldar Fǫður míns er á himnum er, en allt þat er þú batt
mun þér veitt vera. En er Guðs mær heyrði þetta af Dróttni með
fagnaði, þá kom hon til staðar píslar sinnar ok lauk þar dýrligri
145 þraut, svá sem hon hafði beðit af Guði, þvíat hon var í þeim stað
hǫggvin af fǫður sínum, ok endi hon líf sitt í játningu Krists tveim

119–120 kom Dróttinn at hjálpa henni ok sendi] AM 429 12mo; sendi Dróttinn Stock. 2 .   122   hræddiz] AM 429 12mo; reiddiz Stock. 2.   hana] AM 429 12mo; Barbaram Stock. 2.   125   er hann tók við hana] AM 429 12mo; –Stock. 2.   130–131   er gekk] AM 429 12mo; gekkt Stock. 2.   135   þinni] + Dróttinn Stock. 2.   136   við þá menn] AM 429 12mo; –Stock. 2.   141   við hana] AM 429 12mo; –Stock. 2.

wicked people. And as she prayed in this manner, the Lord came to help her and sent His angel, who covered her with a white shift. Then the earl's men became blind, so that they could not see God's virgin because of the light that accompanied her. Then the
135 earl became afraid and had her taken back to her father Dioscorus.

[V] About Barbara's passion
But her father became very angry when he received her and led her to the mountain again. But Saint Barbara hurried joyfully to the final reward of her victory, and she prayed to the Lord that
140 she might end her torments in this place and said: Lord Jesus Christ who created heaven and made earth and closed the bottomless pit and fixed the sea's boundaries, you who command clouds to rain on good and bad people, you who walked over the sea and stopped its raging waves, you who stretched out your holy arms
145 on the cross and performed many other miracles. Hear me, your handmaid, because all things obey your command. Lord Jesus Christ, my refuge in my youth. Grant me the wish that my struggle comes to a good end, and bestow on your handmaid such grace that you show your gentleness to those people, who with all their
150 heart commemorate me in their afflictions and especially on the day of my passion. Forget, Lord, on the Day of Judgment the sins of those who faithfully invoke me, and grant them forgiveness for their sins, because you know that we are feeble in flesh. And when she ended her prayer, a voice from heaven said to her: Come, my
155 most beautiful virgin, to my father's joyous place of rest which is in heaven, and you will be granted all that you prayed for. And when God's virgin with gladness heard this from the Lord, she came to the place of her passion and there ended her glorious struggle just as she had asked God, because in that place she was
160 executed by her father, and she ended her life professing Christ

náttum fyrir Nikulásarmessu biskups. En er faðir hennar sté ofan
af fjalli með sínum mǫnnum, þá kom eldr ór lopti ok brendi hann
svá at þatki var at aska hans fyndiz. En nǫkkurr heilagr maðr kom
150 leyniliga ok tók á braut líkam innar helgustu meyjar Barbare ok
gróf í þeim stað er kallaðr er Sólarstaðr, ok lét hann þar gera
bœnahús í minningu hennar, ok verða þar margar jarteignir til lofs
ok dýrðar Dróttni várum Jesú Kristi þeim er með Feðr ok Helgum
Anda lifir ok ríkir, einn Guð í þrenningu um allar aldir alda.
155 Amen.

---

154 einn] AM 429 12mo; –Stock. 2.   í þrenningu] AM 429 12mo; –Stock. 2.

two nights before the feastday of Bishop Nicholas. But when her father descended the mountain with his men, fire came from the air and burned him, so that his ashes were nowhere to be found. But a holy man came in secret and took away the body of the virgin Saint Barbara and buried it in a place called the City of the Sun, and there he had built a house of prayer in memory of her, and in that place many miracles happen in praise and honor of our Lord Jesus Christ who with His Father and the Holy Ghost, the Trinity, lives and reigns, in eternity. Amen.

Passio Sancte Barbare
(Douai, Bibliothèque Municipale Codex 838)

Incipit Passio Sancte Barbare virginis et martyris

Temporibvs Maximiani imperatoris, erat quidam satrapa dioscorus nomine, diues ualde, paganus uero existens et colens ydola. Hic habebat filiam unicam, nomine barbaram. Fecit autem pater eius
5 turrim sublimem, ibique reclusit eam, ita ut non [143rb] ab hominibus propter eminentem pulchritudinem eius deciperetur. Loquuti sunt uero quidam de optimatibus patri eius de ea, ut uirum sibi acciperet. Jpse uero ascendens in turrim, persuadebat ei dicens. Filia mea quidam de potentibus commemorati sunt me de te, ut accipi-
10 ant te in coniugio. Quid ergo uelis de hoc, proprio ore *dicto Jpsa intuens in eum cum ira dixit. Ne cogas me hoc agere pater. At ipse secessit ab ea, et descendens permanebat in quo condebatur lauachrum. Jnstituerat enim multitudinem artificum, quatinus hoc cito perficeretur. Jnstituens quoque quomodo deberet fieri et
15 tribuens singulis propriam mercedem ex integro, profectus est in regionem longinquam, faciens ibidem non modicum tempus. Descendens autem famula dei barbara de turri, ut uideret opus quod factum est, uidit contra septentrionem duas solummodo fenestras superastantes, et dicit artificibus. Quare duas tantum fenestras insti-
20 tuistis? Dicunt ei. Pater tuus sic nobis disposuit. Dicit eis beata barbara. Facite mihi et tertiam. Jpsi uero dicunt ei. Timemus domina ne forte indignetur pater tuus aduersum nos, et non possimus portare eum. Dicit eis famula dei barbara. Quod uobis dico facite. Ego de hoc adquiescere faciam patrem meum. Jpsi uero adquieu-
25 erunt ei, ut tertiam fenestram facerent, sicut constituit eis. Perambulans uero inquerelosa et immaculosa barbara in natatorio, et abiens contra orientem, instituit marmoribus digito preciosam crucis figuram, quę usque in hodiernum diem permanet ad cognitionem. Jpsa uero in absidem in qua gradiebatur aqua sanctificata,
30 facta est et ibi figura preciose crucis, in quo loco omnes sanationes et sanitates credentes accipiunt. Jn hoc lauacro, domino disponente

10 dicto] dictto.

sancta uirgo suscepit a quodam sanctum baptisma. Ubi per aliquot
tempus locustis ac melle siluestri alita, preconem ac precursorem
domini imitabatur iohannem baptistam. Hoc lauachrum similabatur
35 fonti syloe, in quo a natiuitate cecus lauans lumen recepit. Hoc
lauachrum similabatur probaticę piscinę, in qua paraliticus uerbo
curatus est. Hęc est natatoria, et fons incorruptibilis. Hec est
natatoria et aqua uiua, quam samaritana ad fontem a christo petiuit.
Pertransiens ergo famula christi barbara, et ascendens iterum in
40 turrim, uidit simulachra quę colebat pater eius. Et suscipiens
spiritum sanctum multifarie, bene mobilem, incontaminatum, diser-
tum, luculentum, benignum, acutissimum, beneficum, certum, dili-
gentissimum, securum, cuncta superinspicientem. Circuiuit uapor
dei uirtutis eam, et affluentis omnipotentis glorię ac sinceritatis.
45 Hęc igitur ut premissum est uidens surda simulachra, inspuens in
faciem eorum dixit. Simulachra gentium argentum et aurum, opera
manuum hominum. Similes uestri fiant qui faciunt uos, et omnes
qui confidunt in uobis. Et ascendens in eminentiorem locum, erat
ibidem deprecans deum. Finito autem opere atque perfecto, reuersus
50 est pater eius de peregrinatione. Et contemplatus tres fenestras, dicit
artificibus. Quare tres fenestras instituistis? Dicunt ei. Filia tua sic
nobis precepit. Jpse uero conuocans filiam suam, dicit ei. Filia tu
imperasti tres fenestras statuere? Jpsa uero dicit [143va] ei. Etiam.
Et enim bene feci. Nam tres fenestrę illuminant omnem hominem,
55 at uero duę tenebre sunt. Et sumens eam pater eius, descendit in
natatorio, et dixit ei. Quomodo habundantius illuminant tres á
duabus? Beata barbara dixit. *Hę euidentius patrem et filium et
spiritum sanctum designant, qui est unus et uerus deus, in quem
credere, et quem adorare oportet. Tunc repletus furore pater eius,
60 protulit spatam suam ut occideret eam. Orans ergo beata barbara,
uidit iuxta se scissam petram, quam ingrediens, perrexit usque ad
proximum montem. Et erant duo pastores pascentes oues in eodem
monte, qui uiderunt eam fugientem. Ad quos accedens pater eius,
interrogabat eos de ea. Uolens autem unus saluare eam, constanter

57 Hę] Heę.

65 negauit quod non uidisset eam. Alius uero crudelis, digito demon-
strauit eam. Et maledixit eum beata barbara. Statimque factę sunt
oues eius locustę, quę permane < n > t ad sepulchrum eius usque in
hodiernum diem. Jgitur pater eius repperiens flagellauit eam, et per
capillos capitis eius pertraxit eam ad montem, et reclusit eam in
70 cellulam pauperculam, et muniuit claue, instituitque cathenas ut non
aperiret ei quisquam, constituens et custodes donec nunciaret presidi, ut traderet eam ad torquendum. Adueniens itaque preses, iussit
eam sibi presentari. Jtaque ingressus pater eius una cum gerontio
commentariense eiecit eam de cella, et tradidit eam presidi, adiurans
75 eum per potentiam deorum, quatinus atrocibus tormentis consumeret eam. Et preses sedens pro tribunali, et uidens pulchritudinem
eius, dicit ei. Quid? Vis parcere tibi et *sacrificare díjs, an acerri-
mis tormentis tradi? Respondit beata barbara, et dixit. Ego habeo
sacrificare domino meo ihesv christo, qui fecit cęlum et terram,
80 mare et omnia que in eis sunt. De demonibus namque tuis, propheta
ait. Os habent et non loquentur, oculos habent et non uidebunt.
Aures habent et non audient, nares habent et non odorabunt,
manus habent et non palpabunt, pedes habent et non ambulabunt,
neque enim est spiritus in ore ipsorum. Similes illis fiant qui faciunt
85 ea, et omnes qui confidunt in eis. Tunc preses repletus furore, jussit
eam expoliari et carnes eius sine ulla miseratione neruis taurinis
discerpi, et cilicinis textis defricari. Que cum diu illatas sustinuisset
plagas, ita ut omne corpus eius perfunderetur sanguine, iussit ut
denuo recluderetur in carcere, quousque pertractaret, qualiter per
90 pęnas consumeret eam. Media itaque nocte circumfulsit eam lux de
cęlo, in qua apparuit ei et saluator christus dicens. Confide atque
confortare barbara, quoniam copiosum gaudium fit in cęlo et in
terra, super tua passione. Non ergo metuas minas tyranni. Ego
enim tecum sum. Ego eruam te ab omnibus plagis, quę inferuntur
95 tibi. Et statim plagę omnes nusquam apparuerunt in corpore eius.
Posthęc signauit eam dominus, et ascendit in cęlos. Gaudebat autem
et exultabat uirgo christi barbara inenarrabili gaudio, super uisita-

77 sacrificare] sacrifricare.

tione *et* exhortatione d*o*mini. Mane ita*que* facto, iussit iter*um* preses sibi eam p*re*sen[**143vb**]tari, *et* intuens in ea*m* uidit sanissi-

100 ma*m* *esse* ab om*n*ib*us* plagis qu*ę* illi illat*ę* fuer*unt*. Et dicit ei. Quom*o*do reprop*i*tiati sunt t*ibi* dí*j* *et* diligunt te barbara, q*ui*a plagas tuas sanauerunt? Respondens aut*em* martyr *christ*i barbara, dixit p*re*sidi. Similes tui *sunt* dí*j* tui, surdi *et* ceci et sine intellectu, et immobiles, et quom*o*do potuerunt plagas meas curare? Reme-

105 diu*m* sibi ipsi n*on* possunt afferre, *et* quom*o*do alios possent adiu-uare? Me aute*m* q*ui* curauit ih*esus* est *christus* filius d*e*i uiui, que*m* tu n*on* uides, eo q*u*od cor tuu*m* induratu*m* est a diabolo. Tunc iratus p*re*ses et fremens ut seuus leo, iussit ad latera ei*us* lampadas ardentes applicari, et posth*ę*c malleo caput tundendo ei*us* p*er*cuti. Jpsa

110 *uero* intuita in c*ę*lum dixit. Tu nosti cordis cognitor *christe*, q*uo*-*niam* p*ro* amore nominis tui *sancti* libenter ista sustineo. Ne me *ergo* derelinquas d*o*m*i*ne us*que* in fine*m*, cu*m* p*ro* te tanta supplicia fortiter sustinere n*on* distuli. Tunc iubet iniquissim*us* p*rę*ses claudio carnifici, abscidi mamillas eius. Amputans u*ero* ut iussit uberib*us*,

115 martyr *christ*i barbara aspiciens iteru*m* in c*ę*lum, dicebat ad domi-nu*m*. Ne p*ro*icias me a facie tua d*o*mine, *et* sp*iritu*m s*anctum* tuu*m* ne auferas á me, *et* redde m*ihi* l*ę*ticia*m* salutaris tui. Cum aute*m* et hanc plaga*m* supra memorata*m* fortiter sp*irit*u *sanct*o roborata sus-tinuisset, iussit adhuc insan*us* p*re*ses nuda*m* eam circuire omne*m*

120 regione*m* illa*m*, *et* plagas á ministris inferentib*us*, ubiq*ue* ea*m* flagellari. Qu*ę* cum ad crudelia iussa denudata fuisset, denuo eleuatis oc*u*lis in celos ad d*eu*m dixit. D*o*mine d*eu*s q*ui* operis c*ę*los nubib*us*, protector et adiutor meus in hac hora esto, et tege tegumento mis*ericordi*ę tu*ę* denudatum corpus meu*m*, ut n*on* uide-

125 at*ur* ab ullo uiror*um* impior*um*. Et h*ę*c orante ea, uenit d*o*min*us* in adiutoriu*m* ei*us*, mittens*que* angel*u*m suu*m* coop*er*uit ea*m* stola candida. Jgit*ur* milit*es* cecati, circu*m*dederunt ea*m* cum furore, in p*rę*dio q*u*od uocat*ur* dalasium, in loco solis dicto. T*un*c quoq*ue* p*re*ses confusus, p*er* claudiu*m* precepit illa*m* iam passionib*us* fati-

130 gata*m*, patri suo tradi. T*un*c pater ei*us* furore repletus, suscepit eam á preside, et iteru*m* perduxit ea*m* in montem. At u*ero* martyr *christ*i barbara gaudens sup*er* hoc, festinabat uenire, ut p*er*fectu*m* uictori*ę*

brauium ibidem perciperet. Et ducta ad locum adorabat deum, et
rogabat martyríj sui consummationem dicens. Domine ihesu christe
135 qui cęlos extendisti, et terram fundasti, qui abyssos conclusisti, et
mari murum posuisti, qui precepisti ymbriferis nubibus super bonos
et malos pluere, qui super mare ambulasti, et furentes fluctus eius
sedasti, qui in cruce extendisti manus tuas, et alia multa miracula
fecisti, exaudi me famulam tuam, omnia enim obędiunt iussioni
140 tuę. Domine ihesu christe protector meus á juuentute mea, pręsta
in petitionem hanc, ut iam nunc in consummatione bona consum-
mem agonem meum, et da mihi famulę tuę gratiam hanc, ut si qui
in toto corde memoriam mei fecerunt in necessitatibus suis, facias
misericordiam tuam cum eis, et precipue in die martyríj mei.
145 Domine ne memineris peccatorum meorum in die iudicíj, et qui
fideliter inuocant me, propitiare peccatis eorum. Tu enim domine
scis, quia caro sumus. Et dicente ea amen, [144ra] facta est uox
domini de cęlis ad eam dicens. Ueni pulchra mea, ueni ad lętis-
simam et suauissimam patris mei requiem, quę est in cęlis. De quo
150 autem et de quibus postulasti concessa sunt tibi. Et hęc cum gaudio
magno audiens uirgo christi á domino suo, uenit ad locum superius
memoratum, et illic sicut petierat á domino, peractum est pre-
ciosum eius martyrium. Jn eodem quippe loco á patre suo decollata
est, pridie Nonas decembris, consummans finem uitę in bona con-
155 fessione, in christo ihesu domino nostro. Descendens uero posthęc
pater eius cum suis de monte, ignis cecidit de cęlo et combussit
eum, ita ut nec puluis inueniretur de eo. Quidam autem uir uener-
abilis ueniens, accepit corpus beatę uirginis occultę, et reposuit
illud in loco solis dicto, ubi ędificauit habitaculum modicum, in
160 quo et sanationes plurimę ex tunc et nunc celebrantur in gloriam
omnipotentis dei. Passa est autem beatissima uirgo et martyr christi
barbara imperante Maximiano augusto, et presidente Martiano,
apud nos uero regnante domino deo atque saluatore nostro ihesu
christo, cui est honor et gloria in secula seculorum amen.

Bibliography

Anna Sigurðardóttir. *Allt hafði annan róm áður í páfadóm. Nunnu-klaustrin tvö á Íslandi á miðöldum og brot úr kristnisögu.* Reykjavík: Kvennasögusafn Íslands, 1988.

Anson, John. "The Female Transvestite in Early Monasticism: The Origin and Development of a Motif." *Viator* 5 (1974): 1-32.

Arne Magnussons i AM. 435A-B, 4to indeholdte håndskriftfortegnelser med to tillæg. [Ed. Kr. Kålund.] Copenhagen: Gyldendal, 1909.

Atkinson, Clarissa W. *Mystic and Pilgrim: The 'Book' and the World of Margery Kempe.* Ithaca and London: Cornell University Press, 1983.

Battelli, Guido. *Le più belle leggende cristiane.* Milan: Ulrico Hoepli, 1924.

Beckman, N., and Kr. Kålund, ed. *Alfræði íslenzk.* Samfund til udgivelse af gammel nordisk litteratur 37, 41, 45. 3 vols. Copenhagen: Møller, 1908-1918.

Bede. "Martyrologium de natalitiis sanctorum; cum auctario Flori et aliorum." In *The Complete Works of Venerable Bede* ..., ed. J.A. Giles, 4: 16-172. 12 vols. London: Whittaker, 1843-1844.

Bedjan, Paulus, ed. *Acta martyrum et sanctorum.* 7 vols. Paris: Otto Harrassowitz, 1890-1897.

Bender, H. "Barbara." In *Lexikon für Theologie und Kirche,* 1: 1235-1236. Freiburg: Herder, 1957.

BHG = Bibliotheca Hagiographica Graeca. Subsidia hagiographica 8a. 3 vols. Brussels: Société des Bollandistes, 1957.

BHL = Bibliotheca Hagiographica Latina Antiquae et Mediae Aetatis. Subsidia hagiographica 6. Brussels: Société des Bollandistes, 1898-1899. Rpt. 1992. *Supplementum.* Subsidia hagiographica 12. Brussels: Société des Bollandistes, 1911. *Novum Supplementum.* Subsidia hagiographica 70. Brussels: Société des Bollandistes, 1986.

BHO = Bibliotheca Hagiographica Orientalis. Subsidia hagiographica 10. Brussels: Société des Bollandistes, 1910.

Blume, Clemens. *Thesauri hymnologici hymnarium: Die Hymnen des Thesaurus Hymnologicus H.A. Daniels. 1: Die Hymnen des 5.-11. Jahrhunderts und die Irish-Keltische Hymnodie. 2: Die Hymnen des 12.-16. Jahrhunderts.* Analecta hymnica medii aevi 51, 52. Leipzig: O.R. Reisland, 1908–1909. Rpt. New York and London: Johnson Reprint Corporation, 1961.

—. *Liturgische Prosen zweiter Epoche auf Feste der Heiligen.* Analecta Hymnica Medii Aevi 55. Leipzig: O.R. Reisland, 1922. Rpt. New York and London: Johnson Reprint Corporation, 1961.

Bol, Laurens J. *Jan van Eyck.* Trans. Albert J. Fransella. New York: Barnes & Noble, 1965.

Braun, Joseph. *Tracht und Attribute der Heiligen in der deutschen Kunst.* Stuttgart: Metzler, 1943.

Brun, Frans de. "Anteckningar rörande medeltida gillen i Stockholm." *Samfundet Sankt Eriks Årsbok* (1917): 34–79.

Brun, J. Le. "Martyrologies." In *New Catholic Encyclopedia* 9 [1967]: 317–318. 19 vols. New York: McGraw-Hill, 1967–1989.

Bugge, John. *'Virginitas': An Essay in the History of a Medieval Ideal.* Archives internationales d'histoire des idées, series minor 17. The Hague: Martinus Nijhoff, 1975.

Bullough, Vern L. "Transvestites in the Middle Ages." *American Journal of Sociology* 79 (1974): 1381–1394.

Buur, Chr. "Danske Cisiojanus og andre Kalenderrim." *Sprog og kultur* 5 (1936): 84–102.

Bynum, Caroline Walker. *Holy Feast and Holy Fast: The Religious Significance of Food to Medieval Women.* Berkeley, Los Angeles, and London: University of California Press, 1987.

Børthy, Lissa. "En dansk billedkalender fra 1513." *Folkeminder* 12 (1966): 57–84.

Carlé, Birte. "Structural Patterns in the Legends of the Holy Women of Christianity." In *Aspects of Female Existence*, ed. Birte Carlé et al., pp. 79–86. Proceedings from The St. Gertrud Symposium "Women in the Middle Ages," Copenhagen, September 1978. Copenhagen: Gyldendal, 1980.

—. *Jomfru-fortællingen. Et bidrag til genrehistorien.* Odense University studies in Scandinavian languages and literatures 12. Odense: Odense University Press, 1985.

Carlquist, Jonas. *De fornsvenska helgonlegenderna. Källor, stil och skriftmiljö.* Samlingar utgivna av svenska fornskrift-sällskapet, hf. 262, bd. 82. [Uppsala]: Svenska fornskrift-sällskapet; Stockholm: Graphic Systems, 1996.

Caxton, William: *see* Jacobus de Voragine.

Cazelles, Brigitte. "Introduction." In *Images of Sainthood in Medieval Europe,* ed. Renate Blumenfeld-Kosinski and Timea Szell, pp. 1–17. Ithaca and London: Cornell University Press, 1991.

—. *The Lady as Saint: A Collection of French Hagiographic Romances of the Thirteenth Century.* Philadelphia: University of Pennsylvania Press, 1991.

Cormack, Margaret. *The Saints in Iceland. Their Veneration from the Conversion to 1400.* Subsidia Hagiographica 78. Brussels: Société des Bollandistes, 1994.

Cornell, Henrik, and Sigurd Wallin. *Upsvenska målarskolor på 1400-talet.* Stockholm: Almqvist & Wiksell, 1933.

—. *Uppsvenska kyrkomålningar på 1500-talet.* Stockholm: Humanistiska sällskapet, 1953.

Costelloe, M.J. "Barbara, St." In *The New Catholic Encyclopedia* 1 [1967]: 86. 19 vols. New York: McGraw–Hill, 1967–1989.

Crawford, J.P. Wickersham. *Spanish Drama before Lope de Vega.* With a bibliographical supplement by Warren T. McCready. 1937. Rev. ed., Philadelphia: University of Pennsylvania Press, 1967.

Curnow, Maureen Cheney. "The *Livre de la Cité des Dames* of Christine de Pisan: A Critical Edition." Diss. Vanderbilt University, 1975.

Curman, Sigurd, and Johnny Roosval. *Sveriges kyrkor: Konsthistoriskt inventarium* 4.1 *Gotland: Kyrkorna i Lina och Halla Ting.* Stockholm: Generalstabens litografiska anstalts förlag, 1959–1964.

Dahlgren, F.A., ed. *Skrifter till läsning för klosterfolk.* Samlingar utgifna af svenska fornskrift-sällskapet 20. Stockholm: Norstedt & Söner, 1875.

Delehaye, Hippolyte. *Les légendes hagiographiques.* 3rd rev. ed. Subsidia hagiographica 18. Brussels: Société des Bollandistes, 1927.

Denomy, Alexander Joseph. "An Old French Life of Saint Barbara." *Mediaeval Studies* 1 (1939): 148–178.

Derolez, Albert. "A Devotee of Saint Barbara in a Belgian Beguinage (Marston MS 287)." In *Beinecke Studies in Early Manuscripts* [ed. Robert G. Babcock], *Yale University Library Gazette* 66 Suppl. (1991): 197–218.

DI = *Diplomatarium Islandicum. Íslenzk fornbréfasafn.* 16 vols. Copenhagen and Reykjavík: Möller and Hið íslenzka bókmentafélag, 1857–1952.

Diemer, Joseph. *Kleine Beiträge zur älteren deutschen Sprache und Literatur* 6. Sitzungsberichte der österreichischen Akademie der Wissenschaften. Phil.- Hist. Klasse 11. Vienna, 1853.

Dix mille saints. Dictionnaire hagiographique. Ed. Les Bénédictins de Ramsgate. Brepols: A & C Black, 1988.

DN = *Diplomatarium Norvegicum. Oldbreve til Kundskab om Norges indre og ydre Forhold, Sprog, Slægter, Sæder, Lovgivning og Rettergang i Middelalderen.* Ed. Chr. C.A. Lange, C.R. Unger, et al. 22 vols. Christiania [Oslo]: Malling; Oslo: Kommisjonen for Diplomatarium Norvegicum, 1852–1992.

Dubois, Jacques. *Les martyrologes du moyen âge latin.* Typologie des sources du moyen âge occidental 26. Brepols: Turnhout, 1978.

—, and Geneviève Renaud, ed. *Edition pratique des martyrologes de Béde, de l'anonyme Lyonnais et de Florus.* Édition du Centre National de la recherche scientifique, 1976.

—, ed. *Le Martyrologe d'Adon. Ses deux familles, ses trois recensions.* Paris: Centre National de la recherche scientifique, 1984.

—, ed. *Le martyrologe d'Usuard. Texte et commentaire.* Subsidia hagiographica 40. Brussels: Société des Bollandistes, 1965.

Dunbar, Agnes B.C. *A Dictionary of Saintly Women.* 2 vols. London: George Bell & Sons, 1904.

Eis, Gerhard. "Johannes Kirchschlags Predigt zum Barbaratag 1486." *Beiträge zur Geschichte der deutschen Sprache und Literatur* 81 (1959): 196–200.

Eiríkur Þormóðsson. "Bókaeign Möðruvallaklausturs 1461." *Mímir* 12 (1968): 18–20.

Ernault, Émile, ed. *Le mystère de sainte Barbe, tragédie Bretonne.* Archives de Bretagne 3. Nantes: Société des Bibliophiles Bretons, 1885.

Finnur Jónsson, ed. *Den norsk-islandske Skjaldedigtning.* IA-IIA (tekst efter håndskrifterne) and IB-IIB (rettet tekst). Copenhagen: Gyldendal, 1908-1915.

Fogelklou, Emilia, Andreas Lindblom, Elias Wessén, ed. *Legender från Sveriges medeltid.* 2 vols. Stockholm: [Broderna Lagerström], 1917.

Foote, Peter, ed. *Lives of Saints. Perg. fol. nr. 2 in the Royal Library, Stockholm.* Early Icelandic Manuscripts in Facsimile 4. Copenhagen: Rosenkilde and Bagger, 1962.

Frank, Grace. *The Medieval French Drama.* Oxford: Oxford University Press, 1954. Rpt. 1960.

Franz, Adolph. *Die Messe im deutschen Mittelalter. Beiträge zur Geschichte der Liturgie und des religiösen Volkslebens.* Freiburg im Breisgau: Herder, 1902.

Gad, Tue. *Legenden i dansk middelalder.* Copenhagen: Dansk videnskabs forlag, 1961.

—. *Helgener. Legender fortalt i Norden.* Copenhagen: Rhodos, 1971.

Gaiffier, Baudouin de. "Bulletin des publications hagiographiques." *Analecta Bollandiana* 76 (1958): 469–470.

—. "Le triptyque du Maître de la Légende de Sainte Barbe. Sources littéraires de l'iconographie." *Revue Belge d'archéologie et d'histoire de l'art* 27 (1958): 3–23.

—. "La légende latine de sainte Barbe par Jean de Wackerzeele." *Analecta Bollandiana* 77 (1959): 5–41.

Geete, Robert, ed. *Svenska böner från medeltiden.* Samlingar utgifna af svenska fornskrift-sällskapet 131, 133, 135. Stockholm: Norstedt & Söner, 1907–1909.

Gering, Hugo, ed. *Islendzk æventyri. Isländische Legenden Novellen und Märchen.* 2 vols. Halle: Verlag der Buchhandlung des Waisenhauses, 1882–1884.

Gerould, Gordon Hall. *Saints' Legends.* Boston and New York: Houghton Mifflin Company, 1916.

Gjerløw, Lilli. "Kalendarium II." In *Kulturhistorisk Leksikon for nordisk middelalder* 8 [1963]: 134–147. 22 vols. Copenhagen: Rosenkilde and Bagger, 1956–1978.

—, ed. *Ordo Nidrosiensis Ecclesiae.* Libri Liturgici Provinciae Nidrosiensis Medii Aevi 2. Oslo: Norsk Historisk Kjeldeskrift-Institutt, 1968.

—. *Liturgica Islandica.* Vol 1: *Text*; Vol. 2: *Facsimiles.* Bibliotheca Arnamagnæana 35–36. Copenhagen: Reitzel, 1980.

Goodich, Michael. *Vita Perfecta: The Ideal of Sainthood in the Thirteenth Century.* Monographien zur Geschichte des Mittelalters 25. Stuttgart: Anton Hiersemann, 1982.

Gordini, Gian Domenico, and Renato Aprile. "Barbara." In *Bibliotheca Sanctorum* 2 [1962]: 751–767. 12 vols. Rome: Instituto Giovanni 23, [1961]–1968.

Grágás III = *Grágás. Stykker, som findes i det Arnamagnæanske Haandskrift Nr. 351 fol., Skálholtsbók og en Række andre Haandskrifter.* Ed. Vilhjálmur Finsen. Copenhagen: Gyldendal, 1883. Rpt. Odense: Odense Universitetsforlag, 1974.

Grüneisen, Wladimir de. *Sainte Marie Antique.* Rome: Max Bretschneider, 1911.

Guðbrandur Jónsson. *Dómkirkjan á Hólum í Hjaltadal. Lýsing íslenzkra miðaldakirkna.* Safn til sögu Íslands og ísl. bókmenta 5.6. Reykjavík: Gutenberg, 1919–1929.

Guðrún Kvaran and Sigurður Jónsson frá Arnarvatni. *Nöfn Íslendinga.* Reykjavík: Heimskringla, 1991.

Guðrún P. Helgadóttir. *Skáldkonur fyrri alda.* 2 vols. Akureyri: Kvöldvökuútgáfan, 1961–1963.

Günter, Heinrich. *Legenden-Studien.* Cologne: Bachem, 1906.

—. *Psychologie der Legende. Studien zu einer wissenschaftlichen Heiligen-Geschichte.* Freiburg: Herder, 1949.

Gödel, Vilhelm. *Katalog öfver Kongl. Bibliotekets fornisländska och fornnorska handskrifter.* Stockholm: Norstedt & Söner, 1897–1900.

Görlach, Manfred. *The 'South English Legendary,' 'Gilte Legende' and 'Golden Legend.'* Braunschweiger Anglistische Arbeiten 3. Braunschweig: Institut für Anglistik und Amerikanistik, 1972.

Hallberg, Svante, Rune Norberg, and Oloph Odenius. "Den heliga Barbara i svensk kult och konst under medeltiden." *Med hammare och fackla* 25 (1967): 83–191.

Heffernan, Thomas J. *Sacred Biography: Saints and Their Biographers in the Middle Ages.* New York: Oxford University Press, 1988.

Heilfurth, Gerhard. "St. Barbara als Berufspatronin des Bergbaues." *Zeitschrift für Volkskunde* 53 (1956–1957): 1–64.

Helander, Sven. *Ordinarius Lincopensis c:a 1400 och dess liturgiska förebilder.* Bibliotheca Theologiae Practicae 4. Lund: Gleerup, 1957.

Henning, Sam., ed. *Siælinna thrøst: Førsta delin aff the bokinne som kallas Siælinna thrøst.* Samlingar utgivna av svenska fornskrift-sällskapet 59. Uppsala: Almqvist & Wiksell, 1954.

Hreinn Benediktsson. *Early Icelandic Script, as Illustrated in Vernacular Texts from the Twelfth and Thirteenth Centuries.* Íslenzk handrit: Icelandic Manuscripts, Series in Folio 2. Reykjavík: The Manuscript Institute of Iceland, 1965.

Indrebø, Gustav, ed. *Gamal norsk homiliebok. Cod. AM 619 4°.* Oslo: Dybwad, 1931.

Isidore of Seville. "Etymologiae." PL 82: 73–728.

Jacobus de Voragine. *The Golden Legend [or, Lives of the Saints, as Englished by William Caxton].* Ed. F.S. Ellis. 7 vols. London: Dent, 1900. Rpt. 1934–1939.

—. *Jacobi a Voragine: Legenda Aurea Vulgo Historia Lombardica Dicta.* Ed. Th. Graesse. 3rd ed. Dresden and Leipzig, 1890. Rpt. Osnabrück: Otto Zeller Verlag, 1969.

Janus Jónsson. "Um klaustrin á Íslandi." *Tímarit Hins íslenzka bókmenntafjelagsins* 8 (1887): 174–265.

Jerome. *Commentarius in Epistolam ad Ephesios.* PL 60: 467–590.

Jexlev, Thelma. "Vor Frue Kirkes relikvier. To senmiddelalderlige fortegnelser." *Historiske meddelelser om København* (1976): 26–47.

Johansson, Hilding, ed. *Hemsjömanualet: En liturgi-historisk studie.* Samlingar och studier till svenska kyrkans historia 24. Stockholm: Svenska kyrkans diakonistyrelses bokförlag, 1950.

John Damascene. *Laudatio sanctae Barbarae.* PG 96: 781–814.

John the Deacon. *Sancti Gregorii Magni Vita.* PL 75: 59–242.

Jón Helgason, ed. *Íslenzk miðaldakvæði: Islandske digte fra senmiddelalderen.* Vol. 1.2: Copenhagen: Munksgaard, 1936; Vol. 2: Copenhagen: Munksgaard, 1938.

[Jón Sigurðsson and Guðbrandur Vigfússon, ed.] *Biskupa sögur.* 2 vols. Copenhagen: Møller, 1858–1878.

Jón Þorkelsson. *Om Digtningen på Island i det 15. og 16. Århundrede.* Copenhagen: Høst, 1888.

Jorgensen. Peter A. "Producing the Best Text Edition: Herculean and Sisyphean." *Scandinavian Studies* 65 (1993): 329–337.

Julleville, L. Petit de. *Les Mystères.* 2 vols. Histoire du théatre en France. Paris: Hachette, 1880.

Kirnbauer, Franz. *St. Barbara in der Kunst.* Vienna: Urban-Verlag, 1952.

Kirsch, J.P. "Barbara." In *The Catholic Encyclopedia*, ed. Edward A. Pace et al., 2 [1907]: 284–285. 16 vols. New York: The Encyclopedia Press, Inc., 1907–1912.

Klemming, G.E., ed. *Själens tröst. Tio Guds bud.* Samlingar utgifna af svenska fornskrift-sällskapet 57–60. Stockholm: Norstedt & Söner, 1871–1873.

—, ed. *Klosterläsning: Järteckensbok, Apostla gerningar, Helga manna lefverne, Legender, Nichodemi evangelium. Efter gammal handskrift.* Samlingar utgifna af svenska fornskrift-sällskapet 68–70. Stockholm: Norstedt & Söner, 1877–1878.

—, ed. *Läke- och örte-böcker från Sveriges medeltid.* Samlingar utgifna af svenska fornskrift-sällskapet 82, 84, 90. Stockholm: Norstedt & Söner, 1883–1886.

Knudsen, Gunnar, and Marius Kristensen. *Danmarks gamle Personnavne. I. Fornavne.* 2 vols. Copenhagen: Gad, 1936–1948.

Kolsrud, Oluf, ed. *Messuskýringar: Liturgisk symbolik frå den norsk-islandske kyrkja i millomalderen.* Norsk historisk kjeldeskrift-institutt. Oslo: Dybwad, 1952.

Konráð Gíslason, ed. *Fire og fyrretyve for en stor deel forhen utrykte prøver af oldnordisk sprog og literatur.* Copenhagen: Gyldendal, 1860.

Kristján Eldjárn. "Kapelluhraun og Kapellulág." *Árbók Hins íslenzka fornleifafélags* 1955 (1956): 5–34.

—. *Hundrað ár í Þjóðminjasafni.* Reykjavík: Menningarsjóður, 1973.

—, and Hörður Ágústsson. *Skálholt: Skrúði og áhöld.* [Reykjavík]: Hið íslenska bókmenntafélag, 1992.

Kunze, Konrad. "Überlieferung und Bestand der elsässischen Legenda Aurea." *Zeitschrift für deutsches Altertum und deutsche Literatur* 99 (1970): 265–309.

Künstle, Karl. *Ikonographie der Heiligen.* 2 vols. Freiburg im Breisgau: Herder, 1926– 1928.

Küppers, Leonhard. *Barbara.* Heilige in Bild und Legende 10. Recklinghausen: Bongers, 1968.

Köhler, Reinhold. "Sage, Fabel und Legende." *Zeitschrift für deutsche Mythologie und Sittenkunde* 3 (1855): 298–302.

Kålund, Kr. *Katalog over Den arnamagnæanske Håndskriftsamling.* 2 vols. Copenhagen: Gyldendal, 1889–1894.

Lapparent, Le Comte de. *Sainte Barbe.* L'Art et les Saints. Paris: Henri Laurens, 1926.

Lewis, Agnes Smith, ed. and trans. *Select Narratives of Holy Women, from the Syro-Antiochene or Sinai palimpsest as written above the old Syriac Gospels by John the Stylite, of Beth-mari-qanūn in A.D. 778.* Studia Sinaitica 9, 10. London, C.J. Clay and Sons, 1900.

Liebgott, Niels-Knud. "Rimstav." *Skalk* 1 (1969): 15–18.

—. *Hellige mænd og kvinder.* Højbjerg: Wormianum, 1982.

Lind, E.H. *Norsk-isländska dopnamn ock fingerade namn från medeltiden.* Uppsala: Almqvist & Wiksell, 1905–1915.

Lindblom, Andreas. *Nordtysk skulptur och måleri i Sverige från den senare medeltiden.* Kungl. vitterhets historie och antikvitets akademien. Stockholm: Cederquist, 1916.

Lithberg, Nils. "Kalendariska hjälpmedel." In *Tideräkningen,* ed. Martin Persson Nilsson, pp. 77–94. Nordisk kultur 21. Stockholm: Bonnier; Oslo: Aschehoug; Copenhagen: Schultz, 1934.

—, and Elias Wessén, ed. *Den götländska runkalendern 1328.* Kungl. vitterhets historie och antikvitets akademiens handlingar 45.2. Stockholm: Wahlström & Widstrand, 1939.

Ljunggren, Gustaf. *Svenska dramat intill slutet af sjuttonde århundradet.* Lund: Gleerup; Copenhagen: Falkenberg, 1864.

Lockwood, W.B. "A Manuscript in the Rylands Library and Flemish-Dutch and Low German Accounts of the Life and Miracles of Saint Barbara." *Bulletin of the John Rylands Library, Manchester* 36 (1953–1954): 23–37.

Louis-Jensen, Jonna. "'Seg Hallfríði góða nótt'." In *Opuscula* 2:2: 149–153. Bibliotheca Arnamagnæana 25.2. Copenhagen: Reitzel, 1977.

Magnús Már Lárusson. "Kalendarium II." In *Kulturhistorisk Leksikon for nordisk middelalder* 8 [1963]: 106–109. 22 vols. Copenhagen: Rosenkilde and Bagger, 1956–1976.

—, and Jónas Kristjánsson, ed. *Sigilla Islandica.* Íslenzk handrit: Icelandic Manuscripts, Series in Octavo 1–2. 2 vols. Reykjavík: Handritastofnun Íslands, 1965–1967.

Maliniemi, Aarno, ed. *Zur Kenntnis des Breviarium Aboense.* Suomalaisen tiedeakatemian Julkaisemia pohjoismaiden historiaa valaisevia asiakirjoja / Documenta historica quibus res nationium septentrionalium illustrantur edidit Academia Scientiarum Fennica 9. Helsinki: Suoma-laisen Kirjallisuuden Kirjapaino, 1957.

Mariacher, Giovanni. *Palma il Vecchio.* Milan: Bramante Editrice, 1968.

Martyrologium Romanum. In *Propylaeum ad Acta Sanctorum Decembris.* Ed. Hippolyte Delehaye et al. Brussels: Société des Bollandistes, 1940.

Matthías Þórðarson. "Biskupskápan gamla." *Árbók Hins íslenzka fornleifa-félags* 1911 (1911): 36-59.

McLaughlin, Eleanor Commo. "Equality of Souls, Inequality of Sexes: Woman in Medieval Theology." In *Religion and Sexism: Images of Woman in the Jewish and Christian Traditions,* ed. Rosemary Radford Ruether, pp. 213-266. New York: Simon and Schuster, 1974.

McNamara, Jo Ann. "Sexual Equality and the Cult of Virginity in Early Christian Thought." *Feminist Studies* 3 (1976): 145-158.

Melchers, Erna. *Das Jahr der Heiligen: Geschichte und Legende.* Munich: Südwest Verlag, 1965.

Miles, Margaret R. *Carnal Knowing: Female Nakedness and Religious Mean-ing in the Christian West.* Boston: Beacon Press, 1989; New York: Vintage Books, 1991.

Mombrizio, Bonino. *Sanctuarium seu Vitae Sanctorum.* 2 vols. Paris: Fontemoing, 1910. Rpt. Hildesheim: Georg Olms, 1978.

Morris, William. *Icelandic Journals.* Introductory essay by Magnus Mag-nusson; foreword by Fiona MacCarthy. London : Mare's Nest Pub-lishing, 1996.

Muir, Lynette R. "The Saint Play in Medieval France." In *The Saint Play in Medieval Europe,* ed. Clifford Davidson, pp. 123-180. Early Drama, Art and Music Monograph Series 8. Kalamazoo: Medieval Institute Publications, 1986.

Newman, Barbara. *From Virile Woman to Woman Christ: Studies in Medie-val Religion and Literature.* Philadelphia: University of Pennsylvania Press, 1995.

Nielsen, Karl Martin, ed. *Middelalderens danske bønnebøger.* 4 vols. Copen-hagen: Gyldendal, 1946-1963.

Nielsen, Niels. *Sjælens Trøst ("Siæla trøst").* Universitets-jubilæets Danske Samfund, Skrifter 360, 316. Copenhagen: Schultz, 1937-1952.

Nilsén, Anna. *Program och funktion i senmedeltida kalkmåleri. Kyrkmål-ningar i Mälarlandskapen och Finland 1400-1534.* Stockholm: Kungl. vitterhets historie och antikvitets akademien, 1986.

Nyrop, C., ed. *Danmarks Gilde- og Lavsskraaer fra Middelalderen.* Vol. 1. Copenhagen: Gad, 1899-1900.

Odenius, Oloph. "Cisiojani Latini. Neute Beiträge zur Bibliographie der metrischen Kalendarien des Mittelalters." *Arv* 15 (1959): 61-154.

Olmer, Emil. *Boksamlingar på Island 1179–1490*. Gothenburg: Zachrisson, 1902.

Otterbjörk, Roland. *Svenska förnamn*. 3rd ed. Stockholm: Norstedt, 1981.

Peine, Selmar. *St. Barbara, die Schutzheilige der Bergleute und der Artillerie, und ihre Darstellung in der Kunst*. Freiberg: Gerlach'sche Buchdruckerei, 1896.

Petersen, Henry. *Danske geistlige Sigiller fra Middelalderen*. Copenhagen: Reitzel, 1883.

Petzoldt, L. "Barbara." In *Lexikon der christlichen Ikonographie* 5 [1973]: 304–311. 8 vols. Rome: Herder, 1968–1976.

PG = *Patrologiae cursus completus: Series Graeca*, ed. J.-P. Migne, 161 vols. Paris: Migne, 1857–1866.

PL = *Patrologiae cursus completus: Series Latina*, ed. J.-P. Migne, 221 vols. Paris: Migne, 1844–1864.

Pylkkänen, Riitta. *Sancta Barbara*. Helsinki: Valtionewoston kirjapaino, 1966.

Quentin, Henri. *Les martyrologes historiques du moyen âge: Étude sur la formation du Martyrologe Romain*. Paris, 1908. Rpt. Aalen: Scientia Verlag 1969.

Raasted, Jørgen. "Helgener." In *Kulturhistorisk Leksikon for nordisk middelalder* 6 [1961]: 321–327. 22 vols. Copenhagen: Rosenkilde and Bagger, 1956–1978.

Rabanus Maurus. *De Universo*. PL 111: 9–614.

—. *Martyrologivm*. Ed. John McCulloh. *Corpus Christianorum Continuatio Mediaevalis* 44: 1–161. Turnhout: Brepols, 1979.

Reames, Sherry L. *The 'Legenda aurea': A Reexamination of Its Paradoxical History*. Madison: University of Wisconsin Press, 1985.

Reuter, Elisabeth. "Barbara." In *Die deutsche Literatur des Mittelalters: Verfasserlexikon*, 1: 601–603. 2nd ed. Berlin and New York: de Gruyter, 1977.

Rindal, Magnus, ed. *Barlaams ok Josaphats saga*. Norsk historisk kjeldeskrift-institutt. Norrøne tekster 4. Oslo: Norsk historisk kjeldeskriftinstitutt, 1981.

Robertson, Elizabeth. "The Corporeality of Female Sanctity in *The Life of Saint Margaret*." In *Images of Sainthood in Medieval Europe*, ed Renate Blumenfeld-Kosinski and Timea Szell, pp. 268–287. Ithaca and London: Cornell University Press, 1991.

Rossi, Giovanni Battista de, and Louis Duchesne, ed. *Martyrologium Hieronymianum*. Brussels: Société des Bollandistes, 1894. [Excerpt of *Acta Sanctorum*, Nov. t. II, pars prior.]

Rouanet, Léo, ed. *Colección de autos, farsas, y coloquios del siglo XVI.* Bibliotheca hispanica [5-8]. 4 vols. Barcelona and Madrid: L'Avenç and Librería de M. Murillo, 1901.

Rydbeck, Otto. *Medeltida kalkmålningar i Skånes kyrkor.* Lund: Berling-ska boktryckeriet, 1904.

Saxtorph, Niels M. *Jeg ser på kalkmalerier: En gennemgang af alle kalk-malerier i danske kirker.* Copenhagen: Politikens forlag, 1967.

Schade, Oskar, ed. *Geistliche Gedichte des XIV. und XV. Jarhunderts vom Niderrhein.* Hannover: Carl Rümpler, 1854. Rpt. Amsterdam: Rodopi, 1968.

Schade, Werner. *Cranach: A Family of Master Painters.* Trans. Helen Sebba. New York: Putnam, 1980.

Schmid, Toni, ed. *Liber Ecclesiæ Vallentunensis.* Kungl. vitterhets historie och antikvitets akademien. Stockholm: Wahlström & Widstrand, 1945.

Schmitt, Margarete, ed. *Der grosse Seelentrost. Ein niederdeutsches Erbau-ungsbuch des vierzehnten Jahrhunderts.* Niederdeutsche Studien 5. Cologne and Graz: Böhlau, 1959.

Schreiner, Klaus. "'Discrimen veri ac falsi': Ansätze und Formen der Kritik in der Heiligen- und Reliquienverehrung des Mittelalters." *Archiv für Kulturgeschichte* 48 (1966): 1–53.

Schulenburg, Jane Tibbets. "Sexism and the Celestial Gynaeceum—from 500 to 1200." *Journal of Medieval History* 4 (1978): 117–133.

—. "The Heroics of Virginity: Brides of Christ and Sacrificial Mutilation." In *Women in the Middle Ages and the Renaissance: Literary and His-torical Perspectives,* ed. Mary Beth Rose, pp. 29–72. Syracuse: Syracuse University Press, 1986.

Seefeldt, Paul. *Studien über die verschiedenen mittelalterlichen dramatischen Fassungen der Barbara-Legende nebst Neudruck des ältesten 'Mystère français de Sainte Barbe en deux journées.'* Greifswald: Hans Alder, 1908.

Seip, Didrik Arup. *Palæografi: B: Norge og Island.* Ed. Johs. Brøndum-Nielsen. Nordisk kultur 28:B. Stockholm: Bonnier; Oslo: Aschehoug; Copenhagen: Schultz, 1954.

Seybolt, Robert Francis. "Fifteenth Century Editions of the *Legenda aurea.*" *Speculum* 21 (1946): 327–338.

Shewring, W.H., trans. *The Passion of SS. Perpetua and Felicity, MM: A new edition and translation of the Latin text, together with the Sermons of St. Augustine … .* London: Sheed and Ward, 1931.

Sigurveig Guðmundsdóttir. *Heilög Barbara.* [Reykjavík]: Barbörusjóður, 1981.

Simeon Metaphrastes. *Menologion.* PG 116: 310–316.

SRD = Langebek, Jakob. *Scriptores Rerum Danicarum Medii Ævi.* Copenhagen, 1772–1878. 9 vols. Rpt. Nendeln, Liechtenstein: Kraus Reprint, 1969.

Thorén, Ivar. *Studier över Själens tröst.* Nordiska texter och undersökningar 14. Stockholm: Hugo Gebers Förlag; Copenhagen: Munksgaard, 1942.

Tomner, Lennart, ed. *Christen Skeels Resedagbok 1619–1627.* Malmö: Allhems förlag, 1962.

Þorvaldur Bjarnarson, ed. *Leifar fornra kristinna fræða íslenzkra.* Copenhagen: Hagerup, 1878.

Uldall, F. *Danmarks middelalderlige Kirkeklokker.* Copenhagen: Lehmann & Stage, 1906; 2nd ed. [Højbjerg]: Hikuin, 1982.

Unger, C.R., ed. *Heilagra manna søgur. Fortællinger og legender om hellige mænd og kvinder.* 2 vols. Christiania [Oslo]: Bentzen, 1877.

Vilhjálmur Örn Vilhjálmsson. "Af heilagri Barböru og uppruna hennar." *Árbók Hins íslenzka fornleifafélags* 1982 (1983): 171–175.

Villemot, Justin (Abbé). *Histoire de sainte Barbe, vierge et martyre.* Besançon: Jacquin, 1864.

Viteau, Joseph, ed. *Passions des saints Écaterine et Pierre d'Alexandrie, Barbara et Anysia.* Paris: Librairie Émile Bouillon, 1897.

Weale, James. "Iconographie chrétienne sainte Barbe." *Le Beffroi* 4 (1872–1873): 5–44.

Wegener, Philipp "Drei mittelniederdeutsche Gedichte des 15. Jarhunderts mit kritischen Bemerkungen." *Jahrbuch des Pädagogiums zum Kloster unser lieben Frauen in Magdeburg* 42. Magdeburg: Königl. Hofbuchdruckerei von Carl Friese, 1878.

Weibull, Lauritz, ed. *Necrologium Lundense: Lunds domkyrkas nekrologium.* Monumenta Scaniæ Historica. Lund: Berling, 1923.

Weyh, Wilhelm. *Die syrische Barbara-Legende. Mit einem Anhang: Die syrische Kosmas- und Damian-Legende in deutscher Uebersetzung.* Programm des K. humanistischen Gymnasiums Schweinfurt für das Schuljahr 1911–1912. Schweinfurt: Druck der Fr. J. Reichardt'schen Buchdruckerei, 1911–1912.

Widding, Ole. "AM 672, 4°—en skyggetilværelse." In *Opuscula* 1: 344–349. Bibliotheca Arnamagnæana 20. Copenhagen: Munksgaard, 1960.

—, Hans Bekker-Nielsen, and L.K. Shook. "The Lives of the Saints in Old Norse Prose: A Handlist." *Mediaeval Studies* 25 (1963): 294–337.

Williams, Harry F. "Old French Lives of Saint Barbara." *Proceedings of the American Philosophical Society* 119:2 (1975): 156–185.

—. "A Saint Neglected." In *Voices of Conscience: Essays on Medieval and Modern French Literature in Memory of James D. Powell and Rosemary*

Hodgins, ed. Raymond J. Cormier, pp. 95–103. Philadelphia: Temple University Press, 1977.

Williams-Krapp, Werner. *Die deutschen und niederländischen Legendare des Mittelalters. Studien zu ihrer Überlieferungs-, Text- und Wirkungsgeschichte.* Tübingen: Niemeyer, 1986.

—. "German and Dutch Translations of the *Legenda aurea*." In *'Legenda aurea': Sept siècles de diffusion*, ed. Brenda Dunn-Lardeau, pp. 227–232. Actes du colloque international sur la *Legenda aurea* texte latin et branches vernaculaires à l'Université du Québec à Montréal 11–12, mai 1983. Cahiers d'études médiévales: Cahier spécial 2. Montreal: Éditions Bellarmin, 1986.

Wimmer, E. "Barbara." In *Lexikon des Mittelalters* 1.7 [1980]: 1432–1433. 10 vols. Munich and Zürich: Artemis, 1977–1999.

Wirth, Albrecht, ed. *Danae in christlichen Legenden*. Vienna: Tempskh, 1892.

Wolf, Kirsten. "Old Norse—New Philology." *Scandinavian Studies* 65 (1993): 338–348.

—. "The Severed Breast: A Topos in the Legends of Female Virgin Martyr Saints." *Arkiv för nordisk filologi* 112 (1997): 97–112.

—, ed. *The Icelandic Legend of Saint Dorothy*. Studies and Texts 130. Toronto: Pontifical Institute of Mediaeval Studies, 1997.

Wolpers, Theodor. *Die englische Heiligenlegende des Mittelalters*. Tübingen: Max Niemeyer, 1964.

Wormald, F. "An Early Carmelite Liturgical Calendar from England." *Bulletin of the Institute of Historical Research* 39 (1966): 174–180.

Zaccaria, F.A. *De rebus ad historiam atque antiquitates ecclesiæ pertinentibus*. 2 vols. Foligno: P. Campana, 1781.

Index of Sources

This index includes the principal sources cited, and is divided into two sections. The index of manuscripts contains a brief list of codices cited by their familiar or older names in the early secondary literature (for example, *Codex Pii papae II 22*), followed by conventional manuscript citations organized by city, collection, and shelfmark. References to printed collections (such as the *Bibliotheca Hagiographica Latina [BHL]*) are listed separately. For other literary and liturgical works, see the General Index.

MANUSCRIPTS

Codex Augiensis XXXII 15
Codex Bernensis 12
Codex Epternacenis 12
Codex Messinensis 76 6, 8, 10
Codex Ottobonianus 1 11
Codex Ottobonianus 223 20
Codex Pii papae II 22 10, 11
Codex Vaticanus 803 10, 11
Codex Vaticanus 866 9, 11
Codex Vindobonensis hist. 61 6, 8, 10, 11
Codex Wissenbergensis 12
Paris. 770 10, 11

The Arnamagnaean Collection (Det arnamagnæanske Institut, Copenhagen; Stofnun Árna Magnússonar, Reykjavík)
AM 238 fol. VIII: 80
AM 241a fol.: 66
AM 249a fol.: 66
AM 249b fol.: 66
AM 249c fol.: 64, 65
AM 249d fol.: 65

AM 249e fol.: 65
AM 249f fol.: 65
AM 249g fol.: 66
AM 249h fol.: 67
AM 249i fol.: 66
AM 249k fol.: 67
AM 249l fol.: 66
AM 249m fol.: 65
AM 249n fol.: 65
AM 249o fol.: 66
AM 249p fol.: 66
AM 249q fol. I–VIII: 66, 67
AM 351 fol. (*Skálholtsbók*): 67

AM 435a 4to: 92, 113
AM 621 4to: 90
AM 624 4to: 68
AM 625 4to: 68
AM 672 4to: 73, 111–114
AM 721 4to: 90
AM 727 4to: 68
AM 782 4to: 55
AM 784 4to: 55, 57

PRINTED COLLECTIONS

General Index